MW01141978

Insert

Break...	
Page N**u**mbers...	
Foot**n**ote...	
Book**m**ark...	Ctrl+Shift+F5
Annotation	
Date and **T**ime...	
Fiel**d**...	
Symbol...	
Index **E**ntry...	
Index...	
Table of **C**ontents...	
Fi**l**e...	
Frame	
Picture...	
Object...	

(Format)

Character...	
Paragraph...	
Tabs...	
Border...	
Language...	
St**y**le...	Ctrl+S
Page Set**u**p...	
C**o**lumns...	
Section Layout...	
Frame...	
Pi**c**ture...	

Tools

Spelling...	
Grammar...	
Thesaurus...	Shift+F7
Hyphenation...	
Bullets and Numbering...	
Create **E**nvelope...	
Revision Mar**k**s...	
Compare **V**ersions...	
Sor**t**ing...	
Calculate	
Re**p**aginate Now	
Record Macro...	
Macro...	
Options...	

Table

Insert Table...	
Delete Columns	
Merge Cells	
Convert **T**ext to Table...	
Select **R**ow	
Select **C**olumn	
Select Ta**b**le	Alt+NumPad 5
Row **H**eight...	
Column **W**idth...	
Split Table	
√ **G**ridlines	

Window

New Window
Arrange All
√ **1** Document1

Computer users are not all alike. Neither are SYBEX books.

We know our customers have a variety of needs. They've told us so. And because we've listened, we've developed several distinct types of books to meet the needs of each of our customers. What are you looking for in computer help?

If you're looking for the basics, try the **ABC's** series. You'll find short, unintimidating tutorials and helpful illustrations. For a more visual approach, select **Teach Yourself**, featuring screen-by-screen illustrations of how to use your latest software purchase.

Mastering and **Understanding** titles offer you a step-by-step introduction, plus an in-depth examination of intermediate-level features, to use as you progress.

Our **Up & Running** series is designed for computer-literate consumers who want a no-nonsense overview of new programs. Just 20 basic lessons, and you're on your way.

We also publish two types of reference books. Our **Instant References** provide quick access to each of a program's commands and functions. SYBEX **Encyclopedias** and **Desktop References** provide a *comprehensive reference* and explanation of all of the commands, features, and functions of the subject software.

Sometimes a subject requires a special treatment that our standard series don't provide. So you'll find we have titles like **Advanced Techniques, Handbooks, Tips & Tricks**, and others that are specifically tailored to satisfy a unique need.

We carefully select our authors for their in-depth understanding of the software they're writing about, as well as their ability to write clearly and communicate effectively. Each manuscript is thoroughly reviewed by our technical staff to ensure its complete accuracy. Our production department makes sure it's easy to use. All of this adds up to the highest quality books available, consistently appearing on best-seller charts worldwide.

You'll find SYBEX publishes a variety of books on every popular software package. Looking for computer help? Help Yourself to SYBEX.

For a complete catalog of our publications:

SYBEX, Inc.
2021 Challenger Drive, Alameda, CA 94501
Tel: (510) 523-8233/(800) 227-2346 Telex: 336311
Fax: (510) 523-2373

SYBEX is committed to using natural resources wisely to preserve and improve our environment. As a leader in the computer book publishing industry, we are aware that over 40% of America's solid waste is paper. This is why we have been printing the text of books like this one on recycled paper since 1982.

This year our use of recycled paper will result in the saving of more than 15,300 trees. We will lower air pollution effluents by 54,000 pounds, save 6,300,000 gallons of water, and reduce landfill by 2,700 cubic yards.

In choosing a SYBEX book you are not only making a choice for the best in skills and information, you are also choosing to enhance the quality of life for all of us.

The ABC's of Microsoft Word
for Windows, Version 2.0

The ABC's of Microsoft® Word for Windows,™ Version 2.0

Second Edition

BY ALAN R. NEIBAUER

SYBEX®

San Francisco
Paris
Düsseldorf
Soest

ACQUISITIONS EDITOR: *Dianne King*

EDITOR: *Marilyn Smith*

PROJECT EDITOR: *Kathleen Lattinville*

TECHNICAL EDITOR: *Nick Dargahi*

WORD PROCESSORS: *Ann Dunn, Susan Trybull*

BOOK DESIGNER: *Amparo Del Rio*

CHAPTER ART AND LAYOUT: *Charlotte Carter*

SCREEN GRAPHICS: *Cuong Le*

DESKTOP PUBLISHING SPECIALIST: *Deborah Maizels*

PROOFREADER/PRODUCTION ASSISTANT: *Arno Harris*

INDEXER: *Julie Kawabata*

COVER DESIGNER: *Ingalls + Associates*

COVER PHOTOGRAPHER: *Mark Johann*

Library of Congress Card Number: 91-67704

ISBN: 0-7821-1052-5

Manufactured in the United States of America

10 9 8 7 6 5 4 3 2 1

To Barbara, Adam, and

Joshua

ACKNOWLEDGMENTS

Completing a new edition of a book such as this is no less difficult than producing the original. This is particularly true when the new version of the software contains many spectacular and powerful features. But through temperance, planning, and good editing, SYBEX has again produced a book that is best suited for its readers. I would expect no less of SYBEX and could not envision a publisher doing any more.

Marilyn Smith, who edited this book, deserves a lion's share of the credit. She knows her job, and does it with professionalism and grace. We were helped unmeasurably by Kathleen Lattinville, who served as project editor of this book. Her role was similar to a field commander overseeing the movement of troops, ready to personally lead the charge.

My thanks to technical editor Nick Dargahi, word processors Ann Dunn and Susan Trybull, typesetter Deborah Maizels, proofreader Arno Harris, and indexer Julie Kawabata. The work of chapter designer and layout artist Charlotte Carter and book designer Amparo Del Rio guaranteed a readable and attractive product. Thanks also to Dianne King for her continued support, as well as the other people at SYBEX whose efforts contributed to this book.

No matter how many words I write in a book such as this, I can never find enough words to thank my wife, Barbara. She constantly amazes and amuses me. Her support and understanding are unflinching and unequalled, even when unrewarded and undeserved. The celebration of our silver wedding anniversary is a remarkable testimony to her fortitude and patience.

Contents AT A GLANCE

PART FIVE   **Desktop Publishing**   **345**

APPENDICES   **383**

Table of Contents

PART ONE   Word for Windows Fundamentals

Lesson 1

Lesson 2

Lesson 3

PART THREE   Formatting Your Documents

PART FOUR   Advanced Features

Lesson 31

Searching for Text and Formats   246

Lesson 32

Replacing Text and Formats   253

Lesson 33

Using Advanced Printing Features   258

Lesson 34

Recording and Using Macros   268

PART FIVE   Desktop Publishing

APPENDICES

Just when you thought that word processing programs could not get any better, along comes Word for Windows. Word applies the full potential of Windows to a powerful word processor. You will see on your screen exactly how your document will appear when it is printed, including font styles and sizes, graphics, and formats.

But Word goes much further by providing many built-in capabilities that other programs don't include. Here are some examples of what you can do with Word for Windows:

- Automatically format and print envelopes.

- Create customized graphs by typing information into tables.

- Create PostScript-like special type effects with any Windows-supported printer.

- Create presentation-quality graphics.

Yet, with all of these powers, Word for Windows is remarkably easy and even fun to use.

Who Should Read This Book

If you are switching from the DOS version of Word, or never used Word at all, this book is ideal for you. You will learn how to create and print documents in short, easy-to-follow lessons. Each lesson takes only a short time to teach you a complete and useful task. Because the lessons are *task oriented*, you will be able to immediately apply them to your own documents. You can complete the lessons individually, or go through several lessons in one session to build your Word expertise quickly and painlessly.

As your skills increase, the lessons will start to cover more sophisticated functions, including the powerful macro, merge, and desktop publishing features. But even these more advanced lessons are clear and concise.

With each lesson, you will also learn more about Windows itself, such as how to work with multiple windows and use the Clipboard to copy and move text. So even if you are new to Windows, you will be "up and running" with this sophisticated word processing program in minutes.

What This Book Contains

The lessons in Part 1 show you how to type, print, and save a simple document in the quickest amount of time. Not every detail of editing, saving, or printing is given in these beginning lessons, just the basics you need to start using Word for your own work.

Part 2 is devoted to building your editing skills. You will learn how to recall documents from the disk, and how to insert, delete, move, and copy text. In this part of the book, you will also learn how to have Word check your spelling and grammar and look up synonyms and antonyms.

The lessons in Part 3 focus on formatting—arranging the appearance of your document for maximum visual impact. You will learn how to format characters, paragraphs, and pages. One lesson describes how to automatically format and print envelopes with the click of the mouse.

Part 4 covers Word's power-user features. You will learn how to use a wide variety of sophisticated functions, including templates, spreadsheet tables, fields, macros, form documents, and styles. You will also find lessons on working with windows and panes, adding headers and footers, finding and replacing text, using printing options, and customizing the toolbar and menus.

Desktop publishing is the focus of the lessons in Part 5. After completing these lessons, you will be able to add rules, boxes, and graphics to your documents, and to produce newsletters with columns. You will also learn how to create drawings, charts, graphs, and special text effects.

How to Use This Book

If you have not yet installed Word, go directly to Appendix A. There you will learn how to make a copy of your disks and install Word on your computer.

Appendix B explains how to use the mouse and keyboard to interact with Windows and Windows applications. The lessons in this book assume you have a fundamental understanding of how to use the mouse, Windows menus, and dialog boxes. If you a new Windows user, read Appendix B before starting the lessons. It will make your work with Word much easier.

The lessons themselves are organized in a logical progression based on the skills you will need to become productive with Word for Windows. Most of the lessons include a series of easy-to-follow steps. To learn how to use Word, just sit down at your computer and do what each step instructs.

While there is a natural progression of the lessons, you can jump ahead to a more advanced lesson if you need that information to complete your work. For example, you might be typing a rather straightforward document that should be printed in two columns. Look in the table of contents or index, and go directly to that lesson.

Within the steps, when you are asked to type something in from the keyboard, what you are to type will appear in boldface. For example, you may see "Type **Collect**." In some cases, your entry will consist of an entire brief document, which will all be in boldface.

Read all the information in the step before performing it. In some instances, a step may include optional instructions for mouse and keyboard users. Even if you have a mouse, you may find several of the keyboard alternatives more efficient.

In a few instances, you will see a series of steps that give generic instructions. These are designed as an aid for you to follow when performing your own work—you do not have to perform them to complete the lesson.

PART 1

Word For Windows Fundamentals

FEATURING

Starting Word

Understanding the Word screen

▼

Starting Word for Windows

Word for Windows is designed to use the graphic interface of Microsoft Windows. This means that you'll see on the screen exactly how your document will appear when it is printed, including the character formats and graphics. Word for Windows provides many features for controlling the format of your text. Because you can see the effects of your formatting on the screen, you can perfect your documents before printing them.

In this book, you will learn the fundamentals of using Word for Windows, a remarkably robust and versatile program. We will begin by starting Word and examining the Word screen.

Starting Up

You can use one of these methods to start Word for Windows:

- Start Windows and Word at the same time by typing **WIN WINWORD**.

- If you are already in Windows, you can start Word by double-clicking on the Microsoft Word icon in Program Manager. (See Appendix B if you are not familiar with the techniques for using Windows.)

Use one of these methods to start the program now. In a few seconds, you'll see the Word screen, as shown in Figure 1.1.

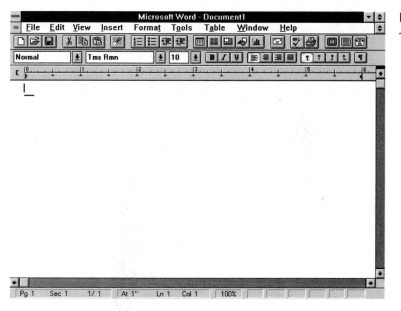

FIGURE 1.1:

The Word screen

The Word Screen

Each part of the Word screen provides useful information or tools. Before you start working with the program, take a few minutes to become familiar with the main sections of the Word screen, starting from the top.

THE TITLE BAR

The line on top of the screen is the title bar, which shows the name of the document in the window. It says *Document1* because you have not yet given the document a name. If you divide the screen into more than one window, the title bar of each one lets you know which document that window contains. (You will learn how to divide the screen into windows in Lesson 28.)

The title bar also contains three control boxes that are provided by Windows:

- The *Control menu*, or *close box*, on the left (the rectangle) lets you exit Word, reduce the program to an icon (so you can work with another program while Word is still running), or switch to another application.

- The *restore box* on the far right (the two triangles) changes the size of the Word window.

- The *minimize box* (single triangle) on the left side of the restore box reduces Word to an icon.

THE MENU BAR AND TOOLBAR

The menu bar, which is just below the title bar, displays the menus from which you select options to work with your documents. You will be using the menu bar constantly to give commands to the program.

Under the menu bar is the toolbar. If you have a mouse, you can use the toolbar to perform the most frequently used Word functions with a single click of the mouse. You can customize the toolbar to include the commands that you use most often, or turn it off so it doesn't appear on the screen. You'll learn how to use the menu bar and the toolbar in Lesson 2.

THE RIBBON AND THE RULER

The ribbon contains options for formatting characters. You'll learn how to use the ribbon in Lesson 12.

The ruler is a graphic representation of a ruler marked in inches, like an actual ruler laying across the top of your paper. You can use it to judge spacing, visualize how your document will appear when printed, and set and move tab stops. You will learn how to set tab stops in Lesson 15.

You can turn off the ribbon, ruler, and toolbar to display more lines of your own document on the screen and to speed up Word's operation (see Lesson 2).

THE TEXT REGION

The text region is where your document will appear as you type. Even before you enter any text, the text region will contain a few items.

The blinking vertical line is the *cursor*, or *insertion point*, which shows where the next character typed will appear. You can use the mouse or directional arrow keys to move the insertion point to where you want to type, insert, or delete characters.

The horizontal line beneath the insertion point is the *end mark*. The end mark is always located at the end of your document; it moves down or up as you enter or delete characters. You cannot delete the end mark or place the insertion point after it. When you use the directional arrow keys to move the insertion point, the end mark remains after the last character in the document; it does not move to the insertion-point location. As you'll learn later, in some views, the end mark does not appear on the screen.

If you have a mouse, you'll also see the mouse pointer. The shape of the mouse pointer depends on where it is located on the screen. When the mouse pointer is in the text region, it is shaped like an I-beam.

You use the I-beam to position the insertion point when you want to edit your document.

On the right and bottom sides of the text region are scroll bars. Lesson 7 describes how to use the scroll bars to move from place to place in your document, as well as how to move the insertion point.

THE STATUS BAR

The status bar, below the text region, gives you information about the current status of Word and your document. Table 1.1 explains what each of the status bar indicators means.

INDICATOR	MEANING
Pg 1	Current page number
Sec 1	Current section number
1/1	Current page/total pages in the document
At 1"	Position of the insertion point from the top of the page
Ln 1	Line number where the insertion point is located
Col 1	Character position of the insertion point from the left margin
100%	Magnification of the displayed image
REC	Macro record mode
EXT	Extend mode
COL	Column select mode
OVR	Overlay mode
MRK	Mark revisions function is on
CAPS	Caps Lock function is on
NUM	Num Lock function is on

TABLE 1.1:

Indicators on the Word Status Bar

2 LESSON

FEATURING

Using the menu bar

Making dialog box selections

Working with the toolbar

▼

Giving Commands to Word

As you work with Word, you will need to communicate with the program. You will give it instructions and respond to its questions and requests, and sometimes the program will guide you through procedures and tasks. When you select an option and instruct the program to perform that option's function, you are giving Word a *command*. You can issue commands using either the mouse or the keyboard.

In this lesson, you will learn how to give commands to the program.

The techniques and procedures for giving commands to Word are the same as those used with other Windows applications. This means that if you are familiar with one Windows application, you already know how to communicate with Word. However, if you are a new Windows user, you should refer to Appendix B for basic information about using the mouse and keyboard with Windows applications. Then return to this lesson to practice your Windows skills.

Using the Menu System

The menus on the menu bar give you access to Word's functions. Table 2.1 lists the menus on the menu bar and the functions they control.

As an example of using these menus to communicate with Word, we will explore the Help menu.

OPTION	PURPOSE
File	Opens, saves, and prints documents; changes document summary; exits Word
Edit	Inserts, deletes, finds, and replaces text
View	Changes the way the document appears on the screen; inserts headers and footers
Insert	Adds dates, times, graphics, footnotes, and page numbers
Format	Modifies the appearance of characters, paragraphs, and pages
Tools	Starts the spelling checker, grammar checker, thesaurus, and hyphenation; creates envelopes; records and plays macros; customizes Word operations
Table	Creates, edits, and formats spreadsheet-like tables
Window	Displays multiple windows or documents on the screen
Help	Provides help on using Word and access to the on-line tutorial

TABLE 2.1:

Menu Bar Options

GETTING HELP

If you need help when typing, editing, or formatting a document, you can use Word's comprehensive Help feature. The Help option on the menu bar displays windows that explain each command and function. Let's use the Help menu and see what information is provided about opening a document (recalling a saved document to the screen).

1. Click on Help or press Alt-H to display the Help pull-down menu.

This menu lists five options: Help Index displays the Help Index, Getting Started runs an on-line tutorial on Word's basic functions, Learning Word runs an on-line tutorial that covers all aspects of Word, WordPerfect Help shows the Word for Windows equivalent of Word-Perfect commands, and About reports the version of Word you are using and the amount of memory and disk space available.

2. Click on Help Index or press I to display the screen shown in Figure 2.1.

All the Help windows in Windows applications contain the same menu bar and command buttons (see Appendix B for a description of Help window controls). To quickly locate Help information on a topic, use the Search command button.

3. Click on Search or press S to display the Search dialog box, which lists Help topics alphabetically. You can scroll through the list of topics, but it's faster to have Word scroll for you.

4. Type **O**. When you type in the text box, the list scrolls to display Help topics starting with the character you typed.

5. Type **P**, the second character of the topic. The topic Opening Documents is now listed in the box.

6. Double-click on Opening Documents. With the keyboard, press Tab to select the list box, then ↓ to highlight the topic,

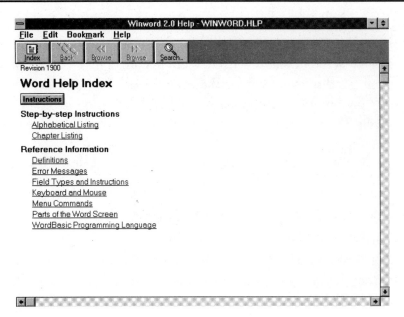

then ↵. A list of topics appears in the bottom list box, as shown in Figure 2.2.

7. Double-click on the topic Opening an Existing Document. With the keyboard, press ↓ to highlight it and press Alt-G to select Goto. The Search dialog box disappears, and you now see a Help window explaining how to open an existing document.

8. Press Alt-F4 to close the Help window.

If you need information about the menu, dialog box, or function you are currently working with, rather than going through the Help menu, press F1. This displays *context-sensitive* help about the part of Word from which you pressed F1.

If you press F1 while you are working in the text region, the Help Index will appear. To get context-sensitive help from the text region,

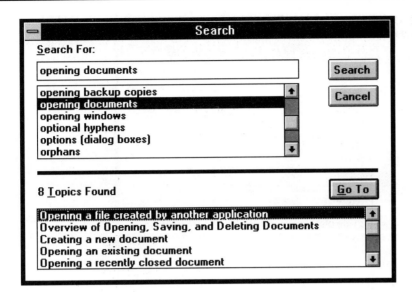

FIGURE 2.2:

The Search dialog box with found topics displayed

press Shift-F1. The I-beam becomes a small pointer connected to a question mark. Select the menu option or dialog box about which you want information (press Esc to return to the text region).

NAVIGATING THROUGH A DIALOG BOX

As another example of how to work with Word's menus and dialog boxes, we will explore the Character dialog box, which is accessed through the Format menu. (See Appendix B for more details on working with dialog boxes.)

1. Click on the word Format with the mouse button or press Alt-T to pull down the Format menu.

2. Click on Character or press C to display the dialog box shown in Figure 2.3.

The font name is highlighted in the Font text box, indicating that Word is ready for you to select another font. The arrow shows that a

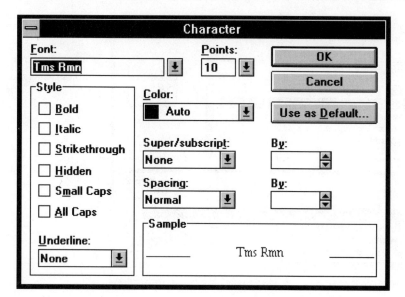

list box is available. It is separate from the text box because you can type a name in the box or select from the list box.

3. Click on the arrow or press ↓ to display the Font list box, which has a scroll bar on its right side. Your screen will look similar to the one shown in Figure 2.4, but the fonts you see in the list depend on your printer.

4. Click on the up or down arrow in the scroll box, or press the ↑ or ↓ key to cycle through the available choices.

5. To move to the Points option, click on the Points text box or press Alt-P. A list box showing available point sizes for the selected font will appear.

6. Select Bold by clicking on it or pressing Alt-B.

7. Select Italic by clicking on it or pressing I.

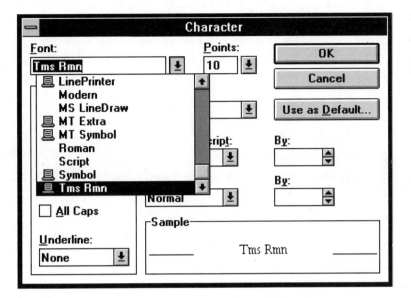

FIGURE 2.4:

A Fonts list in
the Character
dialog box

When a check box is selected, you can select another text box by pressing just its underlined letter; you do not have to hold down the Alt key.

8. Click on Bold or press B to select Bold again. You will see that selecting an option that is already turned on turns it off.

9. Click on Super/Subscript or press Alt-T to display the list box. The scroll box arrow is connected to this text box, which means that you cannot type in the text box.

10. Select Superscript from the list box by clicking on it or by using the arrow keys to highlight it.

Notice the By text box next to the Super/Subscript option. When you select Superscript or Subscript, you can type a number in the text box to indicate the spacing between the text and superscript. The default value is 3 points.

11. Click on Cancel or press Esc to leave the dialog box without using any of its functions.

Now that you know how to choose menu and dialog box options, the steps in this book will simply instruct you to "select" the option, and the key to press if you are using the keyboard will be in boldface type, as in "Pull down the For**m**at menu and select **C**haracter." If there is a shortcut key for the menu option, it will be shown in parentheses, as in "Pull down the **F**ile menu and select **P**rint (Ctrl-Shift-F12)."

If you are using the keyboard, remember not to press ↵ after entering information into a text box unless you have finished selecting options and want to return to the document.

Using the Toolbar

If you have a mouse, you can use the toolbar to work with Word. The *toolbar* contains buttons with icons that represent the most common Word commands. For example, the third button from the left side of the screen shows a picture of a disk, which is the icon for the Save command. Table 2.2 shows the toolbar icons and their functions. To use the toolbar, click on the icon for the command you want to perform.

Removing the Toolbar, Ribbon, or Ruler

Displaying the toolbar, ribbon, and ruler reduces the number of lines that Word displays at one time and consumes some of your computer's memory, which may slow down how Word responds to your typing and commands.

To remove any of these elements from the screen, select **V**iew to pull down the View menu, and then select **T**oolbar, **R**ibbon, or **R**uler to remove the check mark and turn off the option. Note that if you turn off the display of the toolbar, you'll have to use the menus or keyboard to perform the functions.

To return the toolbar, ribbon, or ruler to the screen, select View again and choose the item again to place a check mark next to it. Since you will be using the toolbar, ribbon, and ruler in the lessons that follow, leave them on the screen for now.

TABLE 2.2:

Toolbar Icons

ICON	NAME	FUNCTION
	New Document	Starts a new document
	Open	Opens an existing document
	Save	Saves a document
	Cut	Cuts selection
	Copy	Copies selection
	Paste	Pastes contents of the Clipboard
	Undo	Reverts to version before most recent change
	Numbered List	Numbers paragraphs
	Bulleted List	Adds bullets to paragraphs
	Unindent	Unindents paragraphs
	Indent	Indents paragraphs

ICON	NAME	FUNCTION
	Table	Creates tables
	Column	Creates columns
	Frame	Inserts frames
	Draw	Runs Microsoft Draw
	Graph	Runs Microsoft Graph
	Envelope	Creates an envelope
	Spelling	Checks spelling
	Print	Prints the document
	Zoom Whole Page	Reduces the image so the whole page is displayed on the screen
	Zoom 100 Percent	Returns to the normal view, with 100 percent magnification
	Zoom Page Width	Magnifies the image so you can see the full width of the page

TABLE 2.2:

Toolbar Icons (continued)

Creating a Document

Using a word processor such as Word for Windows to type text is a lot like using a typewriter. All the letter, number, and punctuation keys on the four middle rows of the keyboard work the same as they do on a typewriter keyboard. However, unlike a typewriter, Word makes it easy to correct your typing errors. This is just one of the many advantages of word processing.

In this lesson, you will create a Word for Windows document and work with some basic word processing features.

Typing the Text

Our sample document will be a short business letter. Follow these steps to create it:

1. Start Word for Windows (see Lesson 1).

2. Type **Dear Mr. Reynolds**: and press ↵ to move the insertion point to the next line.

3. Press ↵ again to double-space between the salutation and the first paragraph.

4. Type the following text. Do not press ↵ when the cursor reaches the right edge of the screen; just continue typing. If you make a mistake, press the Backspace key. This will move the insertion point back through your text, erasing characters as it goes.

   Your account is now two months overdue and we would appreciate payment within the week. Although we value your business, we are a small company that cannot afford to carry receivables more than one month.

5. Press the ↵ key twice.

6. Type the following paragraphs, double-spacing between paragraphs.

   Please contact your sales representative, Harvey Satitch, if you will have difficulty making the payment. Unfortunately, we will be unable to process any further orders until the full amount due has been paid.

   We have had a mutually beneficial relationship for some time now. It is our earnest desire to continue our business relationship into the future.

7. Press the ↵ key twice.

8. Type **Sincerely,** and then press ↵ three times to leave room for your signature. At this point, your document should look like the one shown in Figure 3.1.

9. Type your name.

That's how easy it is to create a Word document. We will work with this letter in the next lesson, so keep it on your screen.

Basic Word Processing Features

As you saw while typing the sample document, Word knows when the word you are typing will not fit on the remainder of a line, and it moves the word down to the next line. This is *word wrap*, which allows you to continue typing without worrying about line breaks. You press ↵ only to end short lines or paragraphs or to insert blank lines. The exact place

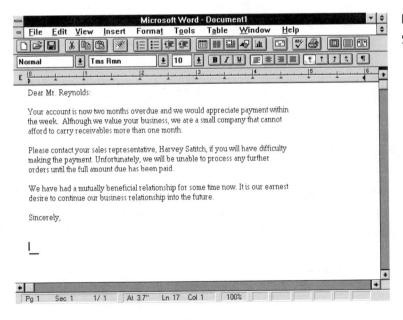

FIGURE 3.1:

Sample document

where your lines wrap depends on your monitor and printer, so it may be different on your screen than the wrap shown in the figures in this book.

As you type, the insertion point moves down the page. When you reach the last line on the screen, the lines at the top will *scroll* up and out of view. Although you can't see those lines, they are still in the computer's memory, and you can scroll them back onto the screen.

As your text grows even longer, you just continue typing, without worrying about ending one page and starting another. When you print the document, Word divides it into pages. This is called *autopagination*, and it enables you to add or delete text anywhere without running out of room on the page.

These basic word processing features will become very familiar to you as you work with Word. Table 3.1 provides descriptions of common word processing terms.

TERM	DEFINITION
Autopagination	The division of text into pages during printing.
Copy	Duplicate a section of existing text and paste it elsewhere, leaving the original text intact.
Default	The preset value of format or command settings.
Delete	Remove text from the document.
Edit	Change or correct the document by deleting, inserting, or rearranging text.
Format	Adjust the appearance of text or its position on the page.
Insertion point	The on-screen indicator showing the position of typing or editing actions.
Move	Remove a section of text from one location and paste it elsewhere.
Open	Retrieve the stored copy of the document from disk.

TABLE 3.1:

Basic Word Processing Terms

TERM	DEFINITION
Paginate	Divide the document into pages.
Replace	Search for specific text within the document and put other text in its place.
Save	Store a copy of the document on disk.
Scroll	Display different portions of the document on the screen.
Search	Locate specific text within the document.
Word Wrap	The automatic division of text into lines.

TABLE 3.1:

Basic Word
Processing Terms
(continued)

FEATURING

**Printing
documents**

**Selecting your
printer**

▼

Printing Your Documents

Most people want a printout, or hard copy, of their word processed documents. When you installed Word and Windows, you copied files that contain the information necessary for you to use your printer with Word. In this lesson, you will see how easy it is to print your Word documents. We will use two methods to print the sample letter you typed in Lesson 3.

Make sure your printer is turned on and ready and the paper is loaded properly before continuing.

Printing with the Toolbar

If you have a mouse, follow these steps to print the sample document using the toolbar:

1. Locate the Print button, which is the fourth icon from the right on the toolbar (refer to Table 2.1).

2. Click on the Print button in the toolbar.

You will see a dialog box showing the page being printed, the document name, and the printer being used. To cancel printing, select the Cancel button in the dialog box. After the document is printed, the dialog box disappears.

You now have a printed copy of your document. You'll learn how to save it onto your disk in the next lesson.

Printing through the toolbar is very convenient, but if you want to control the printing process, you must use the Print command in the File menu, which is described in the next section.

Using the Print Command

The Print command on the File menu provides another way to print your documents. Follow these steps to print the sample letter by using the menu command:

1. Pull down the File menu and select Print (Ctrl-Shift-F12) to display the Print dialog box.

Figure 4.1 shows the dialog box for a Hewlett-Packard LaserJet printer. In Lesson 33, you will learn how to use this dialog box to control the appearance of the printout.

2. Select OK to start printing.

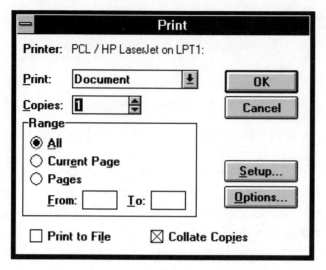

You will see a dialog box showing the status of the print job. After the document is printed, the dialog box disappears.

Selecting Your Printer

If your document did not print, you may have to select a printer. You only need to do this the first time you use Word or if you change printers. It is not necessary to follow these steps every time you print a document.

Selecting the printer is particularly important if you have more than one printer connected to your system or if you plan to take advantage of Word's special formatting powers. If the wrong printer is selected, the document might not print, or the printout may not resemble what appears on the screen.

Follow these steps to select a printer:

1. Pull down the File menu, and then choose Print Setup to display the Print Setup dialog box, shown in Figure 4.2.

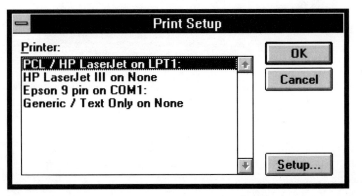

FIGURE 4.2:

The Print Setup dialog box

The available printers will be listed with the ports selected for them, such as

PCL/HP Laserjet on LPT1:
PostScript printer on COM1:

If your printer is connected to a port other than the one shown, or if the port is shown as *none*, you must change the port. Select Cancel, exit Word, and then follow the instructions in Appendix A for setting up Word for Windows.

2. Select the printer that is connected to your system, and then select OK.

If you did not set up your printer when you installed Word or Windows, or if you have any trouble printing your document, refer to Appendix A for information about setting up Windows printers.

Saving, Clearing, and Exiting

FEATURING

Saving your document on disk

Clearing the document window

Ending a Word session

▼

Saving a document means storing the text of the document on disk. Unless you save the document, when you turn off the computer or exit Word, it is lost forever. If you save a document, then make some changes to it, you must save it again. This way, the revisions you made to the original version will be recorded on disk.

After you have saved your document, you will either want to work on another document or exit Word. In this lesson, you will learn how to save a document, clear the document window, and exit Word and Windows.

Saving a Document the First Time

When you save a document for the first time, you must give it a file name. Document file names can be from one to eight characters. Let's save the document you just created under the name COLLECT:

1. Click on the Save button on the toolbar (the third button from the left; the one with an icon of a disk) to display the Save As dialog box, shown in Figure 5.1. With the keyboard, pull down the File menu and select Save (Shift-F12).

2. The insertion point is in the File Name text box. Type **Collect**, and then press ↵.

Since this is the first time you've saved the document, the Summary Info dialog box will appear, as shown in the example in Figure 5.2. The name you entered when you installed Word appears in the Author box. You will see this dialog box the first time you save a document and when you save a document under a different name.

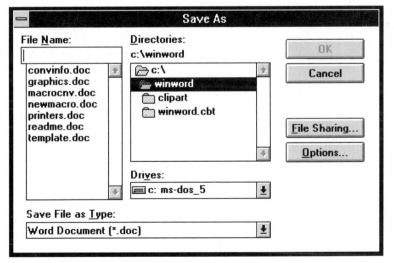

FIGURE 5.1:

The Save As dialog box

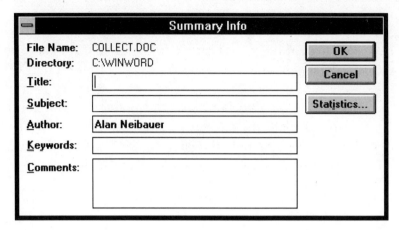

3. The insertion point is in the title text box. Type **Reynolds Automotive Past Due**.

4. Press Tab to reach the Subject text box, and then type **Reynolds Automotive**.

5. Press Tab twice to reach the Keywords text box and type **Reynolds Overdue Bill**.

6. Press Tab to reach the Comments text box and type **Follow up next month**.

7. Select OK to save the document.

In the status bar, Word briefly displays the number of characters in the document, such as

COLLECT.DOC: 610 chars

After the document is saved, its file name appears in the title bar. The document remains on the screen so you can continue working on it.

When Word saves a document, it automatically adds the extension .DOC to the document's name; COLLECT is stored on disk as COLLECT.DOC. This makes it easy for you to distinguish between the document and other files on your disk. Word assumes that your documents have the .DOC extension.

You can give the file a different three-character extension by typing it in the Save As dialog box when you name the file. However, if you do use another extension, you will have to go through a few more steps to recall the file later. Note that you cannot use certain extension names that are reserved for special types of programs: .EXE and .COM are used for program names, .BAT is for batch files, and .SYS is for system files used by the operating system.

WORKING WITH SUMMARY INFORMATION

The Summary Info dialog box helps identify your document, which is especially useful if you have several versions of the same document on your disk.

If you want to review or edit summary information, pull down the File menu and select Summary Info to display the Summary Info dialog box. You can edit the information and select OK, or select Statistics to see a report on the document, including the last revision date, document size, and total editing time. You can also use the Summary Info data to locate specific files on your disk when you use the Find File command in the File pull-down menu.

Saving an Edited Document

When you save a document for the first time, you give it a file name and have the opportunity to fill out the Summary Info dialog box. When you use the Save command again to save the same document (click on the Save button in the toolbar, select Save from the File menu, or press Shift-F12), the Save As and Summary Info dialog boxes do not appear, but the file is saved.

If you selected Read Only when you opened the document you are saving, you will see a dialog box with the message

This file is read-only

which means that you cannot change the document and save it under the same name. Select OK to display the Save As dialog box, type another file name, and then select OK to save the document.

Renaming a Document

If you don't like the name of your document, or you want to keep the original version unchanged, save the document under a new name by using the Save As command.

Pull down the File menu and select Save As (F12) to display the Save As dialog box. Type the new name you wish the file to have, and then select OK. A Summary Info dialog box will appear because you gave the document a new name.

Making Backup Copies

When you save an edited document under the same name as the original version, the original copy will be deleted. If you want to keep the original version on the disk unchanged, set Word to make backup copies. Then when you save a document, Word gives the original copy the extension .BAK and saves the new version with same name and the default .DOC extension.

But sometimes, even backup copies are not enough. Someone may accidentally turn off your computer or pull the plug, or some hardware or software glitch may send your computer back to the DOS prompt or off into never-never land. Whatever you've typed since last saving the document will be lost forever. To prevent such losses, you can set up Word to automatically save your work at regular intervals. Here's how to turn on the backup options:

1. Pull down the File menu and select Save As (F12).

2. Select **O**ptions to display the dialog box shown in Figure 5.3.

If you want Word to make backup copies of your edited documents, select Always Create **B**ackup Copy. Backup copies can take up a great deal of disk space, however, so you might decide not to select this option. The Fast Save option speeds the saving process by saving just the sections of the document that you edited. Turn off the Prompt for Summary Info option if you do not want to see the Summary Info dialog box when you save a document for the first time or under a new name.

3. To turn on automatic backup, select Automatic **S**ave Every.

The number 10 appears in the Minutes text box. To select another time period, enter the number of minutes in the text box or click on the up or down arrows.

4. Select OK to save your settings and redisplay the Save As dialog box.

5. Select **C**lose to return to the document window.

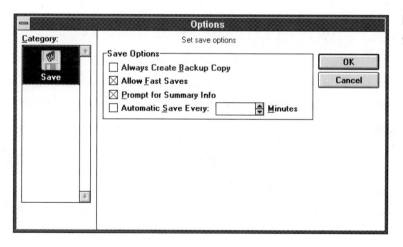

FIGURE 5.3:

Save As options

Clearing the Document Window

When you are ready to clear a document from the screen and erase it from the computer's memory (after you have saved it to disk), use the Close command in the File menu. Follow these steps to close our document:

1. Pull down the File menu. You will see that the document COLLECT.DOC is listed at the bottom of the menu, next to the underlined number 1.

Word adds the names of the last four documents you worked on to the File menu, which makes it easier to work with them. For example, you can use this feature to recall documents, as you will learn in Lesson 6.

2. Select Close.

The document window will be replaced by a blank background. The ruler will disappear, and only the options File and Help will appear in the menu bar. You cannot type in this window; Word is waiting for you to select an option from the menu bar.

If you had selected to close the document before saving it, Word would have warned you that you must specify that changes to the document be stored on the disk:

Do you want to save changes to Document1?

Whenever you have made changes to a document since the last time it was saved and then choose to close it, you'll see a dialog box asking if you want to save the document. It allows you to take one of the following actions:

- Select Yes to save the document, and the Save dialog box will appear if you have not yet named it.

- Choose No to clear the screen without saving the document (for example, if you have changed your mind about what you've already typed and want to erase all the text).

■ Select Cancel to leave the document on the screen without saving it.

Note that you do not have to close a document in order to exit Word for Windows. After saving or printing a document, close it so you can open another document or start a new one.

Leaving Word for Windows

When you are finished using Word, you should always exit the program and return to the Windows environment. Before turning off your computer, you should also exit Windows. If you turn off your computer before leaving Word and Windows, you could damage files that you will need later. To exit Word, follow these steps:

1. Double-click on the rectangle on the left side of the title bar (the close box). Using the keyboard, press Alt-F4, or pull down the File menu and select Exit.

The Windows Program Manager screen will appear. If Program Manager appears as an icon at the bottom of the desktop, double-click on it to restore it to a window. With the keyboard, press Alt-Tab until the Program Manager window is restored.

2. To exit Windows, double-click on the Program Manager control box or press Alt-F4. A dialog box will appear with the message

This will end your Windows session

3. Select Yes or press ↵. (Select Cancel or press Esc if you want to remain in Windows.)

Now you can turn off your computer without risking damage to your files. In the next lesson, you'll learn how to open documents so that you can continue working on them.

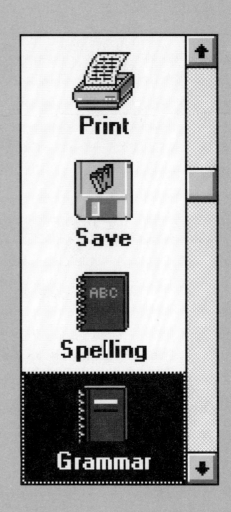

PART 2

Editing Your Documents

Opening Documents

ou can edit new documents as you type them or existing documents already saved on disk. To edit an existing document, you must first open it, or *recall* it from the disk on which it was stored.

When you open a document, you load the text from the disk into your computer's memory to display it in the text region of the document window.

Opening an Existing Document

Word makes it easy to open one of the last four documents you opened or created and saved. As you saw in the last lesson, the document COLLECT.DOC is listed at the bottom of the File menu, next to the underlined number 1. You can open a document by selecting it from the File menu.

Follow these steps to open the COLLECT document, which you saved in the last lesson:

1. Start Word for Windows.

2. Pull down the File menu and select COLLECT.DOC or press **1** to open the document and recall it to the text region.

Opening Other Documents

To open a document that is not listed on the File menu, click on the Open button in the toolbar (the second button on the left) to display the Open dialog box shown in Figure 6.1. With the keyboard, pull down the File menu and select **O**pen (Ctrl-F12).

The Open dialog box lists the files in the current directory that have a .DOC extension. Select the document you want to open, and then select OK. You can also double-click on the file name to open the document without clicking on OK.

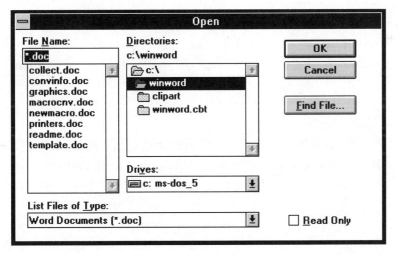

FIGURE 6.1:

The Open dialog box

The current directory will be shown highlighted in the Directories list box, and the drive will appear in the Drives text box. The default is drive C, the WINWORD directory. To open a file located in another drive or directory, type the drive letter and path, along with the file name, in the File Name text box, such as

D:\BUDGET\REPORT.DOC

To list files in another drive and directory, pull down the Drives list box and select the drive, then select the directory in the Directories list box.

If you saved your file with an extension other than .DOC, type *. followed by the extension in the File Name box, and then select OK to list the files with that extension in the dialog box.

If you want to open a document just to review or print it, select the Read Only option in the dialog box (the lower-right corner) before selecting OK. In this mode, Word will not allow you to resave the document under the same name, so the original is kept intact. If you make changes, you'll have to save the edited version with a different name, as explained in Lesson 5.

Opening a New Document

If you want to start working on a new document, either while a document is on the screen or after you have cleared a document, you can open an empty document window. Click on the New Document button on the toolbar (the first button on the left) to display a new, blank document.

With the keyboard, pull down the File menu and select New. Unlike the toolbar command, the menu command displays the New dialog box, shown in Figure 6.2.

This dialog box gives you the choice of creating a new document or a new template. Select OK to display an empty document window. (As you will learn in Lesson 24, a template is a special type of document that contains format instructions.)

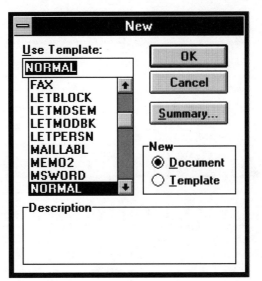

FIGURE 6.2:

The New dialog box

Moving the Insertion Point and Selecting Text

I n order to work with existing text, you must move the insertion point to the place where you want to make changes. For editing operations, you must first select the text that you want to affect. In this lesson, you will learn how to move the insertion point from place to place within a document and how to select text.

Moving the Insertion Point

You can move the insertion point by using the mouse, arrow keys, or certain key combinations. As you review these techniques described in the following sections, practice using them with the COLLECT document, which should still be on your screen. If you closed the document, open it now, as described in Lesson 6.

MOVING THE INSERTION POINT WITH THE MOUSE

If you have a mouse, you can move the insertion point by moving the I-beam. Place the I-beam where you want to enter, delete, or revise text, and then click the left button.

To move the insertion point to a part of the document that is not visible on the screen, you must first use the scroll bar on the right side of the window. Similar scroll bars appear in list boxes when there are more options than can be displayed at one time.

On the ends of the scroll bars are up- and down-pointing arrows, which are used to scroll up and down through the document. The box inside the scroll bar is called the *scroll box*, which can be dragged to scroll to a position within the document. Use the scroll bar as follows:

- To scroll line by line, click the up or down arrow on the ends of the scroll bar.

- To scroll screen by screen, click above or below the scroll box.

- To scroll to a specific position in the document, drag the scroll box to the relative position of the text. For example, drag the scroll box to the middle of the scroll bar to display text in the middle of the document.

The horizontal scroll bar at the bottom of the text area scrolls the text to the right or left, which is useful when you are working with documents that are too wide to fit on the screen.

After you scroll to another place in the document, use the mouse to position the I-beam where you want the insertion point to go in the displayed text and click the left button. If you just start typing after scrolling, the screen will scroll back to the position of the insertion point.

MOVING THE INSERTION POINT WITH THE KEYBOARD

The four basic insertion-point movement keys are the directional arrows. Your keyboard may have separate numeric and arrow-key keypads, or the number and arrows might be combined on a keypad. If they are on the same keypad and a number appears on the screen when you try to move the insertion point, you should see the letters NUM on the status bar. Press the Num Lock key to switch to the arrow-key function.

The arrow keys work as follows:

- The ↑ key moves the insertion point up one line. If the insertion point is on the first line in the window, lines above it will scroll down into view. Pressing the key has no effect when the insertion point is on the first line of the document.

- The ↓ key moves the insertion point down one line, except when it is on the last line of the document. (To move beyond the last line, press ↵.) If the insertion point is on the last line in the window, lines below it will scroll up into view.

- The → key moves the insertion point one character to the right. When it reaches the right margin, the insertion point will move to the first character of the next line.

- The ← key moves the insertion point one character to the left. When it reaches the left margin, the insertion point will move to the last character of the line above.

To move more than one line or character at a time, hold down any of the arrow keys. Its function will be repeated until you release the key.

There are many key combinations you can use to move the insertion point to specific places in a document. Table 7.1 lists these key combinations.

LOCATION	KEYPRESS
Previous word	Ctrl-←
Bottom of window	Ctrl-PgDn
Top of window	Ctrl-PgUp
Next paragraph	Ctrl-↓
Previous paragraph	Ctrl-↑
Next screen	PgDn
Previous screen	PgUp
Next page	F5 ↵
Previous page	F5, −1, ↵
Specific page	F5, *page number*, ↵
Next section	F5 S ↵
Specific section	F5, *section number*, ↵
Beginning of line	Home
End of line	End
Beginning of document	Ctrl-Home
End of document	Ctrl-End

TABLE 7.1:

Key Combinations for Moving the Insertion Point

Selecting Text

For many editing functions, you must select text, or highlight it to make the characters appear white on a black background. You can select any amount of text by using the mouse or keyboard. The selection always takes effect from the position of the insertion point. After text is selected, you can easily delete it, copy it, move it to another location, or change its appearance.

By default, Word will replace, or overtype, the selected text with the next character you type. So after you've selected some text, be careful not to press any character keys unless you intend to replace the selected text with those other characters.

SELECTING TEXT BY DRAGGING

To select text with a mouse, you drag from one end of the text to the other end, moving the I-beam or insertion point across the characters.

Follow these steps to select the first paragraph of the COLLECT document:

1. Position the I-beam at the beginning of the first paragraph.

2. Press and hold down the left mouse button, and then drag the pointer to the end of the paragraph. As you drag the mouse pointer, the text under it becomes highlighted, as shown in Figure 7.1.

3. Release the mouse button.

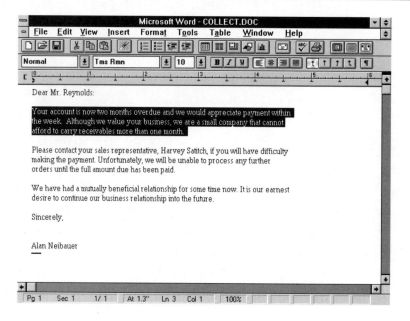

FIGURE 7.1:

Selected text

SELECTING PORTIONS OF TEXT WITH A MOUSE

You can also use the following methods to select portions of text with a mouse:

- To quickly select a single word, move the I-beam to the word and double-click the left button.

- To select an entire sentence, move the I-beam to a word within the sentence, hold down the Ctrl key, and then click the left button.

- To select sections of text without holding down the mouse button, place the insertion point at one end of the text, position the mouse pointer at the other end, hold down the Shift key, and then click the left button.

- To select sections of text by dragging without holding down a mouse button, position the insertion point at the start of the text and press F8. The letters EXT will appear in the status bar, indicating that Word is in extend mode. Move the pointer to the end of the text and click the left button. Press Esc to turn off extend mode.

USING THE SELECTION BAR WITH A MOUSE

The blank area in the left margin, between the text and the left edge of the screen, is called the *selection bar*. With a mouse, you can use the selection bar to quickly select portions of text.

Move the pointer to the area in the selection bar that is next to the text that you want to select, and then proceed as follows:

- To select one line, click the left button once.

- To select multiple lines, drag the pointer down.

- To select the paragraph, click the left button twice.

- To select multiple paragraphs, double-click and drag down on the second click.

- To select the entire document, hold down the Ctrl key and click the left button.

SELECTING TEXT WITH THE KEYBOARD

To quickly select text with the keyboard, press and hold down the Shift key while you move the insertion point with the arrow keys.

You can select portions of text by using the F8 function key. Press F8 to turn on extend mode, and the characters EXT will appear in the status bar. In extend mode, each time you press the F8 key, the selection increases to include the word, sentence, paragraph, section, then document, starting at the position of the insertion point. For example, to select the paragraph in which the insertion point currently appears, press F8 four times: once to change to extend mode, and then three more times to select the entire paragraph. Press Esc to turn off extend mode.

You can use the arrow keys in extend mode to select portions of text without holding down the Shift key.

Deselecting Text

You may need to *deselect* text, or remove the highlighting so your editing operations will not affect it. To quickly deselect all highlighted text, click the mouse. If you used the Shift key and arrow keys to select text, release the Shift key and press any arrow key to remove the highlighting. Deselect text highlighted in extend mode by pressing Esc to turn off extend mode, and then pressing any arrow key.

If you selected more text than you intended to, you can deselect the extra characters by dragging the pointer back over them. If you back up past the position where you originally started, the selection will extend in that direction.

Try out this feature now by deselecting the highlighted paragraph on your screen: click the mouse; release Shift and press an arrow key; or press Esc to turn off extend mode, and then press an arrow key. The highlighting will disappear.

Inserting and Deleting Characters and Page Breaks

As you revise a document, you will need to insert and delete text. You may also need to add or remove formatting characters (such as tab spaces), split or join paragraphs, and insert or delete page breaks. In this lesson, you will learn how to make these basic changes.

Inserting Text and Spaces

Inserting new text or tab spaces is as easy as placing the insertion point and typing or pressing the Tab key. Using the techniques for moving the insertion point that you learned in Lesson 7, you can easily add text and formatting to your COLLECT document. Follow these steps:

1. Make sure that the letters OVR are not on the status bar, indicating that Word is in overtype mode. If they do appear, press the Ins key (with the Num Lock function turned off).

2. Place the insertion point at the start of the first sentence, on the Y in *Your*.

3. Press the Tab key.

This indents the first line ½ inch. The remaining text shifts to the right and down, adjusting automatically to the inserted spaces, as shown in Figure 8.1.

4. Move the insertion point to the beginning of the next paragraph of the document and press the Tab key to insert a tab space at the beginning of the second paragraph.

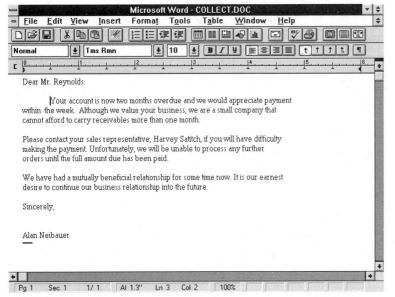

FIGURE 8.1:

A tab space inserted to indent a sentence

5. Move the insertion point to the beginning of the third paragraph and press Tab to indent this line.

6. Move the insertion point to just after the word *small* in the first paragraph and type **privately owned**. The rest of the paragraph will adjust to accommodate the new characters.

Deleting Text

Word provides many ways to delete characters, or erase mistakes. The simplest methods involve using the Backspace and Del keys.

To erase a character to the left of the insertion point, press the Backspace key. To erase several characters, hold down the Backspace key, and the characters to the left will continue to be deleted until you release the Backspace key. Press Ctrl-Backspace to delete the word to the left of the insertion point.

To erase a character to the right of the insertion point, or to erase selected text, press the Del key. To delete several characters to the right of the insertion point, hold down the Del key; or first select the characters with the mouse or keyboard, and then press Del once. Press Ctrl-Del to quickly erase characters from the insertion point to the end of the word.

Let's try these techniques now to erase text from the COLLECT document. You will delete the words *your sales representative* from the second paragraph.

1. Place the I-beam just before the word *your* in the second paragraph of the document.

2. Hold down the left mouse button and drag the pointer to just before the name *Harvey*.

3. Release the button, and then press Del.

To delete these words using the keyboard, position the insertion point just before the word *your* and then press and hold down the Del key. Release the Del key when the comma before the name *Harvey* is erased.

4. To delete the comma after the name *Satitch*, move the insertion point to just after the comma and press Backspace.

Replacing Characters as You Type

So far, you've learned how to edit text by first deleting incorrect characters, then inserting new ones in their place. This type of editing is done in insert mode. You can also replace text by selecting it, and then typing the new characters. The selected text will be deleted when you start typing.

Another way to replace text is to *overtype* characters. In overtype mode, the new characters you type replace existing ones. To enter overtype mode, press Ins. The characters OVR will appear on the status bar. Now one character will be deleted for every one you type. To return to insert mode, press Ins again. The characters OVR will disappear from the status bar, and any text you type will be added to existing text rather than replacing it.

Overtyping is a fast way to change mistakes. However, it has limited value because you can easily erase words accidentally as you continue typing. It is most useful when you are replacing characters with the same number of new ones.

Let's try using overtype mode:

1. Place the insertion point in front of the letter *o* of the word *one* in the first paragraph.

2. Press the Ins key, and the characters OVR appear on the status bar.

3. Type **30 days**. Because Word is in overtype mode, the new characters replaced the ones that were there.

4. Press Del twice to delete the remainder of the word *month*. Figure 8.2 shows the document at this point.

5. Press the Ins key to turn off overtype mode.

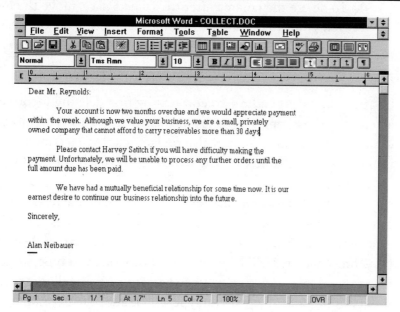

FIGURE 8.2:

Edited document

Remember, in many cases it is better to edit text in insert mode. Even changing a single character is just as fast in insert mode. You simply type the new character, and then press Del.

Splitting and Combining Paragraphs

The basic editing methods you use to insert and delete characters are also used to divide one paragraph into two, or combine two paragraphs into one.

To combine two paragraphs into one, position the insertion point immediately after the first paragraph you want to combine and press Del. The paragraph below will move up one line. If one Del press doesn't do the trick, there might be some extra spaces between the end of the sentence and the paragraph code. Keep pressing Del until the second paragraph moves up. Also, if you double-spaced paragraphs by pressing ↵ twice, or indented the second paragraph by pressing Tab, you'll have to press Del more than once.

You can just as easily split one paragraph into two. Place the insertion point at the beginning of the sentence you want to start the new paragraph, and then press ↵. The text of that paragraph, from the insertion-point position down, will move to the next line. If you have indented the other paragraphs, press Tab to insert a tab space. If you double-spaced between paragraphs, press ↵ again.

Undoing Mistakes

Word provides the Undo command for reversing certain editing operations. For example, if you just deleted an entire paragraph by accident, you can use the Undo command instead of retyping all the text. The Undo command can be used to both restore text and delete it.

To use the Undo command, click on the Undo button in the toolbar (the icon of an eraser). With the keyboard, pull down the Edit menu and select Undo, or press Ctrl-Z. If you reversed a deletion, the text you removed will reappear in its original position, even if you have moved the insertion point. When you use Undo after inserting text, the new text will disappear. Undo works on any text you typed since you last moved the insertion point or used the Undo command.

On the Edit menu, the full name of the Undo command depends on the action you took just before pulling down the menu, although the shortcut key is always Ctrl-Z. For example, it may appear as Undo Typing, Undo Formatting, Undo Cut, or Undo Edit Clear.

Now we will edit the COLLECT document and see how helpful the Undo command can be:

1. Move the insertion point to the first character in the beginning of the document and press ↵ twice to insert two blank lines at the top.

2. Move the insertion point to the first blank line and type the following:

March 14, 1993

Mr. Paul Reynolds
Reynolds Automotive
45 Locust Lane
Mount Carmel, NJ 18985

3. Select and delete the entire last paragraph by clicking twice in the selection bar next to the paragraph and then pressing Del. With the keyboard, press F8 four times, then press Del.

4. Move the insertion point to the beginning of the document and click on the Undo button in the toolbar. With the keyboard, pull down the Edit menu and select Undo Edit Clear (Ctrl-Z). The last paragraph will reappear in its original position, just as it was before you deleted it, even though you moved the insertion point.

5. Click the mouse button or press an arrow key to deselect the text.

Now let's see how Undo can be used to quickly delete text without selecting it first.

6. Place the insertion point just before the period at the end of the last paragraph, press the spacebar, and then type this phrase:

because we need the money.

7. Click on the Undo button in the toolbar or select Undo Typing from the Edit menu (Ctrl-Z). The characters you just entered will be erased.

8. Save the edited document by clicking on the Save button or pulling down the File menu and selecting Save (Shift-F12).

Inserting and Deleting Hard Page Breaks

As you already know, Word divides the document into pages as you type. When you reach the end of one page, Word displays a row of dots across the screen and increments the page number indicator in the status bar. This type of page break is called a *soft break* because its position can change as you insert or delete text. However, if you do not want to wait until Word ends the page, you can insert a hard page break.

Suppose that you are typing a short memo or letter and a second page to which it refers. You want the memo printed on a page by itself, so you need to tell Word to end the page. This is called a *hard page break*, and it is entered by pressing Ctrl-↵. A solid line will appear across the screen, indicating that a new page will begin at this point, and the page number indicator on the status bar will increase.

As an example, we'll add another page of information to the COLLECT document and separate it from the letter with a hard page break.

1. Place the insertion point at the end of the document and press ↵ to insert a blank line.

2. Press Ctrl-↵ to insert a hard page break, as shown in Figure 8.3.

The line across the screen shows that Word will always start a new page at this location, no matter how much text you add or delete in the document.

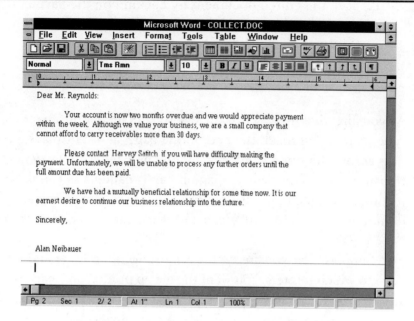

3. Type the following text:

Unpaid Invoices

December 1992	$875.98
January 1993	$563.87
February 1993	$834.76

4. Click on the Print button in the toolbar to print the document. With the keyboard, pull down the File menu and select Print (Ctrl-Shift-F12) and then choose OK. The letter now appears on its own page.

You can remove a hard page break if you change your mind about ending the page at that location. Simply delete the page break line using the Del or Backspace key.

5. Double-click on the page break line to select it, or place the insertion point on the line, and then press Del.

6. Press ↵ five times to separate the letter from the list of unpaid invoices.

7. Click on the Save button in the toolbar to save the edited document. With the keyboard, pull down the File menu and select Save (Shift-F12).

This lesson has covered some common editing techniques. The other revisions commonly made to documents involve moving and copying text. You will learn how to move and copy text in the next lesson.

FEATURING

Changing the location of text
Duplicating text
▼

Moving and Copying Text

You've seen how easy it is to insert and delete characters in your document. It is just as easy to make major changes in the text by moving and copying entire sections of text from one location to another. In this lesson, you will learn more about editing your documents with Word.

Moving Text with the Mouse

Word allows you to move text using a technique called *drag and drop*. With this method, you select the text you want to move and place the mouse pointer over the selected area. The I-beam will change to a small arrow. Hold down the left mouse button and drag the mouse to the new location. The pointer will change to include a small dotted box, and a dotted insertion point will move along with it in the text. When the dotted insertion point is where you want the text to appear, release the mouse button.

Now we will improve our COLLECT document by rearranging the text:

1. If you quit Word, start the program and open COLLECT.

2. To select the second sentence in the first paragraph, place the I-beam in the sentence, hold down the Ctrl key, and click the left mouse button.

3. Hold down the left mouse button and drag the pointer until the dotted insertion point is at the end of the last paragraph.

4. Release the mouse pointer, and the highlighted text will appear at the new location.

5. Click the mouse button to deselect the text.

6. To insert a space to separate the two sentences, place the pointer just in front of the word *Although*, click the left mouse button, and press the spacebar.

Copying Text with the Mouse

By using the *right* mouse button, you can easily copy text from one location to another. Follow these steps to copy text in the COLLECT document:

1. In the first paragragh, select *we would appreciate payment within the week.*

2. Place the I-beam at the end of the last paragraph.

3. Hold down the Ctrl and Shift keys, and then click the *right* mouse button. A copy of the highlighted text will appear at the location of the I-beam.

4. Add a space to separate the sentences, and change the *w* in *we* to uppercase.

5. Click on the Print button in the toolbar to print a copy of the letter. With the keyboard, pull down the File menu and select Print (Ctrl-Shift-F12), and then select OK.

6. Click on the Save button in the toolbar to save the edited document. With the keyboard, pull down the File menu and select Save (Shift-F12).

7. Double-click on the close box. With the keyboard, press Alt-F4.

Another way to quickly move and copy text is by using the Repeat command. Pull down the Edit menu and select Repeat (F4) to duplicate the last action you took, whether it was typing, inserting, deleting, or formatting text.

Moving and Copying Text Using the Clipboard

You can also move and copy text with or without using the toolbar through the Clipboard. The *Clipboard* is a special area in the computer's memory where Word temporarily stores text. The Clipboard can even store text and pictures so that you can move them between Word and other applications, such as Microsoft Excel.

To move text, select the text and then click on the Cut button in the toolbar (with the scissors icon). With the keyboard, pull down the Edit menu and select Cut (Ctrl-X or Shift-Del). The text will disappear from the screen. Place the insertion point where you want to insert the text and click on the Paste button in the toolbar (the sixth one from the left).

With the keyboard, pull down the Edit menu and select Paste (Ctrl-V or Shift-Ins).

To copy text, select the text and then click on the Copy button in the toolbar (the fifth one on the left). With the keyboard, pull down the Edit menu and select Copy (Ctrl-C or Ctrl-Ins). Place the insertion point where you want to insert the copied text and click on the Paste button, or select Paste from the Edit menu (Ctrl-V or Shift-Ins).

Any text already in the Clipboard will be erased when you add new text to it, so do not select Cut or Copy again until you are finished with the text that is currently stored. If you do, the characters originally deleted will be erased from the computer's memory, and you won't be able to insert them elsewhere.

If you have to delete something before you complete the move operation, use the Del or Backspace key instead. These keys delete text without placing it in the Clipboard, so the characters you deleted will not affect the text that is stored there. You can also use Ctrl-Del (to delete the word after the I-beam) or Ctrl-Backspace (to delete the word before the I-beam) to delete text without placing it in the Clipboard.

Moving and Copying Text with Function Keys

With the keyboard, you can move and copy text using the F2 key and the Shift-F2 key combination. To move selected text, press F2 to see the prompt

Move to where?

in the status bar. Place the insertion point where you want to position the text. The insertion point will appear as a dotted vertical line at the new position. Press ↵ to move the text to that location.

You can also move text by first positioning the insertion point, and then pressing F2 to display the prompt

Move from where?

Select the text you want to move, and it will be underlined with a dotted line rather than highlighted. Press ↵ to move the selected text to the original position of the insertion point.

To copy selected text, press Shift-F2 to see the prompt

Copy to where?

Position the insertion point and press ↵. You can also position the insertion point at the new location first, press Shift-F2, select the text you wish to copy, and press ↵.

Using the Spelling Checker and Thesaurus

Even if you win spelling bees and are an excellent typist, typing errors will find their way into your documents. You can use Word's spelling checker to correct many of them. Another writing and editing tool provided by Word is a thesaurus, which is useful for looking up synonyms (or antonyms) for words. In this lesson, you will learn how each of these features works.

Checking Your Spelling

When you start the spelling checker, Word compares each word in your document with those stored in its own dictionary. If it encounters a word that is not in its list, it reports the word as not found, but not necessarily incorrect. For example, names, technical terms, and foreign words that are spelled correctly will be reported as possible errors because they are not in Word's dictionary. If you frequently use words that are not in the dictionary, you can add them to a supplemental dictionary.

You should be aware that Word cannot determine if you used the wrong word when it is correctly spelled. For instance, it won't report that you used *too* instead of *to* or *two*, or typed *doing* instead of *going*. However, it will find repeated words, such as *the the*.

RUNNING THE SPELLING CHECKER

In the following steps, you will enter a short document that includes some misspelled words, and then use the spelling checker to find and correct errors.

1. Start Word and type the following paragraphs. Be sure to include the errors.

   > **Nellie Watson, former burlesq leading lady and wife of show operator and star SLiding Billy Watson, was shot and killed at at the Three Hundred Club on April 7, 1926.**
   >
   > **Mrs. Watson, who retirred from burlesque in 1918, appeared with her husband in Girls from Happyland between 1910 and 1911.**

2. Place the insertion point at the start of the document.

3. Click on the Spelling button in the toolbar (the one to the left of the Print button). With the keyboard, pull down the Tools menu and select Spelling. The first time you use the spelling checker, Word displays a dialog box asking if you

want to create a custom dictionary to store your own words. Select Yes to start the checking process.

Word finds the first possible error and displays the dialog box shown in Figure 10.1. In this case, the name *Nellie* is not in Word's dictionary. The word is highlighted in the text and appears in the Not in Dictionary text box. Suggested spellings appear in the Suggestions list box, with the first word in the list also displayed in the Change To text box. If the correct spelling is not shown in the text box, select the word in the list.

4. Since the word is spelled correctly, select Ignore All to accept the word as spelled for the remainder of the current checking session and continue the spelling check.

5. At the next unknown word, *Watson*, select Ignore All.

The spelling checker moves to the word *burlesq.* The correct spelling of the word is shown in the Change To text box.

6. Select Change to replace the word in the document with the word in the Change To text box.

FIGURE 10.1:

The Spelling dialog box

The next error located is *SLiding* because of the incorrect capitalization. Notice that Not in Dictionary has changed to Capitalization.

7. Select Change to correct the typing error.

Next, Word detects the repetition of the word *at*. Now the text box showing the error is labeled Repeated Word.

8. Select the Delete button (which replaced the Change button) to remove the extra word from the text.

9. At the next word, *retirred*, select Change to accept the correct spelling in the text box.

The next word to appear is *Happyland*. Suppose that this is a word that you will use often. You can speed up your spelling checks by adding this word to Word's dictionary.

10. Select Add to add the word to the supplemental dictionary shown in the Add Words To text box, CUSTOM.DIC.

Since the entire document has now been checked, a dialog box will appear with the message

The spelling check is complete.

11. Select OK.

There are several other choices you can make during a spelling check. Choose Ignore to indicate that the word is spelled as you want it in this one instance. The program will look for the next misspelled word. Change All changes each occurrence of the word in the document to the word in the Change To text box. Undo Last reverses up to the last five changes. If you want to close the dialog box and stop the spelling check, choose Cancel or press Esc. This button changes to Close once you perform an action that cannot be reversed.

Sometimes none of Word's alternate spellings are the correct word. To have Word look up other possible spellings for you, select Change To, enter the word, then select Suggest. You can use the wild-card characters * and ?. A *wild-card* character is one that stands for any character or several characters. Each ? will be replaced in the search by a single character, each * by any number of characters. For example, looking up *f?r* will display *far, fir, for,* and *fur.* If you entered *f*r*, you would see words that begin with *f* and end with *r,* such as *fabricator,* and *f-number.*

CHECKING PORTIONS OF A DOCUMENT

Word begins the spelling process at the position of the insertion point. If the insertion point was not at the start of the document when you began the process, when Word reaches the end of your text, you will see a dialog box with the message

Do you want to continue checking at the beginning of the document?

Select Yes to wrap around to the beginning of the document and complete the check, or choose No to stop.

If you select text before beginning the spelling check, Word checks the words in the selection. To check a single word, place the insertion point in the word and press F7. When the spelling check of the selected text or word has been completed, a dialog box will appear with the question

Do you want to continue checking the remainder of the document?

Select Yes if you want Word to check the other text, or choose No to stop checking.

USING OTHER SPELLING CHECKER OPTIONS

When you select Options in the Spelling dialog box, Word displays a dialog box with options for customizing the spelling check process, as shown in Figure 10.2. (This dialog box can also be displayed by pulling down the Tools menu, selecting **O**ptions, and then choosing the Spelling category.)

Select Words in **U**ppercase to have Word skip over words that are all capital letters, such as acronyms and special technical terms. Select Words with **N**umbers to have Word skip works that contain numbers, such as F12 or C3PO.

If you turn off the Always **S**uggest option, Word will not automatically display suggested spellings for words not found in the dictionary. Then, during a spelling check, you will have to select Suggest to see suggested words.

Setting Up Special Dictionaries

If you purchase a special computer dictionary, such as one that includes legal or medical terms, you may wish to use it as the primary spelling reference. You might also want to create specialized custom dictionaries to store technical words, names, and foreign words that you use often.

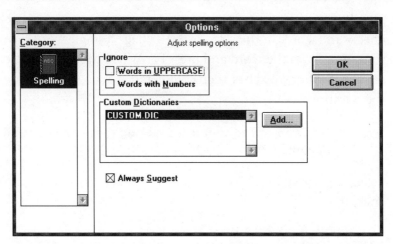

FIGURE 10.2:

The Options dialog box for the Spelling category

To create or use another dictionary, pull down the Tools menu, select Options, and then choose the Spelling category (or start the spelling check and select the Options button in the dialog box). Select Add, and you will be asked to enter the name of the custom dictionary you want to create or open. Type the dictionary name, and then select OK.

Working with Foreign Languages

If you work in a language other than English, your document will contain many words that are not in the English-language dictionary. Rather than have these words reported as spelling errors, you can have Word use the correct foreign-language dictionary (if you have it available) for your document.

Before typing text in a foreign language, pull down the Format menu and select Language to display the dialog box shown in Figure 10.3. Select the language you will be using, and then choose OK. Select Use as Default if you want to type every document in that language.

When Word reaches that section of text during the spelling check process, it will use the appropriate dictionary. If it cannot find the language's dictionary on your disk, you will see a dialog box with a message to this effect.

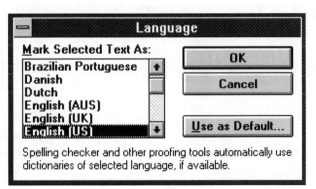

FIGURE 10.3:

The Language dialog box

Using the Thesaurus

When you are looking for just the right word, or want to avoid repeating the same word or phrase, use Word's thesaurus to look up alternative words. This not only builds your vocabulary, but it also enhances the quality of your documents.

In the following steps, you will use the thesaurus on the document you entered at the beginning of this lesson. Let's start by looking for a synonym for the word *former* in the first paragraph.

1. Place the insertion point anywhere in the word *former*.

2. Pull down the Tools menu and select Thesaurus (Shift-F7) to see the dialog box shown in Figure 10.4.

Two meanings, or definitions, of the word *former* are listed in the Meanings list box. Since the highlighted definition is correct in this case, you can select one of the alternatives shown in the Synonyms list box.

Sometimes the Meanings list box will include the options Related Words and Antonyms. Related Words usually shows the root of the selected word, such as *form* for *former*. Antonyms lists words with opposite meanings.

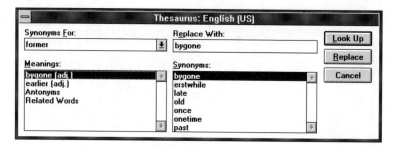

FIGURE 10.4:

The Thesaurus dialog box

3. Select Synonyms, then the word *onetime.*

4. Select the Replace button (on the right side of the dialog box) to insert it in place of *former* in the text.

5. Place the insertion point cursor on the word *operator,* and then pull down the Tools menu and select Thesaurus (Shift-F7).

None of the suggested synonyms for the highlighted meaning, *user,* seem appropriate, so let's see synonyms for the meaning *director.*

6. Select *director* in the Meanings list box. With the keyboard, press Alt-M, then ↓.

Synonyms for that definition now appear in the list box. However, none of these are correct either. You can use the Look Up option to list additional choices for the word highlighted in the Synonyms box.

7. Select the Look Up button (on the right side of the dialog box). A list of additional meanings and synonyms will appear in the dialog box.

8. Select *moving-picture director* in the Meanings list box, and the words change in the Synonym list box.

9. Select *producer* from the Synonyms list box, and then choose Replace.

10. Pull down the File menu and select Exit (Alt-F4), and then choose No to exit Word.

If you are trying to think of a word but don't know where to begin, type a word with a similar meaning in the Synonyms For text box, even if you know it's not the one you want. This will be a starting place for your search. If a suitable replacement doesn't appear, select other definitions from the Meanings list box, or highlight an alternative in the

Synonyms list box and select Look Up. If your search takes you too far from your original word, pull down the Synonyms For list box and select your original word.

One of the common mistakes people make when using a thesaurus is to select a word listed as a synonym but whose definition just doesn't fit, such as substituting *driver* for *operator* in the previous example. Be sure to refer to the Meanings list box to verify that the replacement word means exactly what you intended.

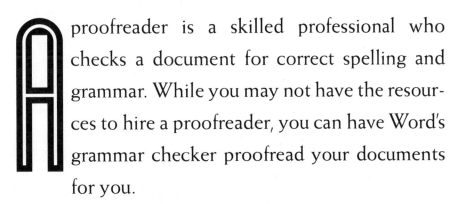

FEATURING

Correcting grammatical errors

Checking reading levels

Customizing grammar checking

▼

Proofing Your Documents

A proofreader is a skilled professional who checks a document for correct spelling and grammar. While you may not have the resources to hire a proofreader, you can have Word's grammar checker proofread your documents for you.

To further help ensure that your document will be understood by those who will be reading it, after proofreading your document, Word will analyze it according to grade level and reading ease, letting you know how easy or difficult the document is to read. In this lesson, you will learn how to use Word's grammar checker.

Checking Your Grammar

The Grammar option in the Tools menu checks your document for spelling errors and for sentences that violate standard rules of grammar. It will suggest actions that you can take to improve the grammar in your document, and it can automatically correct certain types of errors, such as mismatched tenses.

Let's see how this powerful feature works by proofreading the COLLECT document.

1. Start Word and open COLLECT.

2. Pull down the Tools menu and select **Grammar**.

Word begins to check your document for spelling and grammatical errors. The first error detected is the possible misspelled word *Carmel* in the address. Word highlights the sentence and displays the Spelling dialog box.

3. Select Ignore.

4. When the next possible error, *Satitch* appears in the Spelling dialog box, select Ignore again.

Word now finds a sentence that violates one of its grammatical rules. It highlights the entire sentence and displays the dialog box shown in Figure 11.1.

The sentence containing the error is shown in the Sentence list box and the word *orders* appears in boldface. The Suggestions text box includes two possible actions you can take to correct the sentence.

5. Select Change to accept the highlighted suggestion, replacing the word *orders* with *order*.

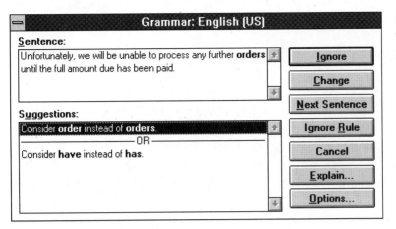

FIGURE 11.1:

The Grammar dialog box

Word now detects another problem in the same sentence and displays the words *has been paid* in boldface. The suggestion includes the comment

This verb group may appear in the passive voice

In this case, Word cannot make the correction for you, so you have to return to the document to enter it yourself.

6. Click in the document window or press Ctrl-Tab to return to the document without closing the Grammar dialog box.

7. Deselect the text, and then edit the sentence to read

Unfortunately, we will be unable to process any further order until you pay the full amount that is now due.

8. Continue the grammar checking process by clicking on the Start button, which replaced the Ignore button. With the keyboard, pull down the Tools menu and select **G**rammar.

Word now stops at the word *receivables* and displays the Spelling dialog box.

9. Press the Backspace key to delete the word in the Change To text box, type **unpaid invoices**, and then select Change.

10. When Word stops at your name in the closing, select Ignore to continue.

Since the entire document was checked, Word displays the Readability Statistics dialog box, shown in Figure 11.2. This dialog box displays statistics about your document and evaluates it according to several standard readability indexes. It reports on the complexity of your sentence structure, so you can edit the document to increase or decrease its level to better match the intended audience.

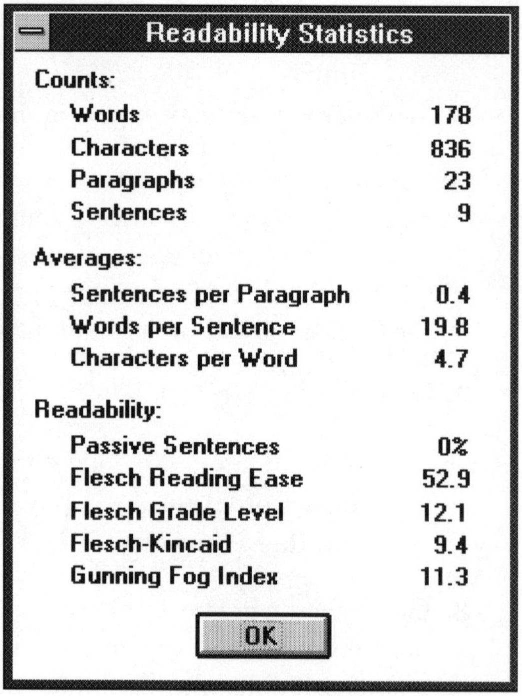

Readability Statistics

Counts:	
Words	178
Characters	836
Paragraphs	23
Sentences	9

Averages:	
Sentences per Paragraph	0.4
Words per Sentence	19.8
Characters per Word	4.7

Readability:	
Passive Sentences	0%
Flesch Reading Ease	52.9
Flesch Grade Level	12.1
Flesch-Kincaid	9.4
Gunning Fog Index	11.3

[OK]

FIGURE 11.2:

The Readability Statistics dialog box

11. Select OK.

12. Pull down the File menu and select Exit (Alt-F4), and then choose Yes to exit Word and save the edited document.

There are several other buttons in the Grammar dialog box that you can use during the grammar checking process. Choose Ignore to make no changes and continue. The Next Sentence option skips this and any other error in the sentence and continues checking with the next sentence in the document. Choose Ignore Rule when you want to ignore the grammatical rule violated in this sentence for the remainder of the document. If you select Explain, you will see a dialog box explaining the grammatical rule that was violated. Choose Cancel or press Esc to end the grammar checking process.

Customizing the Grammar Checker

You can customize the way Word checks for grammatical errors using the dialog box shown in Figure 11.3. To display this dialog box, pull down the Tools menu, select Grammar, and then select the Options button in the Grammar dialog box (or pull down the Tools menu, select Options, and then choose the Grammar category).

First, select a rule group that you want to apply generally to your document:

- Strictly (All Rules): Applies all of Word's grammatical rules when checking your document. This process will take the longest but will catch all possible errors.

- Business Writing: Applies the rules that are most important or common in business documents (fewer than All Rules).

- Casual Writing: Applies the fewest rules. Use this option for personal, informal correspondence.

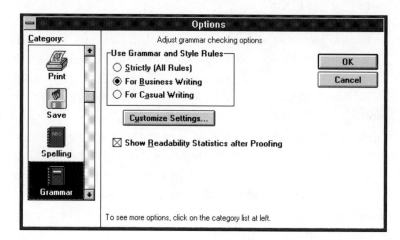

FIGURE 11.3:

The Options dialog box for the Grammar category

If you do not want to see the Readability Statistics dialog box after a grammar check, select Show Readability Statistics after Proofing. This option is turned on by default.

Legal, technical, and some literary writing styles may include certain conventions that violate strict grammatical rules. For example, legal documents often include standard clauses in the passive voice; literary works may include colloquialisms and dialogue. You can turn off specific rules by selecting Customize Settings to display the dialog box shown in Figure 11.4.

Select the check boxes to turn off or on specific grammatical and style rules. For information about a rule, highlight it and select Explain.

If you prefer to use the spelling checker and grammar checker separately, scroll through the Grammar list box and select Spelling Errors. When you check your documents for grammar, possible spelling errors will be ignored.

In the Catch section of the dialog box, the options control how Word applies the following rules:

- Split Infinitives: Designate the number of words between *to* and the verb that will trigger a split infinitive error. The

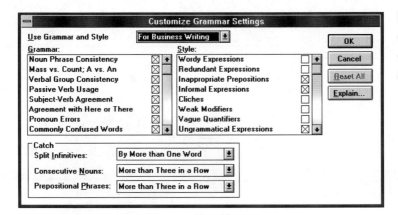

FIGURE 11.4:

Customization options for the grammar checker

options are Always, By More Than One Word, By More Than Two Words, By More Than Three Words, and Never. Selecting two words, for example, will allow *to strongly demand* but not *to very strongly depend*. Select Never to accept all split infinitives.

- Consecutive Nouns: Specify the number of consecutive nouns that will trigger an error. The options are By More Than Two in a Row, By More Than Three in a Row, By More Than Four in a Row, and Never.

- Prepositional Phrases: Designate the number of prepositional phrases that will cause an error. The options are the same as those for consecutive nouns.

This concludes our lessons on basic editing with Word. In the following lessons, you will learn how to use Word's formatting features to change the appearance of your documents.

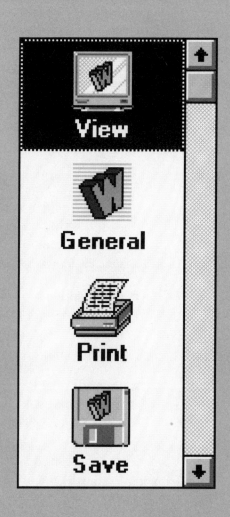

PART 3

Formatting Your Documents

FEATURING

Boldfacing, underlining, and italicizing

Changing type styles

Changing cases

▼

Formatting Characters

To make your documents more attractive and effective, you will want to use different character styles and typefaces for particular text. In this lesson, you will learn how to use Word's ribbon, as well as it's other commands, for formatting your characters.

Selecting Character Styles

With Word, you can format characters as boldfaced, underlined, double-underlined, italic, superscripts, subscripts, and small capital letters. Word can display most of these effects on the screen, as shown in Figure 12.1. If some of the effects do not appear on your screen, it is because your printer is not capable of producing them in the selected font. In this case, Word will display and print the characters normally.

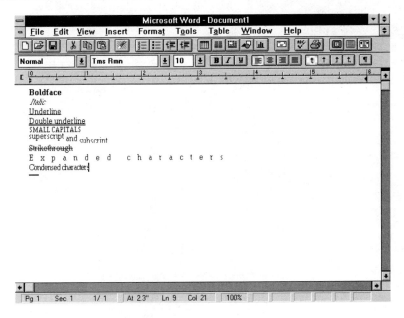

FIGURE 12.1:

Special character effects are displayed on screen

FORMATTING WITH THE RIBBON AND KEY COMBINATIONS

The *ribbon* contains text boxes and option buttons for formatting characters. You select the character formats you want from the ribbon, and then type the text. Table 12.1 shows the ribbon icons and text boxes and their functions.

To use the ribbon, click on the button that represents the format you want to select. With the keyboard, press Ctrl and the letter in the option box. For example, use Ctrl-B to boldface, and Ctrl-U to underline.

In this book, the instructions for using the ribbon will give the button name along with the key combination, as in "select the Underline button (Ctrl-U)." This means to move the mouse pointer to the Underline button in the ribbon (the button with the U), and then click the left

TABLE 12.1:

Ribbon Icons

ICON	NAME	FUNCTION	KEY COMBINATION
Normal ⏷	Style	Selects a style	Ctrl-S
CG Times (WN) ⏷	Font	Selects a font	Ctrl-F
10 ⏷	Point Size	Selects a point size	Ctrl-P
B	Bold	Boldfaces text	Ctrl-B
I	Italic	Italicizes text	Ctrl-I
U	Underline	Underlines text	Ctrl-U
≡	Left	Left justifies text	Ctrl-L
≡	Center	Centers text	Ctrl-E
≡	Right	Right aligns text	Ctrl-R
	Full Justify	Justifies text	Ctrl-J
↑	Left Tab	Creates a left tab stop	
↑	Center Tab	Creates a centered tab stop	
↑	Right Tab	Creates a right tab stop	
↑	Decimal Tab	Creates a decimal tab stop	
¶	Show All	Toggles special characters on and off	

mouse button. Even if you have a mouse, you should become familiar with the Ctrl keystrokes since they can be used even when the ribbon is not displayed.

When one of the buttons is selected, or turned on, it appears pressed down. (With lower resolution and two-color monitors, the button will appear in reverse.) In Figure 12.1, the ribbon reflects the default format used by Word: left-aligned text and left-aligned tab stops. As you move the insertion point or format text, the appropriate icons will appear pushed in or become highlighted to indicate the formats you selected.

You can change the appearance of characters as you type them or by selecting them afterward. You can format characters using the ribbon, Ctrl-key combinations, or the Character dialog box. However, the dialog box is the only method that provides access to all the available formats.

Let's start by formatting characters using the ribbon and Ctrl-key combinations.

1. Start Word for Windows.

2. Type **I subscribe to the**, then press the spacebar.

3. Select the Underline button on the ribbon (Ctrl-U) to underline the next text you type.

4. Type **New York Times**. The words and the spaces between them will be underlined as they appear, as shown in Figure 12.2.

5. Select the Underline button (Ctrl-U) again to turn off underlining.

6. Type **and** in normal text, and then press the spacebar.

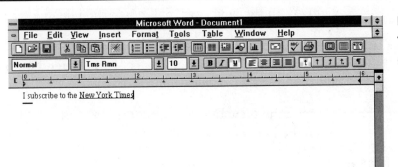

FIGURE 12.2:

Text underlined on screen

7. Select the Bold button on the ribbon (Ctrl-B) to turn on boldface for the next characters.

8. Type **I read it daily**.

9. Select the Bold button (Ctrl-B) again to turn off boldface.

10. Type the period (.) in normal text.

Now let's combine styles by selecting two character formats. We'll add a sentence in underlined italics.

11. Press ↵.

12. Select the Underline button on the ruler (Ctrl-U), and then select the Italic button (Ctrl-I) to turn on both underline and italics.

13. Type **Reading this much makes me smart**. The text will appear in both formats. If the characters do not appear italic on your screen, you do not have an italic font available.

14. Press Ctrl-spacebar. This turns off both character formats at one time.

Now let's see how your formatted characters appear on the page.

15. Click on the Print button in the toolbar to print the document. With the keyboard, pull down the File menu and select Print (Ctrl-Shift-F12), then OK

16. Pull down the File menu and select Close, then No to clear the document without saving it.

17. Click on the New Document button. With the keyboard, pull down the File menu and select New, and then select OK.

If you have already typed the text and want to add formatting, first select the characters, and then choose the format from the ribbon or press the Ctrl-key combination. To immediately format other characters in the same way, highlight them, and then press F4 or pull down the Edit menu and select **R**epeat Formatting (F4).

To remove a character format, highlight the text you want to change, and then select the formats you want to remove to turn them off. Press Ctrl-spacebar to cancel all character formats.

There are other character formats that are not available in the ribbon. The key combinations that select them are listed in Table 12.2.

FORMATTING CHARACTERS THROUGH MENU COMMANDS

As an alternative to using the ribbon or Ctrl-key combinations, you can add the same character styles through the Character dialog box (which you saw in Lesson 2).

As with the ribbon, the Character dialog box options can be used to format text about to be typed as well as existing text. Select the characters to be formatted, or type until you are ready to enter formatted

TABLE 12.2:

Other Formatting Key Combinations

KEY COMBINATION	FORMAT
Ctrl-W	Underline words, not spaces
Ctrl-D	Double underline
Ctrl-K	Small capital letters
Ctrl-A	All capital letters
Ctrl-H	Hidden text—text that you can hide from display (see Lesson 36)
Ctrl-Shift-Equal	Superscript, 3 pts
Ctrl-Equal	Subscript, 3 pts

characters. Then pull down the Format menu and select Character to display the Format Character dialog box (see Figure 2.3), make your selections, and choose OK.

You can also remove character formats through the Character dialog box. Highlight the text, select Character from the Format menu, and then choose the formats you want to turn off to remove the X from the option box. The text in the Sample box will show how your characters will appear.

The Character dialog box provides access to all character formats, even those not available in the ribbon or through Ctrl-key combinations. With the dialog box, you can also select the following character formats:

- Select Strikethrough to indicate text you want to delete.

- Change the color of text.

- Expand character spacing to spread out text to fit a specific area, such as widening a headline to fill a column. Choose Expanded in the Spacing box, then enter the number of points in the By text box. You can expand spacing as much as 14 points between individual characters.

- Condense spacing between characters by up to 1.75 points. This is useful for headlines that would not normally fit between the margins or across a column.

- Change the default typeface and style used for new documents (which you can also do with the ribbon, as described in the next section).

Changing Typefaces and Point Sizes

If your printer can reproduce different typefaces and sizes, you can use Word to give your documents a desktop-published, professional look. Keep in mind that not all printers have this capability; only certain types, such as laser printers, can print in several type styles and sizes.

Font refers to the general shape or design of the characters. Some common fonts are Courier, Times Roman, and Helvetica. Fonts come in many sizes. They usually are measured in points, which designate the height of the characters. There are about 72 points to an inch, so if you're using a 12-point font, you can print six lines of type in 1 inch. Larger type sizes are usually used for titles and headlines.

The default font used by Word depends on your printer, but it usually results in approximately six lines per inch on the printed page. The fonts available for your documents depend on your printer. Refer to your printer manual to see which styles and sizes you can print.

As with other character formats, you can change type styles and sizes by using the ribbon, Ctrl-key combinations, or the Character dialog box.

CHANGING TYPE STYLES WITH THE RIBBON AND KEY COMBINATIONS

As shown in Table 12.1, the ribbon contains Font and Point Size text boxes. Follow these steps to select fonts using the ribbon:

1. In a new document window, type **This is the default font**, and then press ↵. When you print this document, the line will appear in your printer's default font.

2. Click on the arrow in the ribbon's Font box to display a list of fonts available for your printer. With the keyboard, press Ctrl-F, then ↓ to display the Font list box.

Figure 12.3 shows an example of the list of fonts. Your fonts may be different.

Fonts that have a printer icon on the left are available in your printer. The other fonts listed are *screen fonts*. Depending on your printer, Word may be able to print these fonts, but their printed quality might be unsatisfactory.

3. Select one of the fonts available on your printer.

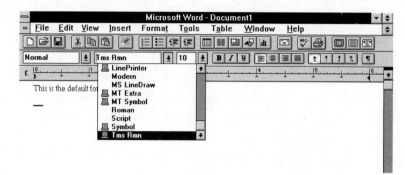

FIGURE 12.3:

The Font list box

4. Click the arrow in the ribbon's Point Size box to display a list of available sizes for the font. With the keyboard, press Ctrl-P, then ↓ to display the Point size list box.

5. Select one of the point sizes.

6. Type the name of the font you just selected, and press ↵. Depending on your system, the text may appear displayed in the selected font.

7. Select other fonts and sizes, if they are available, and type their names to see how they appear on the screen.

8. To see how your printer reproduces the fonts, click on the Print button in the toolbar. With the keyboard, pull down the File menu and select Print (Ctrl-Shift-F12), then OK.

9. Click on the Save button in the toolbar, or pull down the File Menu and select **S**ave (Shift-F12). Then type **Fonts** and select OK twice (once to save the document and another time to close the Summary Info dialog box).

10. Double-click on the close box or press Alt-F4 to exit Word.

If you want to return the characters to the default font and size, press Ctrl-spacebar, which will also remove any other character formats, such as boldface or underline.

To change the font of existing text, first select the text, and then select a new font or font size from the ribbon or Character dialog box.

If you do not have a mouse, use these methods to change fonts and sizes:

- Press Ctrl-F or Ctrl-P when the ribbon is not displayed, and a message will appear in the status bar asking for the name of the font or point size. Type the font name or point size desired and then press ↵.

- Press Ctrl-F or Ctrl-P twice to quickly display the Character dialog box.

- Press Ctrl-F2 to select the next largest available point size.

- Press Ctrl-Shift-F2 to select the next smallest available point size.

- Select text and press Ctrl-Q to return the text to the default font.

CHANGING THE DEFAULT FONT

If the default font used by Word is not a font available in your printer, you should select a new default font that is. Pull down the Format menu and select Character. Select the font and size in the Character dialog box, choose Use as Default to display a dialog box similar to the one shown in Figure 12.4, and then select Yes.

When you exit Word, you'll see the dialog box shown in Figure 12.5. Select Yes in this dialog box, and the selected font will now be used in all new documents.

Converting the Case of Characters

You enter uppercase characters from the keyboard in Word either by pressing the Shift key or the Caps Lock key. You can also quickly change the case of existing characters.

To change the case of characters, select the text and press Shift-F3 until the characters are in the case you want. Each time you press Shift-F3, text will cycle between lowercase, uppercase, and initial capitals, also called *mixed* (the first letter of each word is capitalized).

The order of the three formats depends on the state of the selected characters, but the cycle follows this pattern:

UPPERCASE TEXT   Mixed Text   lowercase text

The first time you press Shift-F3, the characters will change to the next format in the cycle, then the next, then back to their original condition, with the exception of mixed characters.

For example, if the text is all lowercase, it will first change to uppercase, then initial capitals, then back to all lowercase. If text is a mixture of cases, it will change to the case of the first selected character and then cycle through the other cases. All uppercase characters will first change to initial capitals, lowercase, then back to uppercase.

However, mixed characters may not be returned to their original state even if you cycle all the way through. For example, the following sentence:

I read the New York Times

would appear as

I READ THE NEW YORK TIMES

after Shift-F3 is used once, as

I Read The New York Times

after the second press, and as

i read the new york times

after the third Shift-F3.

Notice that in mixed format, the first character of every word is capitalized, not just those in the original sentence. After you select mixed characters and press Shift-F3, you will have to manually edit them to return them to their exact original condition.

You can also capitalize characters by selecting All Caps in the Character dialog box (displayed by the Character command on the Format menu), or by pressing Ctrl-A. However, text capitalized with this option will not be affected by the Shift-F3 command.

FEATURING

Draft and page layout views

Previewing the printed page

Modifying Word for Windows

▼

Changing the Document Display

By default, Word begins in the normal display mode, showing boldface, italic, underlining, and other character formats. You do not see the headers, footers, page numbers, or multiple columns (all covered in later lessons). Excluding these features from the screen reduces the time Word needs to display images.

Changing Views

You can change the way the document appears on the screen by using the toolbar or View menu. In addition to normal view, you can select draft view and page layout view, and you can change the magnification of the displayed image.

Now, let's take a look at the FONTS document, which you created in the last lesson, in each view.

1. Start Word and open the FONTS document. If necessary, place the insertion point at the start of the document.

2. Pull down the View menu and select Draft to switch to draft view.

In draft view, character formatting is removed and all characters appear the same size on the screen. Although you do not see the formatting, it is still stored with the document and will be used when the document is printed. In draft view, Word works even faster than it does in normal view.

3. Pull down the View menu and select Page Layout to turn on page layout view. Your display should look similar to the one shown in Figure 13.1.

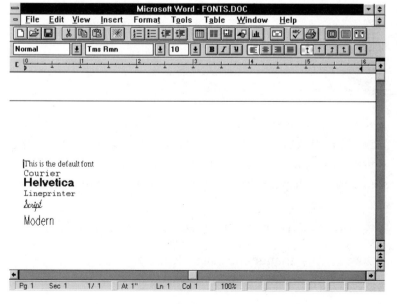

FIGURE 13.1:

Document in page layout view

Page layout view shows the text and graphics as they will appear when printed, including any headers, footers, and multiple columns. The line about an inch above the text represents the top edge of the page. The document's end mark is no longer visible. If you scroll through the document, you will be able to see the lines that represent the bottom, left, and right edges of the page.

The double triangles at the bottom of the scroll bar are for moving from page to page. Click on the up-pointing triangles to see the previous page; click on the down-pointing triangles to see the next page.

4. Pull down the **V**iew menu and select Normal.

In normal and page layout views, you might notice some delay in response to your keystrokes as Word refreshes the display of your text. This delay will be more pronounced if you add lines and graphics to your documents.

Page layout view offers the most accurate representation of how your printed document will appear, but it is the slowest view in which to work. If you are an average typist, use normal view for most of your work. Draft view provides the quickest keyboard and screen response. If you are a fast typist, switch to draft view when you are entering long sections of text.

Changing the Magnification

So far, you've been viewing your document at 100 percent magnification. This means that the text and graphics appear about the same size on the screen as they do on the printed page. You can change the magnification to display the entire page or to enlarge sections of the page.

USING THE TOOLBAR TO MAGNIFY

You can easily change the magnification using a mouse and the toolbar. If you do not have a mouse, review this section anyway because you can get the same results using the View menu, as described in the next section.

1. Click on the Zoom Whole Page button in the toolbar (the third button from the right).

Word changes to page layout view and reduces the image so the whole page is displayed on the screen, as shown in Figure 13.2. Notice that magnification indicator in the status bar now shows 30%. This means that the displayed page is 30% of the actual printed size. Also notice that the measurements in the ruler changed to reflect the magnification of the displayed text.

2. Click on the Zoom Page Width button in the toolbar (the first button on the right).

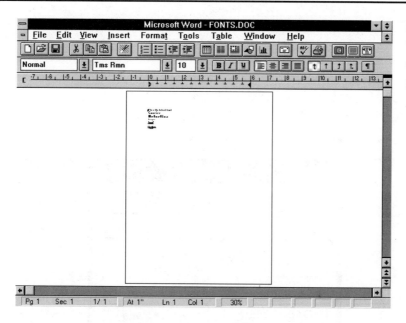

FIGURE 13.2:

Whole page of the document in page layout view

Still in page layout view, Word magnifies the image so you can see the full width of the page on the screen. The lines along the left and right mark the left and right edges of the page.

3. Click on the Zoom 100 Percent button (the second button from the right end of the toolbar).

The screen returns to normal view, with 100 percent magnification of the display.

Using the Zoom Command

When you use the Zoom command in the View menu instead of the toolbar buttons to change the magnification, you have more control over the amount of magnification. Follow these steps to see the magnification options:

1. Pull down the View menu and select Page Layout to change to page layout view.

2. Pull down the View menu and choose Zoom to see the dialog box shown in Figure 13.3.

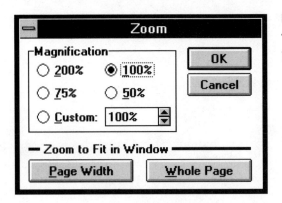

FIGURE 13.3:

The Zoom dialog box

The two options in the Zoom to Fit in Window section, at the bottom of the dialog box, perform the same functions as the Zoom toolbar buttons. Selecting **W**hole Page reduces the image so the whole page is displayed on the screen, like clicking on the Zoom Whole Page button. Selecting **P**age Width magnifies the image so you can see the full width of the page on the screen, like clicking on the Zoom Page Width button. When you select either of these options, the dialog box disappears and the screen changes immediately (you do not have to select OK).

The options in the Magnification section of the Zoom dialog box let you change the magnification to 200, 100, 75, or 50 percent. Select Custom and scroll through the box to change to some other magnification. You can change the magnification in any view. However, in draft view, the ruler adjustment is the only indication of the magnification; the size of the characters will not change.

3. Select 200%, then OK. The text will enlarge to twice its printed size, as shown in Figure 13.4.

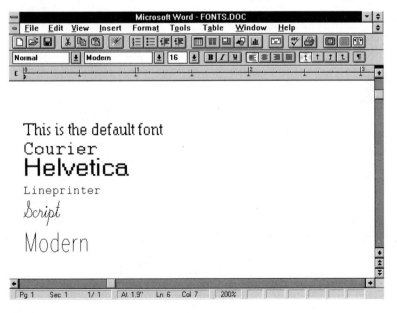

FIGURE 13.4:

Text enlarged to 200% magnification

4. Pull down the View menu, choose Zoom, then 100%, then OK.

5. Pull down the View menu and select Normal.

6. Pull down the File menu and select Exit (Alt-F4) to leave Word.

Previewing Printed Documents

Another view of your document provided by Word displays a preview, or detailed facsimile, of the printed document. To preview the document, pull down the File menu and select Print Preview. The display changes to a graphic representation of the printed document, similar to how it appeared as a whole page in page layout view.

In preview mode, however, you cannot add or change text, zoom in or out, or change the magnification, as you can in page layout view. There are two main advantages of the preview display: you can view two side-by-side pages at one time and you can adjust the page margins by dragging them with the mouse.

WORKING IN PREVIEW MODE

In preview mode, four command buttons appear under the menu bar:

- Print: Prints the page or pages displayed on the screen, selected pages, or the entire document.

- Margins: Turns off and on the display of *boundaries*, which are dotted lines around the page that indicate the margin areas. Boundaries also mark headers, footers, page breaks, and designated positioned objects, such as pictures and tables. With the margins displayed, you can change the page margins, move and copy objects, and change page-break lines while in preview mode.

■ Two Pages: Displays two pages side by side. When two pages are currently displayed, this button changes to One Page.

■ Close: Exits preview mode (you can also press Esc).

If you are previewing a multipage document, you can use the scroll bar or press PgUp and PgDn to move from page to page. The number of the page on the screen will appear to the right of the command buttons.

Setting Display Options

Keys such as Tab and ↵ format your text by inserting special codes into the document. To display these codes, click on the Show All button in the ribbon (the first button on the right). With the keyboard, select Tools to display the Tools menu, and then choose Options to display the dialog box shown in Figure 13.5. In the Nonprinting Characters section (on the right side of the dialog box), select All, and then select OK.

In this display mode, spaces will be indicated with bullets (•), Tabs with →, and the end of paragraphs with ¶. Turn off the special character

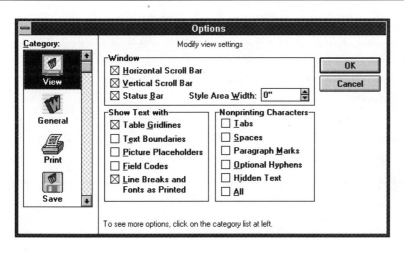

FIGURE 13.5:

Options dialog box for customizing Word

display by selecting the Show All button again or by choosing **All** from the Options dialog box to remove the check mark.

CUSTOMIZING THE VIEW

The other options in the Options dialog box for modifying view settings allow you to customize the appearance of the document window.

The Window options let you turn off and on the display of the scroll bars and status bar. You can also have Word show styles on the screen (you will learn about the style area in Lesson 40). Most of the Show Text With options let you display lines and field codes, which are covered in later lessons.

By default, the Line Breaks and Fonts as Printed option is selected, and Word will display only the fonts and character formats that your printer is capable of reproducing. Lines will also word wrap on the screen exactly as they will on the printed page. With some proportionally spaced fonts, however, this setting may cause the text to appear to wrap too far to the left or right of the margin indicated in the ruler. If the text scrolls past the right edge of the screen, you will have to use the horizontal scroll bar at the bottom of the screen to bring it into view.

In other cases, the text may wrap before reaching the right margin (as in many of the figures in this book). The text will still print correctly, wrapping at the right margin of the page.

If you find either of these situations bothersome, turn off the Line Breaks and Fonts as Printed option. Then text will wrap at the right margin on the screen and appear according to the font and character formats you select, but not necessarily as when printed. Before printing the document, turn this option on to see how your document will appear, or change to page layout view, which shows the document as it will appear when printed, regardless of how the Line Breaks and Fonts as Printed option is set.

CUSTOMIZING OTHER WORD FEATURES

The Category section (on the left side of the dialog box) lets you select other sets of options for customizing Word, as summarized in Table 13.1. The options in the Options dialog box will change when you select a new category.

CATEGORY	PURPOSE
View	Changes the appearance of the document window.
General	Controls general editing features.
Print	Sets default print options.
Save	Determines default save options such as backup copies and fast saves.
Spelling	Sets the dictionary and rules to use with the spelling checker.
Grammar	Determines the grammatical styles used by the grammar checker.
User Info	Changes the user name, initials, and mailing address inserted when Word when installed.
Toolbar	Customizes the functions available on the toolbar.
Menus	Determines the commands and macros on menus.
Keyboard	Assigns and changes shortcut keys.
WIN.INI	Customizes Word for Windows startup options in the Windows initialization file.

TABLE 13.1:

Options Dialog Box Customization Categories

Aligning Text

ou can center, right align, or justify text by using the buttons on the ribbon, Ctrl-key combinations, or the Paragraph dialog box (accessed through the Format menu). Like character formats, alignment formats can be applied to text that you are about to type or to existing text.

Centering Text

A typical use of centered text is for title pages. As an example, we will use the buttons on the ribbon to center a title on the page. (The alignment buttons in the ribbon are shown in Table 12.1.)

1. Start Word.

2. Press ↵ six times to leave six lines at the top of the page.

3. Select the Center button in the ribbon (the eighth button from the right) or press Ctrl-E. The button will appear pushed down (or in reverse), and the insertion point will move to the center of the screen.

4. Type **My Life and Times**. As you type, the characters will move alternately to the left and right, for centered text.

5. Press ↵ to move to the next line. You will notice that the insertion point remains in the center.

6. Type **by** and press ↵.

7. Type your name and press ↵.

8. To turn off centering, select the Left button (the one to the left of the Center button) or press Ctrl-L. The insertion point will return to the margin for left alignment.

9. Click on the Print button in the toolbar to see how the title appears when printed. With the keyboard, pull down the File menu and select Print (Ctrl-Shift-F12), then choose OK.

10. Pull down the File menu and select Close, then No to clear the document window without saving the text.

11. Click on the New Document button in the toolbar. With the keyboard, pull down the File menu and select **New**, then choose OK.

CENTERING EXISTING TEXT

To center existing text, place the cursor anywhere in the paragraph to be centered, and then select the Center button in the ribbon (Ctrl-E).

If you want to center several paragraphs, highlight them first, then select the Center button.

Let's type another title page and then center the text:

1. Type

> **The History of Earth**
> **by**
> **Alvin A. Aardvark**
> **A startling new theory proposing that the Earth was**
> **created as an outpost of the planet Pluto.**

2. Press ↵.

3. To select all the text, press Ctrl and click the left mouse button in the selection bar, or drag the I-beam or insertion point.

4. Select the Center button on the ribbon (Ctrl-E). The entire block of text will be centered on the screen, and it will still be selected.

5. Click the left mouse button or press an arrow key to deselect the text.

6. Click on the Save button in the toolbar. With the keyboard, pull down the File menu and select Save (Shift-F12).

7. Type **Earth**, and then select OK twice.

If you choose Center without selecting any existing text in a document, Word will center the entire paragraph in which the insertion point is located. A paragraph is the text ending with a carriage return, so you can center a single line, such as a report title, by just placing the insertion point in the line and selecting the Center button.

To change a centered line to left aligned, place the insertion point anywhere in the centered line and select the Left button in the ribbon (Ctrl-L). To left align several centered lines, select them, and then choose the Left button.

Aligning Text on the Right

Right-aligned, or flush-right, text is aligned on the right margin with an uneven margin on the left, just the opposite of left-aligned text.

To see how right-aligned text looks on the page, follow these steps:

1. In the EARTH document, select the first three lines, with the title and author.

2. Select the Right button on the ribbon (the seventh one from the right) or press Ctrl-R. The text will shift to the right, as shown in Figure 14.1.

3. Select the Center button (Ctrl-E) to return to centered alignment.

4. Click the mouse or press an arrow key to deselect the text.

If you want to right align several lines at a time, select them before choosing the Right button. To realign the text at the left margin, place

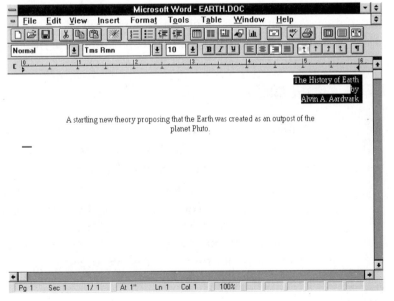

FIGURE 14.1:

Right-aligned text

the cursor on the line (or select several lines), and then select the Left button (Ctrl-L).

To right align new text, select the Right button in the ribbon (Ctrl-R). The insertion point will move to the right margin, and as you type the text, the characters will move to the left. Select the Left button (Ctrl-L) to return the insertion point to the left margin.

Fully Justifying Text

Another alignment option is *full justification*. In this format, the text is aligned along both margins at the same time.

When you justify text, extra spaces are inserted between words in word-wrapped lines to spread out the line to the right margin. Lines that end with a carriage return will not be affected.

There are times, however, when the extra spaces needed to justify a line are unsightly. In Lesson 19, you'll learn how to improve spacing by using hyphenation.

To see how justification works, we will add some text to the EARTH document and fully justify it.

1. Place the insertion point in the paragraph of text beneath the author's name and select the Left button in the ribbon (Ctrl-L) to left align the text.

2. Add the following text to the paragraph:

> **Millions of years ago, the people of Pluto sought a new world as a colonial outpost. Finding no planet suitable for their habitation, they fused together several comets and placed the resulting planet in orbit around the sun. Today, we know this planet as Earth.**

3. Place the insertion point anywhere in the paragraph and select the Justify button in the ribbon (the sixth button from the right) or press Ctrl-J.

Figure 14.2 shows the completed document. Each line except the last one is even along the left and right margins. In some cases, several extra spaces had to be inserted. If you had selected the entire document, the centered lines would have moved to the left margin because choosing an alignment cancels any other alignment.

CANCELING JUSTIFICATION

If you decide you do not want the text justified, select the Left button in the ribbon (Ctrl-L) to make it left aligned. Let's do this now.

1. Place the insertion point in the final paragraph and choose the Left button (Ctrl-L) again.

2. To save the edited document, click on the Save button in the toolbar. With the keyboard, pull down the File menu and choose **Save** (Shift-F12).

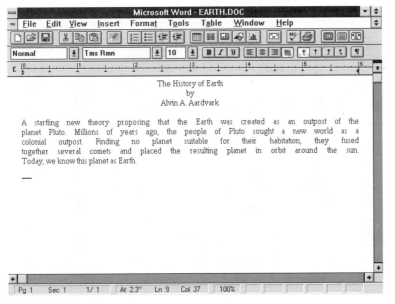

FIGURE 14.2:

Justified text

3. Pull down the File menu and choose Close.

4. Click on the New Document button in the toolbar. With the keyboard, pull down the File menu and select New, then choose OK.

Aligning Text through the Paragraph Dialog Box

As an alternative to using the ribbon buttons or Ctrl-key combinations, you can align text through the Paragraph dialog box, which is displayed by the Paragraph option on the Format menu.

First, select the text to be formatted or type until you are ready to enter the formatted line. Then pull down the Format menu and select Paragraph to display the dialog box shown in Figure 14.3.

Select the format you want from the Alignment drop-down list box: Left, Centered, Right, or Justified. The example in the Sample box will illustrate the selected alignment. You will learn about the other options in the Paragraph dialog box in later lessons.

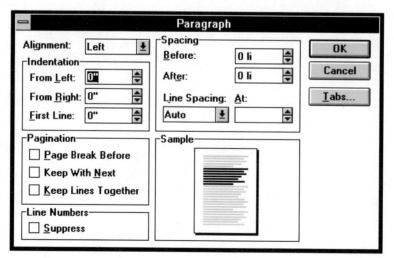

FIGURE 14.3:

The Paragraph dialog box

15 LESSON

FEATURING

Using different tab types

Formatting with leaders

Rearranging tabs

▼

Setting and Using Tabs

I f you've ever used a typewriter, you know the purpose of a tab stop. By setting a tab stop, you can move the cursor directly to a specific position on the line. Actually, you've already used tab stops in earlier lessons. When you press the Tab key to indent the first line of a paragraph, you move the cursor to the first tab stop on the line, $1/2$ inch from the left margin. This is one of Word's default tab stops.

Whenever you start Word, tabs are automatically set every $1/2$ inch. So each time you press the Tab key, the insertion point moves another $1/2$ inch to the right. If the default tab stops are not suitable for your document, you can set custom tab stops. In this lesson, you will learn about the types of tab stops Word provides and how to set them.

Types of Tabs

Word for Windows gives you a choice of several types of tabs. Left tab stops, the default, align text on the left:

Hamburger

French fries

Large soft drink

Centered tab stops create centered columns:

Tomatoes

Relish

Sesame seed bun

Right tab stops resemble right-aligned text:

Extra crispy

Regular

No salt

Decimal tab stops align numbers on the decimal point. Numbers aligned this way are easier to read than left-aligned numeric columns:

123.56	123.56
.77	.77
1.89	1.89
8765.76	8765.76

Leaders are characters, such as periods or hyphens, that lead the eye horizontally. They can be inserted between tab stops, as in the following examples:

President..Fred Burger

Vice President------------------------------Pam Frites

Executive Director_____D.P. Pepper

Setting Tab Stops

Setting a tab is a two-step process. First you select the tab's type, if necessary, and then you set the tab-stop position on the ruler.

USING THE RULER

You can use the ruler across the top of the screen to work with tabs whether or not you have a mouse. By default, the ruler is in *indent scale*. In indent scale, each default tab stop is indicated by the upside-down T symbol, every $1/2$ inch. The numbers on the scale represent distance from the left margin, not the left edge of the page. So, the position marked 2 on the ruler represents a position 2 inches from the left margin, or 3 inches from the left edge of the page.

The ruler can also represent *margin scale* and *table scale*. You will learn about table scale, which appears automatically when you create a table, in Lesson 25. You can change to the margin scale, which is for setting margins rather than tab stops, only if you have a mouse, as you will learn in Lesson 20.

SETTING TABS WITH THE MOUSE

With a mouse, you can select the tab's type by selecting one of the four tab buttons on the right side of the ribbon (the ones with the arrow pointing up). From left to right, the icons represent left, centered, right, and decimal tab stops (see Table 12.1).

Let's set several tab stops that you'll use shortly. You'll set a centered tab at 1 inch and a decimal tab at 5 ½ inches.

1. If there are no tab markers on the ruler, you accidentally selected margin scale. Switch to indent scale by clicking on the two triangles to the left of the ruler, then click in the document window. With the keyboard, press Ctrl-Shift-F10 to activate the ruler and change to indent scale, and then press ↵ to return to the document.

2. Click on the Center Tab button in the ribbon.

3. Click on 1 inch. This means to point just below the 1-inch position on the ruler and click the left mouse button.

Setting your own tab automatically clears all the default tab stops up to that position. So, the centered tab indicator, a straight arrow, appears at 1 inch, and the default tab stop is cleared at the ½-inch position, as shown in Figure 15.1.

4. Click on the Decimal Tab button in the ribbon.

5. Click on 5½, halfway between 5 and 6, on the ruler. The default tab stops to the left will be cleared, and the symbol for a decimal tab will appear.

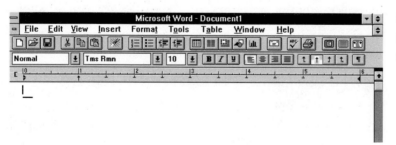

FIGURE 15.1:

Centered tab stop set on ruler

SETTING TAB STOPS WITH THE KEYBOARD

With the keyboard, you enter ruler mode by pressing Ctrl-Shift-F10. You'll see a square box on the left side of the ruler, called the *ruler cursor,* which you can use to set and clear tab stops.

To set a tab stop, enter ruler mode and then press ← or → to place the ruler cursor where you want the tab stop. Press 1 for a left tab, 2 for a centered tab, 3 for a right tab, and 4 for a decimal tab. The numbers correspond to the order of the tab type icons in the ribbon. Notice that the tab icon will change color, or appear to pressed down, to indicate that it has been selected. Finally, press Ins to set the tab stop. When you're finished setting tabs, press ↵ to leave ruler mode.

SETTING TABS AND LEADERS WITH THE TABS DIALOG BOX

If you want to set tabs with leaders, you must use the Tabs dialog box (accessed through the Format menu). You can also use this dialog box to set any type of tab and clear tab stops.

As an example, we will set a right-aligned dot leader tab at the 4-inch position.

1. Pull down the Format menu and choose Tabs to display the dialog box shown in Figure 15.2.

The Tab Stop Position text box is already selected, and your custom tabs are listed in the box beneath it.

2. Type 4.

3. Select Right (Alt-R) in the Alignment section.

4. Select the dot leader option (Alt-2) in the Leader section.

5. Select the Set button (on the right side of the dialog box).

6. Select OK, and a right tab indicator will appear on the ruler.

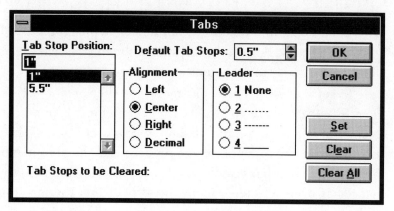

FIGURE 15.2:
The Tabs dialog box

Using Tabs

All tab stops are reached with the Tab key. When you enter text, it will conform to the formatting determined by the tab types you selected.

Now that we have set custom tabs, we can use them to format a three-column list. Follow these steps:

1. Press Tab and type **President**. The word will be centered around the tab-stop position.

2. Press Tab. Dot leaders will appear up to the tab-stop position.

3. Type **Dotti Sugerman**. Since this is a right-aligned tab, the text will move toward the left.

4. Press Tab and type **$45,000.00**. Because this is a decimal tab, the numbers will move to the left until you type the period, or decimal point, the decimal point will remain at the tab-stop position, and the following characters will move to the right.

5. Press Shift-↵.

Shift-↵ inserts a line break. It moves the cursor down to the next line, just like using the ↵ key by itself, but it does not end the paragraph. Using a line break makes it easier to later rearrange the list, since you will be able to handle the entire list as one paragraph.

6. Complete the list with the following text, pressing Shift-↵ after each line except the last one. Press ↵ at the end of the last line.

Vice President	Fran Conti	$41,500.00
Treasurer	Ronald Howard	$36,500.00
Secretary	Marian Oxford	$32,500.00

Your screen should look like the one shown in Figure 15.3.

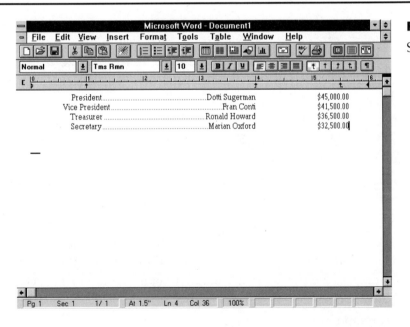

FIGURE 15.3:

Sample table

7. Click on the Print button in the toolbar to print the document. With the keyboard, pull down the File menu and select Print (Ctrl-Shift-F12), then choose OK.

8. Click on the Save button in the toolbar. With the keyboard, pull down the File menu and select Save (Shift-F12).

9. Type **Tabs**, and then select OK twice.

10. Pull down the File menu and choose Close to clear the document window.

11. Click on the New Document button in the toolbar. With the keyboard, pull down the File menu, select New, then choose OK.

Clearing and Moving Tabs

If you want to clear a tab quickly with the mouse, drag its marker up or down away from the ruler. To move a tab stop to another location, drag its marker to where you want it set.

To clear all your custom tabs, restoring the Word defaults, pull down the Format menu, choose **Tabs**, and then select Clear All in the Tabs dialog box. To clear individual tabs, select the positions in the list box of that dialog box, and then choose Clear.

Using the keyboard, press Ctrl-Shift-F10 to activate the ruler, move the ruler cursor to the tab stop you want to delete, and press the Del key. You cannot move a tab stop in one step. You must first delete the one you no longer want, and then set another at the new position.

If you delete or change tab stops, any text already entered at those positions will adjust automatically to the new (or default) tab stop position. So, if you do not like the positions of the columns in existing text, you can move the tab stops, and the columns will move accordingly.

Unless text is selected, any changes to tab stops will affect only the paragraph in which the insertion point is located. However, if you use the Shift-↵ key to end the lines (except the last) in the rows, Word will treat all the text as one paragraph, so you can place the insertion point anywhere within the text with tab stops to change the tabs.

To set or change tab stops for multiple paragraphs, select them first, then set, move, or clear the tab stops.

Using Tabs for Flush Alignment

In an earlier lesson, you learned how to align text along the right margin. The only problem with using right-aligned text is that *all* the text shifts to the right. It isn't possible to have some text left aligned and some right aligned, as in this format:

President.........................Sylvia Chen

Vice President.............Joseph C. Viola

Secretary.............Richard Grysikowski

Treasurer........................Paul Dorfman

To set up this format, use a right-aligned tab (with dot leaders if you want) for the second column. Type the text at the left margin, then press Tab to enter the right-aligned text.

Changing Line Spacing

Each time you press ↵, or when word wrap takes effect, the insertion point moves to the next line. By default, it will move to the very next line, single spacing the document. But there are times when single spacing is not the preferred format.

You might want to double space between paragraphs, or even double or triple space entire sections of text. In this lesson, you will learn how to change the line spacing in your documents.

Using Shortcut Keys to Adjust Spacing

Using the keyboard, you can adjust line spacing with the following commands:

Single spacing	Ctrl-1
1 ½ spacing	Ctrl-5
Double spacing	Ctrl-2
Extra lines between paragraphs	Ctrl-O (letter O)
Remove extra lines between paragraphs	Ctrl-0 (zero)

You can also use the Paragraph dialog box to change line spacing, as described at the end of this lesson.

The line spacing Ctrl-key combinations affect all selected lines in a document. Let's use the COLLECT document, which you created earlier in the book, to experiment with line spacing.

1. Start Word. The ruler should be displayed. If not, pull down the View menu and select Ruler.

2. Click on the Open button in the toolbox. With the keyboard, pull down the File menu and choose Open (Ctrl-F12).

3. Choose COLLECT, and then select OK.

4. Select the entire document by holding down the Ctrl key and clicking the left button in the selection bar. With the keyboard, press F8 until the entire document is selected.

5. Press Ctrl-2. The entire document will be double spaced, including lines between and within paragraphs.

6. Press Ctrl-1 to return the document to single spacing.

7. Click the mouse or press an arrow key to deselect the text.

Inserting Extra Lines Between Paragraphs

The Ctrl-O key combination inserts an extra line at each location where you pressed the ↵ key. This spacing does not affect the single-spaced lines created by word wrap, so the text within the paragraphs remains single spaced. If you press Ctrl-O before typing, the next line will be double spaced every time you press ↵. To cancel this spacing, press Ctrl-0.

Let's see how our COLLECT document looks with extra lines between paragraphs.

1. To select the paragraphs of the letter (without including the salutation or closing), place the insertion point at the start of the first paragraph and drag it to the end of the last paragraph.

2. Press Ctrl-O. An extra line will appear between each of the paragraphs.

3. Press Ctrl-0. Since the text was still selected, the extra lines will disappear.

4. Click the mouse or press an arrow key to deselect the text.

Setting Line Spacing Using the Paragraph Dialog Box

The Ctrl-key combinations provide a quick way to change to 1½ or double spacing, however, if you want wider line spacing, such as triple spacing, you must use the Paragraph dialog box (accessed from the Format menu). You can set any line spacing through this dialog box.

In Lesson 14, you learned how to use the Paragraph dialog box to set text alignment. Now we are interested in the Spacing options (see Figure 14.3):

- Before: Determines the number of extra lines inserted before each paragraph (each time the ↵ key is pressed).

- After: Determines the number of extra lines inserted after each paragraph.

- Line Spacing: Determines the vertical space for each line, or the line spacing used by both the ↵ key and word wrap.

To change any of the settings, select the option, then click on the up or down arrows to increase or decrease the setting. With the Before and After options, you can also type a setting directly in the text box—just make sure you delete the value already there.

You cannot type a setting in the Line Spacing box; instead, select from its drop-down menu, and then enter a value in the At box if necessary. The drop-down menu choices are Auto, Single, 1.5 Lines, Double, At Least, and Exactly.

By default, the Line Spacing option is set to Auto, which sets line height according to the largest font in each line. If you're using different fonts on a line, the Auto setting will ensure that characters will not overlap when printed. When you change line spacing using the Ctrl-key combinations, Word changes the setting here to match what you selected.

Select Exactly for Line Spacing when you want to enter a precise value. For example, to set quadruple line spacing, select Exactly from the list box, then enter 4 in the At text box.

You can also enter measurements in inches, points, and centimeters. To do so, follow the number with IN (or "), PT, or CM, respectively. Word will convert the settings to lines and make the necessary adjustments.

Now we'll reset the spacing for the COLLECT document, which should still be on your screen, to triple space between lines.

1. Select the entire document.

2. Pull down the Format menu and select Paragraph.

3. Pull down the Line Spacing drop-down menu and select Exactly.

4. Select At and enter **3** for triple spacing.

5. Select OK to return to the document, which should now be triple spaced.

6. Press Ctrl-1. Because the text was still selected, the format is restored to single spacing, and the Line Spacing option in the Paragraph dialog box will change to Single.

7. Click the mouse or press an arrow key to deselect the text.

8. Pull down the File menu and select Exit (Alt-F4), then choose No to exit Word without saving the edited version of the document.

FEATURING

Indenting the first line of every paragraph

Indenting text from the left or right margin

▼

Indenting Paragraphs

The default paragraph format used by Word is the block style, where every line starts at the left margin. When you want to indent the first line of a paragraph, you have to press Tab after you press ↵.

But Word provides many other options for paragraph indentation. You can have it indent the first line automatically. Or you might want to indent a whole paragraph from the left margin to make a specific point stand out. You also can indent both the left and right margins.

You can create these indentations by using the ruler, the keyboard, or the Paragraph dialog box.

Indenting the First Line Automatically

In this lesson, you'll be using the ruler to indent paragraphs. In indent scale, you'll see two solid black triangles under the 0 position, on the left side of the ruler. The one on top, called the *first-line indent marker*, controls the indentation of only the first line in a paragraph. The triangle on the bottom, called the *left indent marker*, controls the position of every other line.

If the ruler is in margin scale, the two triangles will be to the left of the ruler. Click on the two triangles to return to indent scale.

You set an automatic indentation for the first line of every paragraph by dragging the first-line indent marker to the indented position. When you set a first-line indentation, every time you press the ↵ key, the insertion point will move down and in to the indented position automatically.

Indenting a Paragraph on the Left or Right

To indent all the lines in a paragraph, click on the Indent button in the toolbar (the eleventh one from the left). Each time you click on the Indent button, the indent markers in the ruler will move to the next tab-stop position toward the right. When you press ↵, or when word wrap takes effect, the insertion point will return to the indented position, the new left margin.

You can also indent paragraphs to any position by dragging the ruler's left indent marker (the bottom triangle). When you drag the left indent marker, the first-line indent marker moves also, but it maintains the same distance. For example, if the markers are 1/2 inch apart when you move the left indent marker, the first-line indent marker will move to remain 1/2 inch from it. To move the left indent marker without changing the position of the first-line indent marker, hold down the Shift key while you drag the left indent marker.

To indent a paragraph at the right margin, drag the right indent marker (the solid black triangle on the right side of the ruler) to the indentation position. Word wrap will adjust to the new right margin.

If the text on the screen does not appear to align with the indentations set on the ruler, it is because the Line Breaks and Fonts as Printed option in the Options dialog box (accessed by selecting Options from the Tools menu) is selected.

Indenting Paragraphs with the Keyboard

To use the keyboard to indent paragraphs, press Ctrl-Shift-F10 to activate the ruler, and then move the ruler cursor to the indentation position. Press F to set the first-line indentation, L for the left indentation, and R for right indentation.

You can also set the left indentation using the Ctrl-N and Ctrl-M key combinations. Each time you press Ctrl-N, the left indentation moves to the next tab stop toward the right. So, for example, you would press Ctrl-N twice to indent a paragraph 1 inch using the default tab stops. Press Ctrl-M to move the indentation back toward the left.

When you press Ctrl-N and Ctrl-M to move the left indent marker, the first-line indent marker also moves to maintain the same distance. For example, suppose you set the first-line indent at the 1-inch position. There will be 1 inch between the first-line and left indent markers. If you press Ctrl-N once, the left indent marker moves to the $\frac{1}{2}$-inch position, and the first-line indent marker moves to the $1\frac{1}{2}$-inch position to maintain the same spacing.

To move the left indent marker without moving the first-line indent marker, press Ctrl-T to indent toward the right, or Ctrl-G to return to the left.

Using Indented Formats in a Document

To see how easy it is to indent paragraphs with Word, you'll create a document with several levels of indentation. Follow these steps:

1. Start Word and select the Center button on the ribbon (Ctrl-E) to center the insertion point.

2. Type the title: **The Impact of Computers on Business**.

3. Press ↵ twice to double space after the title.

4. Select the Left button on the ribbon (Ctrl-L) to cancel the centered format.

5. Drag the first-line indent marker (the top triangle on the left) to the $1/2$-inch position to automatically indent the first line of the next paragraph, as shown in Figure 17.1. With the keyboard, press Ctrl-Shift-F10, move the ruler cursor to the $1/2$-inch position, press F, and then press ↵.

6. Type the following text.

> **High-speed computers allow business organizations to plan future actions and make more informed decisions. By tracking current activities and simulating future circumstances, computers provide managers with the tools needed for financial forecasting.**

7. Press the ↵ key twice. Each time you press ↵, the insertion point will move to the $1/2$-inch position.

8. Hold down the Shift key and drag the left indent marker to the $1/2$-inch position. With the keyboard, press Ctrl-T. Both markers should now be at the $1/2$-inch position.

9. Release the Shift key, and then click on the Indent button in the toolbar. With the keyboard, press Ctrl-N. Both markers will now be at 1 inch.

10. Type the following text.

> **Computers provide a mechanism for control. They allow managers to monitor performance and to measure results against projections. By receiving timely**

and accurate computer-generated reports, the manager can take informed actions to prevent problems that would otherwise develop.

11. Press ↵ twice, and then click twice on the Unindent button in the toolbar (the one to the left of the Indent button). Each time you click on this button, the indent markers in the ruler move to the next tab stop on the left. With the keyboard, press Ctrl-M twice.

12. Type the next paragraph.

The use of computers also promotes more efficient operations. Transaction-oriented systems, automated data input, and electronic mail reduce expenditures and improve employee performance.

13. Press ↵ twice.

Now let's indent the next paragraph 1 inch from both the left and right margins.

14. Click twice on the Indent button in the toolbar, and then drag the right indent marker to the 5-inch position. With the

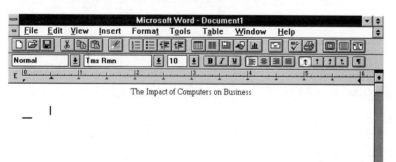

FIGURE 17.1:

First-line indent marker at ½ inch

keyboard, press Ctrl-Shift-F10, move the ruler cursor to the
1-inch position, press L, move the cursor to the 5-inch
position, and press R. Press ↵ to exit ruler mode.

15. Type the following text.

> **Of course, computers may have some negative impact
> on business operations. Employees may have difficulty
> adjusting to automated systems, and the security of
> data may be questioned. In addition, computerization
> often leads to changes in the organizational structure,
> chain of command, and balance of power. These
> issues must be addressed before a business undertakes
> computerization.**

16. Press ↵. The paragraph will be indented 1 inch from both
margins.

Figure 17.2 shows the document at this point. Remember, depending on your printer and font, your lines may appear to wrap and align
differently than shown in the figure.

17. Click on the Print button in the toolbar to print the document.
With the keyboard, pull down the File menu and select Print
(Ctrl-Shift-F12), then choose OK.

Now let's reset all of the paragraphs to the default left margin.

18. Select the text of the document below the title.

19. Press Ctrl-Q to cancel all the formatting.

20. Click the mouse or press an arrow key to deselect the text.

21. Click on the Save button in the toolbar. With the keyboard,
pull down the File menu and choose Save (Shift-F12).

22. Type **Computer**, and then select OK twice.

23. Pull down the File menu and choose Exit (Alt-F4) to exit Word.

Using the Paragraph Dialog Box to Set Indentations

You can also set indentations through the Paragraph dialog box. Pull down the Format menu and select Paragraph, and then choose the type of indent you want from the Indentation section. The From Left option indents from the left margin, the From Right option indents from the right margin, and the First Line option automatically indents the first line of each paragraph. Enter the indentation position in the text box or use the up and down arrows to select the setting.

The settings you used in this lesson are for formatting one or more paragraphs. You will learn how to change the margins of an entire document in Lesson 20.

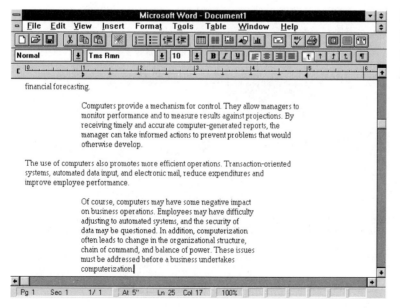

FIGURE 17.2:

Document with indented paragraphs

Creating Hanging Indents

In Lesson 17, you learned how to indent paragraphs from the left and right. Another common type of format is a *hanging indent,* in which the text is indented beneath the first line in the paragraph. The first line usually has a number or bullet at the left margin. In this lesson, you will learn how to set up hanging-indent formats for numbered and bulleted text.

Formatting Numbered Paragraphs

Hanging indents are frequently used for numbered paragraphs and outlines. You create hanging-indent formats by placing the left indent marker to the right of the first-line indent marker. You can also create hanging indents using the keyboard or the Paragraph dialog box.

As an example, we'll create the beginning of a topical outline. Follow these steps:

1. Hold down the Shift key and drag the left indent marker to the $1/2$-inch position. With the keyboard, press Ctrl-T. The first-line indent marker will remain at the 0 position.

2. Type 1., the first number in the outline.

3. Press Tab, and then type the following outline entry.

   The media used for data communications depends upon the speed of the transmission and the distance it must travel. There are two general classifications of media.

Notice that word wrap continues each line at the position of the left indent marker, which is now indented from the hanging numbered list at the first-line indent position.

4. Press ↵.

5. Drag the left indent marker to the 1-inch position. With the keyboard, press Ctrl-N. The first-line indent marker will move to the $1/2$-inch position at the same time.

6. Type a., press Tab, and type the first subtopic.

   Wire media includes open copper wire, twisted pair, and coaxial cable. Fiber optic cable may be included in this category.

7. Press ↵.

8. Type **b.**, press Tab, and type the next subtopic.

>   **Airborne media includes broadcast transmission, microwave, and laser beam transmission.**

9. Press ↵.

10. Drag the left indent marker back to the ½-inch position. With the keyboard, press Ctrl-M.

11. Type **2.**, press Tab, and type the second topic.

>   **The protocol used for data communications depends upon a variety of factors.**

12. Press ↵. Your outline should look like the one shown in Figure 18.1.

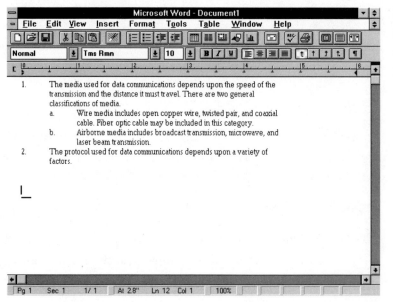

FIGURE 18.1:

Sample document using numbered paragraphs

13. Hold down the Shift key and drag the left indent marker to the 0 position on the ruler to return to the normal paragraph format. With the keyboard, press Ctrl-G.

14. Click on the Print button in the toolbar to print the document. With the keyboard, pull down the File menu and select Print (Ctrl-Shift-F12), then choose OK.

15. Click on the Save button in the toolbar. With the keyboard, pull down the File menu and select Save (Shift-F12).

16. Type **Media**, and then select OK twice.

17. Pull down the File menu and choose Close to clear the document window.

18. Click on the New Document button in the toolbar. With the keyboard, pull down the File menu and select New, then select OK.

If you want to create a paragraph with hanging text instead of numbers, move the left indent marker and then type the paragraph. The second and subsequent lines will be indented.

Using the Paragraph Dialog Box to Set Hanging Indents

You can also create a hanging indent by using the From Left and First Line options in the Indentation section of the Paragraph dialog box. Enter the position for the indented lines in the From Left text box, and then enter the distance of the hanging text as a negative number in the First Line text box.

For example, to create a ¼-inch hanging indent starting at 1 inch, set the From Left option to 1.25 and the First Line option to −.25. These settings will create a hanging indent with the first line starting at the 1-inch position and remaining lines indented at 1¼ inches. The first line will start ¼ inch to the left (the negative value) of the left indent, which is at the 1¼-inch position.

Numbering Paragraphs with the Mouse

If you have a mouse, you can number a paragraph and create a hanging indent in one step by using the Numbered List button in the toolbar. Word will insert a number and move the left indent marker ½ inch to the right. Type the paragraph, then press ↵. Each time you select the button, Word will insert the next consecutive number.

To quickly number existing paragraphs, select them and click on the Numbered List button. Word will add a number to each paragraph and format the text as hanging indents. Let's try this now with the COMPUTER document.

1. Open the COMPUTER document.

2. Select the text of the document below the title.

3. Click on the Numbered List button in the toolbar (the eighth one from the left).

The paragraphs are numbered and formatted as hanging indents.

Adding Bullets with the Mouse

Another toolbar button, Bulleted List, allows you to add bullets to each selected paragraph. You can even use it to replace numbers with bullets. Let's see how this works by changing the numbered paragraphs in the COMPUTER document to a bulleted list.

1. Select the Bulleted List button on the toolbar (the ninth one from the left). You will see a dialog box with the message

   Do you want to replace the existing numbers with bullets?
   Yes   No   Cancel   Help

2. Select Yes to replace each number with a bullet.

3. Click the mouse button to deselect the text. Your list should now look like the one shown in Figure 18.2.

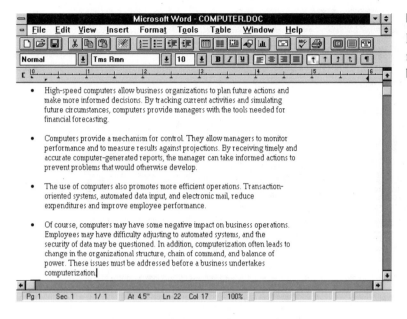

FIGURE 18.2:

Paragraphs formatted as a bulleted list

4. Pull down the File menu and select Exit (Alt-F4), then No to exit Word without saving the changes.

If you would like to change the bullets to numbers, you can click on the Number Paragraph button in the toolbar. You will see a message asking if you want to replace the bullets with numbers.

Inserting Numbers and Bullets with the Keyboard

With the keyboard, type all the text that will have numbers or bullets first, and then select it. Pull down the Tools menu and select Bullets and Numbering to display the dialog box shown in Figure 18.3.

In the Bullets and Numbering dialog box, you can select the format of the numbers, the shape of the bullets, and the amount of indentation for hanging indents. Make your selections and then select OK. You

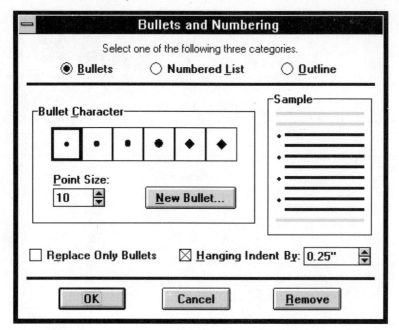

FIGURE 18.3:

The Bullets and Numbering dialog box

could add numbers or bullets as you type, but then you would have to go through the Bullets and Numbering dialog box for each new paragraph.

Removing Numbers and Bullets

If you decide you don't want bullets or numbers, you don't have to delete each one separately. To remove them all, highlight the bulleted or numbered text, pull down the Tools menu, choose Bullets and Numbering, and then select Remove (in the bottom-right corner of the dialog box).

Hyphenating Text

As mentioned in Lesson 14, sometimes a justified paragraph (formatted with the Justified button in the ribbon or the Paragraph dialog box) can have too many extra spaces between words. For example, the following justified column, without hyphenation, has many noticeable gaps:

word   wrap
automatically
returns   the
carriage   to
the   left.

To avoid such problems, you can hyphenate the text. You can either hyphenate the text manually or have Word do it for you automatically, as you will learn in this lesson.

Using Manual Hyphenation

As you type, you can manually hyphenate words at the end of a sentence. But what happens if you later add or delete text? Will word wrap move the word, hyphen and all, down to the next line? When you hyphenate, you must tell Word what to do with the hyphen if editing moves it to another line.

You indicate how the hyphen should be treated by the way that you enter the hyphen character. There are three ways to enter a hyphen in Word:

- Press the hyphen by itself in words that require hyphens, such as mother-in-law. If the paragraph is later reformatted, word wrap will use the hyphen, if necessary, to divide the word between lines.

- Press Ctrl-Shift-hyphen to insert a nonbreaking hyphen. Word wrap will never break a word containing a nonbreaking hyphen between two lines. Use this hyphen when you are typing phone numbers (for example, 555-1212) and other items that should not be divided between lines.

- Press Ctrl-hyphen to enter an optional hyphen. No hyphen will appear on the screen unless word wrap uses it to hyphenate the word between lines. Use the optional hyphen when typing long words that are near the end of the line, and which may later be moved by word wrap.

Hyphenating Automatically

Although manual hyphenation gives you complete control of hyphen placement, it slows down your typing, bypassing the word wrap feature that makes word processing so powerful. As an alternative, you can let Word take care of the hyphenation for you by using the Hyphenation option on the Tools menu.

As an example, we will have Word hyphenate the COMPUTER document. Follow these steps:

1. Start Word and open the COMPUTER document.

2. Pull down the Tools menu and select **H**yphenation to display the dialog box shown in Figure 19.1.

Selecting the **C**onfirm option gives you a chance to approve each hyphenation position. Selecting the **H**yphenate Caps option allows initial capital letters to be hyphenated. Both options are selected by default.

3. Select **C**onfirm to deselect it and have Word make the decisions for you. Note that you must deselect the Confirm option each time you use the Hyphenation dialog box.

4. Select OK.

Word switches into page layout view. Since you selected not to confirm hyphenation, Word scans the document for possible hyphenation

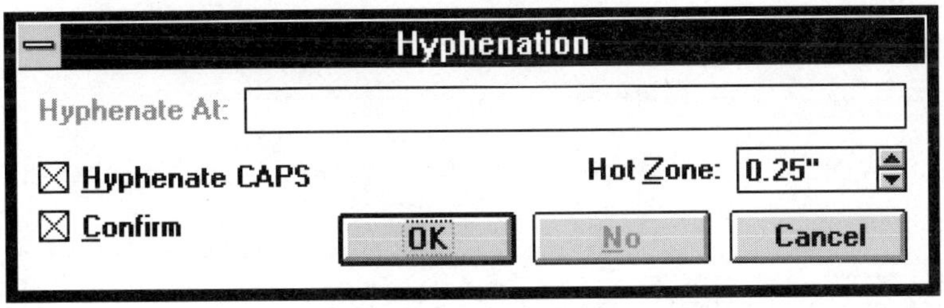

FIGURE 19.1:

The Hyphenation dialog box

points. When it is finished, you will be returned to normal view, and you will see a dialog box with the message

Hyphenation complete

5. Select OK.

6. Pull down the File menu and select Exit (Alt-F4), then No to exit Word without saving the document.

The words hyphenated in your document depend on the font used for the text.

CONFIRMING HYPHENATION

If you want to make the hyphenation decisions yourself, leave the Confirm option in the Hyphenation dialog box selected. When the text reaches a possible hyphenation point, the Hyphenation dialog box remains on the screen, and the word appears in the Hyphenate At text box. The suggested hyphenation point is shown with a hyphen and a blinking box, and the Yes option appears in place of the OK button.

Select Yes to insert the hyphen, No to skip the word, or Cancel to stop the hyphenation process. To select another hyphenation point for the word, click on the position with the mouse, or press the → or ← key to position the insertion point, and then select Yes.

In some cases, several possible hyphenation points will be shown, such as

cir-cum-stances

but Word will still display the blinking box at the suggested location.

SETTING THE HOT ZONE

The Hot Zone option in the Hyphenation dialog box determines which words the program will suggest hyphenating. When the distance between the end of the line and the right indent marker is greater than the Hot Zone setting, Word suggests hyphenating the first word in the next line. Setting the hot zone smaller than the default value results in fewer extra spaces in the line but more hyphenated words.

20 L E S S O N

FEATURING

Using the ruler's margin scale

Setting margins for facing pages

Changing margins in preview mode

▼

Setting Page Margins

In this lesson, you will learn how to set the top, bottom, left, and right margins of your document, either before or after you type the text. If you have a mouse, you can change all the margins (including the top and bottom) in preview mode, and you can set the right and left margins using the markers on the ruler. With the keyboard, you set the margins through the Page Setup dialog box.

The Default Page Settings

All the documents you have created in the previous lessons use Word's default page settings:

- $8\frac{1}{2}$-by-11-inch page size

- 1-inch top and bottom margins

- $1\frac{1}{4}$-inch left and right margins

With these settings and a 10-point font size, each page has 54 lines of text, and each line is 6 inches wide.

Changing the left and right page margins differs from changing the left and right paragraph indentations. Changing indentations affects only the paragraph in which the insertion point is located or a group of selected paragraphs. Changing the page margins, however, affects every paragraph in the document, no matter where the insertion point is placed. (In Lesson 30, you will learn how to change the margins of specific pages.)

Using the Ruler to Change Margins

To change the left and right margins with the mouse, you use the ruler in margin scale. (Without a mouse, you must set all the margins through the Page Setup dialog box, as described shortly.)

As an example we will change the left and right margins on our COMPUTER document to 2 inches.

1. Start Word and open the COMPUTER document.

2. Click on the [symbol on the left side of the ruler to change to margin scale.

The ruler is now in margin scale, as shown in Figure 20.1. In this scale, the [symbol represents the left margin, the] symbol represents

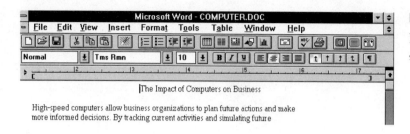

the right margin. Also notice that the ruler has shifted to the left to begin at the 1¼-inch position.

Unlike the ruler's indent scale, in which the measurements represent the width of the printed line, margin scale shows the position of the text relative to the page. Text that is not indented will align with the 1¼-inch position of the ruler, the default left margin. To change the margins, drag the margin indicators to the desired position.

3. Drag the left margin indicator ([) to the 2-inch position on the ruler. The ruler will again shift to the left, and the text lines will be narrower.

4. Drag the right margin indicator (]) to the 6½-inch position. Figure 20.2 shows the new margin settings.

To create narrower margins, drag the left margin indicator toward the left and the right margin indicator to the right. If necessary, keep moving the indicator when it reaches the edge of the screen, and the ruler will scroll. If you have trouble moving the left margin indicator toward the left, first drag it to the right, then without releasing the mouse button, drag it back toward the left until the ruler scale scrolls.

However, moving the indicators too quickly past the edge of the screen may cause some unwanted results. For example, if you move the left margin too quickly toward the left, the ruler and text will shift too far to the right. The end of your lines will scroll past the right

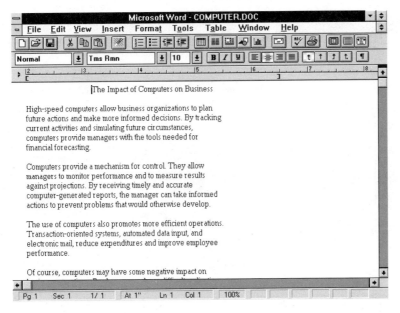

FIGURE 20.2:

Left margin set at 2 inches and right margin set at $6\frac{1}{2}$ inches

edge of the screen, and there will be a blank area along the left. To remove the blank space, move the margin back to the right, place the insertion point on a line that scrolls off the right, and press End.

Your margin changes affect the entire document. The insertion point can be anywhere in the document when you adjust the margins.

Changing the Margins with the Keyboard

With the keyboard, you can change the page margins through the Page Setup dialog box (accessed by selecting Page Setup from the Format menu). Let's use the dialog box now to change the top and bottoms margins in the COMPUTER document from the default 1 inch to 2 inches.

1. Pull down the Format menu and choose Page Setup to display the Page Setup dialog box, shown in Figure 20.3.

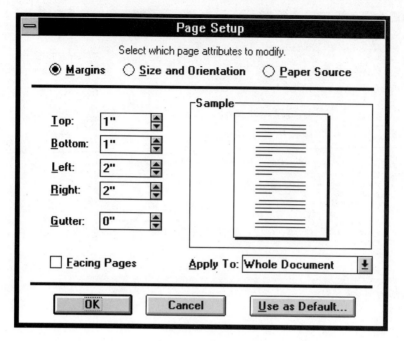

In this dialog box, you can select the margin you want to change—Left, Right, Top, or Bottom—and enter the new measurement. Remember, to change the settings in a text box, make sure the box is highlighted or delete any current setting in it before typing.

2. Select Top and enter 2 to set the new top margin.

Word assumes you mean 2 inches. You can also click the up arrow at the right of the text box to increment the setting. The facsimile of the document in the Sample box changes to reflect the new top margin.

3. Select Bottom and enter 2.

Selecting Use as Default makes the values you entered the new default settings for all new documents. As you'll learn in later lessons, the Page Setup dialog box also provides options for changing the page size and orientation, as well as the paper source.

4. Select OK to accept the changes and return to the document.

5. Pull down the File menu and choose Exit (Alt-F4), then No to exit Word without saving the edited document.

You also can format the document before you enter text. Change the settings on the ruler or in the Page Setup dialog box, and then type the document.

Alternating Margin Settings for Facing Pages

If you will be printing a document on both sides of the page, you may want to set different margins for the right (odd) and left (even) pages. For example, you might set up an extra wide margin to appear along the outside of the page, which would be the left side of even pages, and the right side of odd ones.

To set alternating margins, pull down the Format menu and select Page Setup, and then select Facing Pages (on the bottom-left side of the Page Setup dialog box). The Left and Right margin options change to Inside and Outside, and you can set the size of the inside and outside margins. Figure 20.4 shows two facing pages formatted this way.

Changing the Margins in Preview Mode

If you have a mouse, you can change the top, bottom, left, and right margins in preview mode. Pull down the File menu, choose Print Preview, and select the Margins button (under the menu bar). Figure 20.5 shows how the margins appear on the screen. The dotted horizontal lines represent the top and bottom margins, and the vertical lines show the position of the left and right margins. The small black boxes at the ends of the lines are for adjusting the margins.

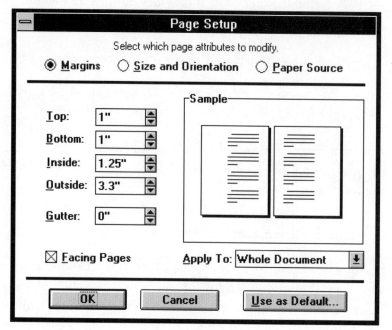

FIGURE 20.4:

Facing pages formatted for alternating margins

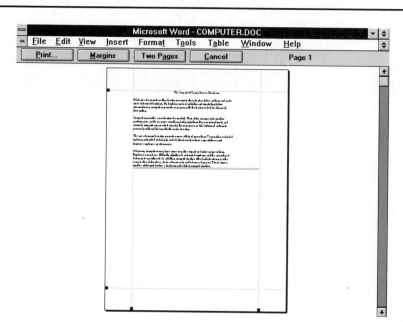

FIGURE 20.5:

Margins in preview mode

To move a margin, drag the black box along the line that represents the margin you want to change. As you drag the box, the position of the margin will be displayed in place of the Page indicator in the status bar. Drag the margin to the new position, and then release the mouse button.

FEATURING

Setting up for legal-sized paper

Handling printer conflicts

Formatting for index cards

▼

Changing Page Length and Width

Y ou need to change the size of the page when you will print the document on paper that is larger or smaller than 8½ by 11 inches. For example, you may want to use 14-inch legal-size paper, smaller personal stationery, or index cards.

To adjust the format for specially sized papers, change the page length and width settings. As you will learn in this lesson, you set custom page sizes through the Page Setup dialog box.

Formatting for Legal-Sized Paper

As an example of changing paper size, let's format the COMPUTER document to print on legal stationery.

1. Start Word and open the COMPUTER document.

2. Pull down the Format menu and choose Page Setup.

3. Select the Size and Orientation button at the top of the dialog box. The dialog box will change to show the size and orientation options, as shown in Figure 21.1.

4. Select Paper Size, and then pull down the list box and select Legal (8½ x 14 in). If your Paper Size box says Custom Size, select Height and enter 14.

5. Select OK.

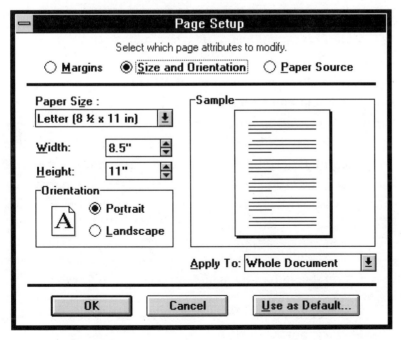

FIGURE 21.1:

The Page Setup dialog box with Size and Orientation options

Although you won't see any change on the screen, the document is now set to print on 14-inch paper. Using the new top and bottom margin settings you set in the previous lesson and the default 10-point font, you can print 60 lines on the page.

Changing the Orientation

If you have a laser printer, you can print in either portrait or landscape orientation. In portrait orientation, the text prints across the width of the page. In landscape orientation the text prints sideways across the length. Landscape orientation is useful for printing large tables and wide graphics.

To change the orientation, pull down the Format menu and select Page Setup. In the Page Setup dialog box, select the Size and Orientation button, and then choose Landscape or Portrait in the Orientation section (on the bottom-left side of the dialog box).

Dealing with Page Size Conflicts

The printer information stored by Windows itself also includes a page size setting. Some printers require this page size to match the page size you set in the Page Setup dialog box. When you print the document formatted for a different page size, you will see a dialog box warning you that the page sizes do not match.

In some cases, the dialog box will contain an option that allows you to continue printing the document, as shown in Figure 21.2. In other cases, the dialog box will not give you the option to continue, and you cannot print the document until you change the page size in the Windows environment.

To change the Windows page size, follow these steps:

1. Pull down the File menu and select Print Setup.

2. Select Setup (Alt-S) to display the dialog box for setting up your printer.

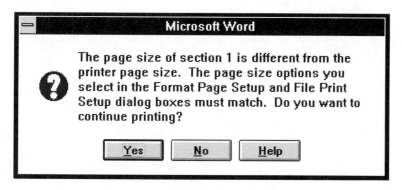

Warning that the
Word and
Windows page
sizes do not match

Figure 21.3 shows the printer setup dialog box for a LaserJet printer. The dialog box for your printer may be quite different. For example, the LaserJet printer setup dialog box has a text box with an associated drop-down list box of paper sizes; other printer setup dialog boxes have separate list boxes for selecting the page width and height.

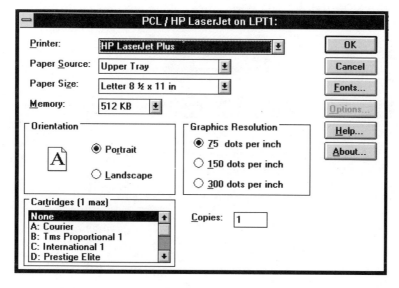

FIGURE 21.3:

A printer setup
dialog box

3. If your printer setup dialog box has a Paper Size drop-down list box, scroll through the list box to select Legal 8½ x 14. If your printer setup dialog box has separate list boxes, select 8½ inches as the width and 14 inches as the length.

4. Select OK twice to return to the document. You will see a dialog box warning you that the Windows page size settings are not used by Word, as shown in Figure 21.4.

5. Select OK.

Formatting for Index Cards

You may want to print some of your documents on index-card size paper. Suppose that you're going to give a speech on computers, using the COMPUTER document for reference. You want to print the document on continuous 3-inch by 5-inch index cards with a dot-matrix printer.

To print on the index cards, you need to set a page length of 3 inches; a width of 5 inches; and top, bottom, left, and right margins of ½ inch. Follow these steps to adjust the settings:

1. Pull down the Format menu and select Page Setup.

2. Select Width and enter 5.

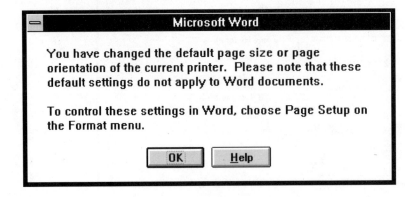

Microsoft Word

You have changed the default page size or page orientation of the current printer. Please note that these default settings do not apply to Word documents.

To control these settings in Word, choose Page Setup on the Format menu.

OK   Help

FIGURE 21.4:

Warning that the Windows page size is not used by Word

3. Select Height and enter **3**.

4. Select the Margins button at the top of the dialog box.

5. Select Top and enter **.5**.

6. Select Bottom and enter **.5**.

7. Select Left and enter **.5**.

8. Select Right and enter **.5**.

9. Select OK to accept the format.

10. To preview the document, pull down the File menu and select Print Preview.

The display changes to a graphic representation of the printed document, as shown in Figure 21.5.

11. Press Esc to exit preview mode.

12. Pull down the File menu and select Exit (Alt-F4), then No to exit Word without saving the edited document.

Saving Your Settings as the Defaults

The format changes you made in this and the previous lesson affect only the current document. But if you want to use these settings for most of the documents you type, you don't have to reset the margins or page size each time you start a new document. Instead, you can save the formats as new default values so they will be used with every document unless you manually change the settings.

Once you adjust the margin settings as you want, select the Use as Default at the bottom of the Page Setup dialog box, and then select OK. If you want other settings for a particular document, adjust its margins. (A more flexible method for adjusting default values, called styles, is discussed in Lesson 40.)

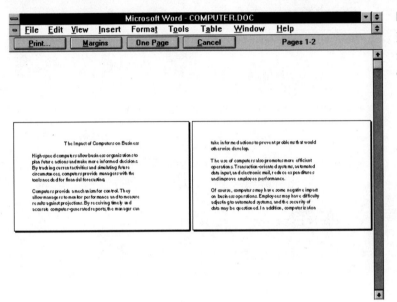

FIGURE 21.5:

Preview of text formatted to print on index cards

22 LESSON

FEATURING

**Creating
envelopes
automatically**

**Printing
envelopes**

Printing labels

▼

Addressing
Envelopes

M any word processor users run back to their typewriter when it's time to address envelopes. This is because envelopes seem to present some special formatting problems. However, Word for Windows makes formatting and printing an envelope as easy as clicking on a button in the toolbar or selecting an option from a menu.

Creating an Envelope

You create an envelope by clicking on the Envelope button in the toolbar or by selecting the Create Envelope option from the Tools menu.

Both display the Create Envelope dialog box, in which you can fill in the address and your return address.

When you create an envelope with a document already on the screen, Word looks for an address at the beginning of the document. Word assumes that an address will be a series of individual lines ending with carriage returns. It also assumes that a single line at the beginning of the document separated from the rest with a blank line, is the date. (If there is an address in the document but it is not in the beginning, select it before creating the envelope.)

As an example, we will create an envelope for the COLLECT document.

1. Start Word and open the COLLECT document.

2. Click on the Envelope button in the toolbar (the sixth one from the right. With the keyboard, pull down the Tools menu and select Create Envelope. You will see the dialog box shown in Figure 22.1.

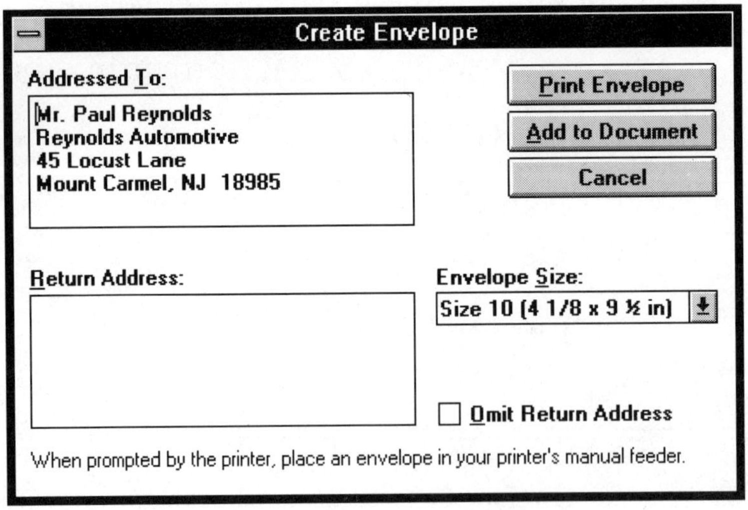

FIGURE 22.1:

The Create Envelope dialog box

The address at the beginning of the COLLECT document appears in the Addressed To box. When the document does not have an inside address, this box will be blank, ready for you to type an address. If you make a mistake, or need to change the inside address from the document, you can edit the address in the Addressed To box.

3. Select Return Address and enter the address that you want to print in the upper-left corner of the envelope.

You can omit the return address from the envelope by selecting Omit Return Address (on the bottom-right side of the dialog box).

The envelope size is a standard number 10 business envelope. To select another size, pull down the Envelope Size drop-down list box.

If you select Print Envelope, Word will print the envelope, then return to the document. Your other choice is Add to Document, which inserts the envelope into the document so that it will print when you print the document.

4. Select Add to Document. Since you edited the return address, Word will display the dialog box shown in Figure 22.2.

5. Select Yes to make the new return address the default.

The document window appears with the envelope inserted at the beginning of the document, separated from the text with a page break,

FIGURE 22.2:

The dialog box for changing the default return address

as shown in Figure 22.3. If you move the insertion point to the next page, you'll see the notation Sec 2 in the status bar. Word uses sections to include pages of different sizes or margins in the same document. You'll learn how to work with sections in Lesson 30.

Printing an Envelope

As noted above, you can print an envelope by selecting Print Envelope in the Create Envelope dialog box (click on the Envelope button in the toolbar, or select Create Envelope from the Tools menu). If you inserted the envelope in the document, as we did, the envelope will print along with the document. Let's print it now.

1. Insert an envelope in your printer. If you have a LaserJet printer, refer to the following section. If you do not have an envelope handy, insert a regular sheet of paper so you can see how Word formats the addresses.

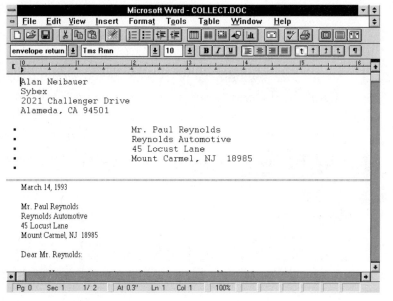

FIGURE 22.3:

Envelope inserted into the document

2. Click on the Print button in the toolbar to print the document. With the keyboard, pull down the File menu and choose **Print** (Ctrl-Shift-F12), and then select OK.

3. Pull down the File menu and choose Exit (Alt-F4), then **No** to exit Word without saving the edited document.

Word for Windows sends all the pages to the Windows Print Manager, which is a special program that controls the flow of work to the printer. If you are using a printer set for manual feed, such as for individual sheets of paper or envelopes on nonlaser printers, the printer will wait until you tell it to print each page. Instructions for using Print Manager are given in Lesson 33.

To select manual feed, pull down the Format menu and select Page Setup. In the Page Setup dialog box, click on the **Paper Source** button. The options available to you depend on your printer. Select the paper source, and then select OK.

PRINTING ENVELOPES WITH LASER PRINTERS

You control laser printers by inserting the envelope into the manual intake tray or through the printer's control panel. The envelope function assumes that you feed the envelopes in the center of the manual input tray. However, older model laser printers, such as the LaserJet Plus, accept envelopes on the left edge of the tray. Before printing envelopes with these printer models, you have to adjust the page size and margins of the envelope.

Place the insertion point in the envelope on the screen, and then make the following changes:

■ Set the top margin at 4.75 inches.

■ Set the left margin at 2.5 inches.

■ Set the paper size at Letter (8½ x 11 in.)

Creating Mailing Labels

To simplify the task of formatting and printing labels, Word provides a template that automatically creates labels for you. A template is a special document that contains formatting information. The template for mailing labels also includes macros that guide you through setting up your labels for printing. In the following steps, you will use these Word features to print mailing labels. You will learn more about templates and macros in later lessons.

1. Start Word, pull down the File menu, and select New. (Do not use the New Document button on the toolbar.)

2. Select MAILLABL in the Use Template list box, and then select OK.

Word will recall the template from the disk, and then display a dialog box showing label forms that are suitable for your printer. Figure 22.4 shows an example of a list of forms displayed for a LaserJet

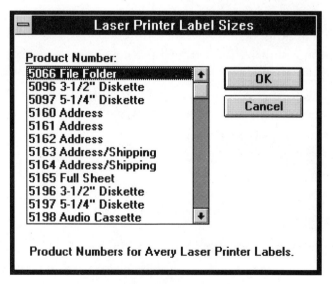

FIGURE 22.4:

A dialog box listing predefined label forms

printer. Use this dialog box to select the type of label you plan to use. If you scroll through the list, you will see that it includes a wide range of label stock, including diskette labels, name tags, badges, and video cassette labels.

3. Select 5160 Address, and then choose OK.

Word automatically displays a table representing the arrangement of the labels on the sheet, and then displays the dialog box shown in Figure 22.5. You use the Multiple Label option to merge addresses from a mailing list, as explained in Lesson 39. Select Single Label to enter the label information manually.

4. Select **S**ingle Label to display the dialog box shown in Figure 22.6.

The **R**ow and **C**olumn options in the Label Location section of the dialog box indicate the location of the label you are about to fill in. By default, it is set at the first label on the sheet. If you want to print a label on a sheet that already contains completed labels, select the row and column of the next blank label.

5. In the Text for Line 1 text box, type **Adam Chesin**.

6. Press Tab to reach the next text box and type **8745 West Avenue**.

FIGURE 22.5:

Select to manually enter labels or merge labels from a mailing list

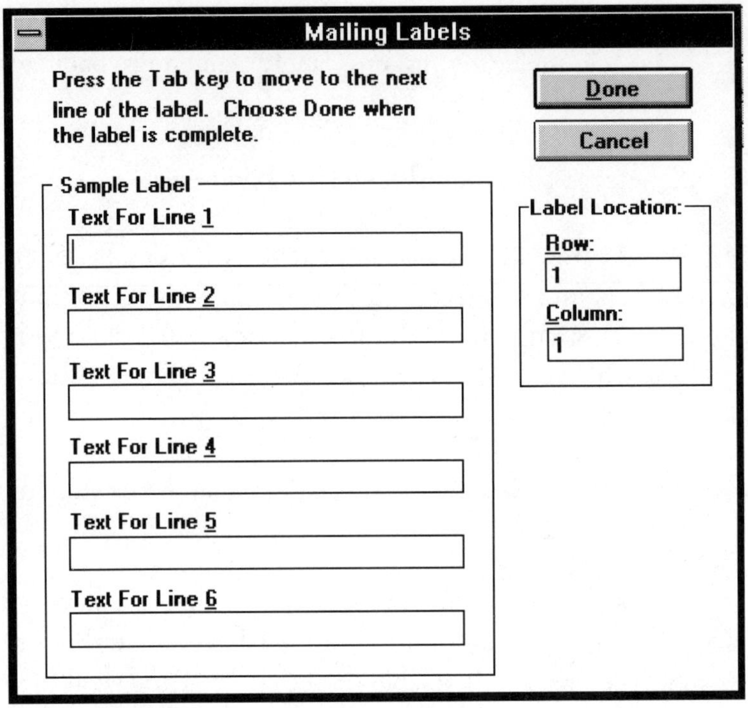

FIGURE 22.6:
Enter the label information and select a label on the page

7. Press Tab to reach the next text box and type **Glenside, PA 19111**.

8. Select Done.

Word displays the label document with the address information inserted, as shown in Figure 22.7. Let's continue and add two more addresses.

9. Press Tab to reach the next label in the row, then type the next label.

Jane Boclair
925 First Avenue
Margate, NJ 08045

10. Press Tab to reach the next label and type the other address.

>   Samuel Adams
>   12 Locust Road
>   Louisville, KY 40233

11. Insert a sheet of label stock in your printer. If you don't want to waste a label sheet, use a plain sheet of paper that is the same size instead.

12. Click on the Print button on the toolbar. With the keyboard, pull down the File menu, select Print, and then choose OK. The document will print with the addresses properly spaced to print on the sheet of labels.

13. Pull down the File menu, select Exit, then No to exit Word without saving the document.

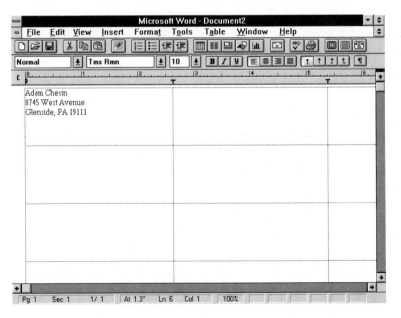

FIGURE 22.7:

Word adds the label information to the table

You can always save the label document to print at a later time or to add labels. To add labels, open the document as you would any other, place the insertion point in the label you want to fill out, and then type the label information.

You have now learned all the fundamental ways to format your documents. In the next lessons, you will learn how to use Word's other features to streamline your work.

Sample

P A R T 4

Advanced Features

Using the Global Glossary

Typing can be tedious, particularly if you must retype the same words or phrase. For instance, you may have to repeat a standard closing, a complex contract term, or some other text in more than one document, or even several times in the same document. In this lesson, you will learn how to avoid retyping text by adding it to Word's global glossary, a special file that is available to all your documents.

Using Boilerplate

Standard text that you use repeatedly is called *boilerplate*. Rather than retype boilerplate text, you can save it as a *glossary*, and then recall it whenever you need to insert it in a document.

Every time you start Word, a default glossary, the *global glossary*, is loaded automatically. This glossary is stored on your disk with the NORMAL.DOT file, which contains Word's default values. Boilerplate stored in the global glossary is available immediately with every document you type.

Adding Text to the Glossary

You should consider placing any text that you type often, such as your name and address or company name, in Word's global glossary. You place text in a glossary by selecting what you want to include, and then using the Glossary option on the Edit menu.

As an example, we will create two glossary entries containing names and addresses. Follow these steps:

1. Start Word and select the Center button in the ribbon (Ctrl-E) to center the text.

2. Type your name and address as you use it in correspondence, such as:

Ms. Martha Ray
1876 Old Farm Road
Turnersville, CA 90461

3. Press ↵ after your address, and then select the Left button on the ribbon (Ctrl-L) to return to left alignment.

4. Select all the text you just typed.

5. Pull down the Edit menu and choose Glossary to display the dialog box shown in Figure 23.1.

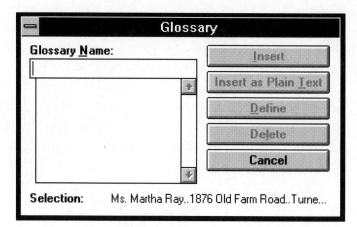

FIGURE 23.1:

The Glossary dialog box

The first 34 characters of the highlighted text appear at the bottom of the dialog box, next to Selection. Carriage returns are indicated by two periods (..).

6. In the Glossary Name box, type **Address**. Glossary names can be up to 31 characters, including spaces.

7. Select **D**efine, and the selected text will be copied into the global glossary.

8. Deselect the text.

9. Type another name and address that you use regularly in correspondence. Include the salutation as well. For example:

Mr. William Smithson
561 Locust Lane
Mt. Pleasant, NJ 09272

Dear Bill:

10. Select the text you just typed. Do not include your own address, which is still on the screen.

11. Pull down the Edit menu and select Glossary. Notice that the name of the boilerplate you just added, ADDRESS, appears in the Glossary Name list box.

12. Type a name for this glossary entry (for example, Smithson for Mr. Smithson) and select **Define**.

13. Pull down the File menu and select Close, then **No** to clear the document window without saving the text.

14. Click on the New Document button in the toolbar. With the keyboard, pull down the File menu and select New, then choose OK.

The text you added to the global glossary can be inserted in any number of documents by pressing a function key or choosing a menu option.

Inserting Boilerplate from the Glossary

In the following steps, you will write a sample letter. But instead of typing your address and the inside address, you will get them from the global glossary. We will use two ways of inserting boilerplate text: with the F3 function key and with the Glossary option on the Edit menu.

1. Type the name of the boilerplate text, **ADDRESS**. Leave the insertion point immediately after the word; do not press the spacebar.

2. Press F3, the Glossary key. Your name and address will appear, centered just as you saved it.

3. Select the Center button in the ribbon (Ctrl-E), type the date, press ↵, then select the Left button in the ribbon (Ctrl-L).

(You will learn how to add the date automatically in Lesson 26.)

4. Pull down the Edit menu and select Glossary to display the Glossary dialog box.

5. From the Glossary Name list box, select the name you gave the other address you typed. The first 34 characters of the highlighted glossary entry appear next to Selection at the bottom of the dialog box.

6. Select Insert, and the text of the glossary entry will be inserted in your document.

The other insertion option is Insert as Plain Text. When you select this button, Word inserts the contents of the entry without any formatting.

7. Type the following letter.

> **Thank you for sending me the materials I requested. I will return them as soon as I've had the opportunity to review the pertinent documents.**
> **If I can be of any assistance, please do not hesitate to call.**
> **Sincerely,**

Your completed document should look like the one shown in Figure 23.2.

8. Click on the Save button in the toolbar. With the keyboard, pull down the File menu and select Save (Shift-F12).

9. Type **Note**, then select OK twice.

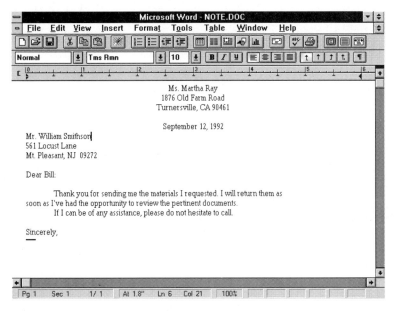

FIGURE 23.2:

Completed letter using glossary boilerplate text

Saving the Glossary

In order for your glossary entries to be available in subsequent Word sessions, you must save the edited NORMAL.DOT file that now contains them. You will have a chance to do so now when you exit Word.

1. Pull down the File menu and select Exit (Alt-F4) to exit Word. A dialog box appears with the message

Do you want to save the global glossary and command changes?

2. Select Yes to save the glossary entries.

The other options are Cancel, to remain in Word; No, to discard the glossary entries; and Help. Choose No when you created the entries for the current session only and will not want to use them again.

SAVING THE GLOSSARY AND DOCUMENT

Instead of saving the glossary entries when you leave Word, you can save the glossary and the document at one time. Pull down the File menu and select Save All. If you made any changes to the document since you last saved it, a dialog box appears, asking if you want to save the changes. Select Yes, No, Cancel, or Help.

Save All also saves any other open documents (in other windows), as well as macros, which are stored sequences of keystrokes. You'll learn about these other features in later lessons.

Printing the Glossary

As you add entries to the glossary, it may become difficult to remember what each entry contains. You can see the first 34 characters of the entry next to Selection in the Glossary dialog box, but this might not be enough to clearly identify longer paragraphs.

For reference, you can print a copy of the glossary, including the name and complete contents of each entry. Let's print a copy now.

1. Start Word, pull down the File menu, and select Print (Ctrl-Shift-F12) to display the Print dialog box.

2. Pull down the Print list box, shown in Figure 23.3.

3. Select Glossary, then OK.

You can also select the text box, press G to select Glossary, and then select OK. You will learn more about using Word's printing options in Lesson 33.

Word will print the glossary entries in alphabetical order, with the name of the entry in boldface.

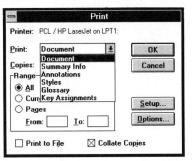

FIGURE 23.3:

The Print list box

Clearing the Glossary

You remove boilerplate from the glossary as easily as you entered it. Now let's erase the sample entries:

1. Pull down the Edit menu and select Glossary.

2. In the Glossary dialog box, select ADDRESS.

3. Select Delete.

4. Select the other entry in the Glossary Name list box.

5. Select Delete.

6. Pull down the File menu and select Close.

7. Pull down the File menu and select Exit (Alt-F4), then Yes to exit Word and save the edited glossary.

Using the Spike

The *Spike* is a special glossary entry used to accumulate text that you want to insert as a group elsewhere. After you insert the contents of the

Spike, they are deleted from the glossary, so you can only use that particular entry once.

For example, suppose you are moving a number of nonconsecutive paragraphs to the same location elsewhere in the document. Without using the Spike, you would have to select and relocate each paragraph separately, moving the insertion point back and forth with each paragraph. Instead, you could just highlight each paragraph and insert it in the Spike. Then move the insertion point to the final location and insert the contents of the Spike—all the paragraphs—at one time.

To insert text into the Spike, select the text, then press Ctrl-F3. Word deletes the selected text from the document and inserts it in the glossary under the name SPIKE, adding a carriage return to the end.

Any other text that you insert in the Spike is added to its current contents, so you can use the Spike to gather sections of text together as a group.

When you want to insert the contents of the Spike in your document, position the insertion point and then use one of the following methods:

- Press Ctrl-Shift-F3.

- Pull down the Edit menu, select Glossary, and then select SPIKE in the Glossary dialog box.

- Type **SPIKE** and press F3.

The contents of the Spike will appear in the document, and the SPIKE glossary entry will be erased.

FEATURING

**Storing
boilerplate in
template
glossaries
Using templates**

▼

Creating Templates

In the previous lesson, you learned how to use Word's global glossary to store and insert boilerplate. If you have certain boilerplate paragraphs that you use for special documents, such as wills, contracts, or leases, you may not want to clutter the global glossary with all these entries. Instead, you can place the entries you don't use for everyday documents in a document template.

A *template* is a special file containing formats and glossary entries. You load it only when needed for the current document. You can create as many different templates as your disk can hold. Your templates will automatically include the global formats and glossary entries in NOR-MAL.DOT. In this lesson, you will learn how to create and use templates.

Setting Up a Template Glossary

As an example, we will create a template that contains boilerplate paragraphs for wills. In Lesson 41, you will learn how to add custom styles, or formats, to templates.

Follow these steps to enter the boilerplate paragraphs and save them in a custom template:

1. Start Word, pull down the File menu, and select New.

2. In the New dialog box, select the Template button, and then choose OK. The document name will appear as Template1.

3. Type the following text. The blank spaces are reserved for the information that will change each time a will is produced. (Use the underline character to enter the lines at the end of the document.)

I,   , of the City of   , in   County, State of   , being of sound and disposing mind, memory, and understanding, do hereby make this my Last Will and Testament and hereby revoke all my prior Wills and/or Codicils.

I give and bequeath my entire estate to my husband,   . If my husband fails to survive me, I give and bequeath the foregoing items to   .

I give and bequeath all of my entire estate to my wife,   . If my wife fails to survive me, I give and bequeath the foregoing items to   .

I give and bequeath my entire estate to   .

I direct that all inheritance and succession taxes, of any kind whatsoever, which may be due as a result of my death, shall be paid out of the principal of my residuary estate. I authorize my fiduciaries to pay such taxes at such time or times as they may deem advisable.

I hereby appoint   as Executor hereunder. Upon the resignation or inability of   to serve as Executor, I appoint   .

In Witness whereof, I have set my hand and seal this day,   .

Signed, sealed, and declared in the presence of us as subscribing witnesses.

_____

Witness   Address

_____

Witness   Address

4. Select the first paragraph. Include the blank line following the text.

5. Pull down the Edit menu and select Glossary to display the Glossary dialog box (see Figure 23.1).

6. Type the name **Sound**.

7. Select Define. Word will display the dialog box shown in Figure 24.1.

In this dialog box, you can select to save the entry in either the global glossary or in your own custom template.

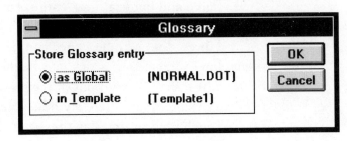

FIGURE 24.1:

The dialog box for saving text in either the global glossary or a template

8. Select In Template to save this entry in your own template instead of NORMAL.DOT, and then select OK.

9. Select, name, and copy each of the remaining paragraphs into the glossary as **Husband**, **Wife**, **Other**, **Taxes**, **Executor**, and **Signed**, respectively. Be sure to select In Template for each entry. For the boilerplate entry named Signed, select all the text shown in Figure 24.2. Be sure to include the blank line following each of the paragraphs.

10. Select all the text in the document, then pull down the Edit menu and select Cut or press Del to delete it.

If you do not delete the text from the screen, it will automatically appear whenever you use the template. In this case, we want to select specific paragraphs from the glossary, not have them all appear at once.

11. Click on the Save button in the toolbar. With the keyboard, pull down the File menu and select Save (Shift-F12).

12. Type **Wills**, and then select OK twice. Word adds the .DOT extension to all templates.

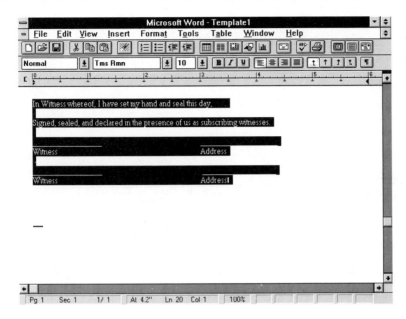

FIGURE 24.2:

Text to select for the Signed boilerplate

Using Your Template Glossary

Before you can insert the text from a custom template, you must first tell Word to use that template when you start a new document. After selecting the template, you can use it with your new document.

SELECTING A TEMPLATE

You can select a template for Word to use from the New dialog box. Let's choose our template so we can create a sample will.

1. Pull down the File menu and select Close.

2. Pull down the File menu and select New.

The names of the available templates are listed in the Use Template list box. In addition to the normal template, which is automatically highlighted, the list contains several templates provided with Word, as well as your own template, WILLS.

3. Scroll through the list until the name WILLS appears.

4. Select WILLS, and then choose OK.

The WILLS template is now associated with the document you are about to create.

INSERTING BOILERPLATE FROM A TEMPLATE

In the following steps, you will use the WILLS template to create the document shown in Figure 24.3.

Last Will and Testament

I, Carlo Hesser, of the City of Llanview, in Montgomery County, State of Pennsylvania, being of sound and disposing mind, memory, and understanding, do hereby make this my Last Will and Testament and hereby revoke all my prior Wills and/or Codicils.

I give and bequeath all of my entire estate to my wife, Stephenie Wilson. If my wife fails to survive me, I give and bequeath the foregoing items to Llanview University.

I direct that all inheritance and succession taxes, of any kind whatsoever, which may be due as a result of my death, shall be paid out of the principal of my residuary estate. I authorize my fiduciaries to pay such taxes at such time or times as they may deem advisable.

I hereby appoint Jamie Johnson as Executor hereunder. Upon the resignation or inability of Ms. Johnson to serve as Executor, I appoint Williard Shelley.

In Witness whereof, I have set my hand and seal this day, October 22, 1993.

Signed, sealed, and declared in the presence of us as subscribing witnesses.

_____   _____
Witness   Address

_____   _____
Witness   Address

FIGURE 24.3:

Document assembled using boilerplate from the WILLS template

1. Select the Center button in the ribbon (Ctrl-E), type **Last Will and Testament**, and press ↵ twice.

2. Select the Left button in the ribbon (Ctrl-L) to cancel centering.

3. Type **Sound**, and then press F3. The first boilerplate paragraph will be inserted into the text, as shown in Figure 24.4.

4. Move the insertion point to the paragraph and type the text **Carlo Hesser, Llanview, Montgomery,** and **Pennsylvania,** respectively, in the blank spaces. Delete any extra spaces.

By leaving blanks to be filled in the boilerplate, you have made the template glossary entries useful for a wider range of documents.

5. Place the insertion point on the second line following the paragraph, type **Wife**, and press F3. The next boilerplate paragraph will appear.

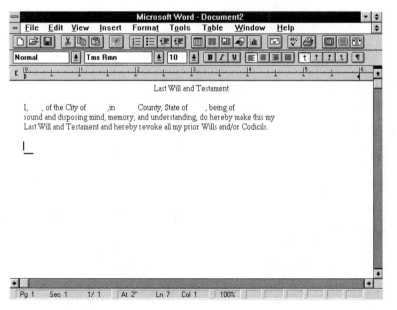

FIGURE 24.4:

First boilerplate entry from the template glossary

6. Add the names **Stephenie Wilson** and **Llanview University** in the blank spaces.

7. Place the insertion point on the second line following the paragraph, type **Taxes**, and press F3.

8. Type **Executor** and press F3.

9. Add the names **Jamie Johnson**, **Ms. Johnson**, and **Williard Shelly** to the paragraph.

10. Place the insertion point on the second line following the paragraph, type **Signed**, and press F3.

11. Enter the date **October 22, 1993**.

12. Click on the Print button in the toolbar to print the document. With the keyboard, pull down the File menu and select Print (Ctrl-Shift-F12), and then choose OK.

13. Pull down the File menu and select Close, then No to clear the document window without saving the text.

14. Click on the New Document button in the toolbar. With the keyboard, pull down the File menu and select New, then OK.

15. If you're not ready to continue with the next lesson, pull down the File menu and select Exit (Alt-F4).

When you print a glossary listing, entries in the template appear first, followed by global entries.

Accessing Other Templates

If you start a document using one template, you can change your mind and use another template with it. To access the glossary in any other template, pull down the File menu and select Template to display the dialog box shown in Figure 24.5. In the Attach Document To list box, select the template you now want to use with the document, and then choose OK.

The other options in the Template dialog box allow you to control how your glossary entries are saved when you are using a template other than NORMAL.DOT. By default, Word is set to display the dialog box shown in Figure 24.1 whenever you define a glossary entry. To add the item to the template glossary or the global glossary without being prompted, select the Prompt for Each New option to turn it off.

FIGURE 24.5:

The Template dialog box

FEATURING

Setting up tables

Calculating in tables and text

Formatting tables

▼

Creating Tables

You can create rows and columns of words and numbers by manually calculating and setting tabs, as you learned in Lesson 15. However, Word provides a much simpler way to produce professional-looking tables. By using the Table button in the toolbar or the Insert Table option on the Table menu, you can have Word set up the table for you, so that all you have to do is type in the data.

As you will learn in this lesson, you can easily create a table, have Word perform spreadsheet-like calculations with the data in the table, and choose formatting options to control the appearance of the printed version.

Creating a Table with a Mouse

If you have a mouse, you can create a table by using the Table button in the toolbar. As an example, we will create the table shown in Figure 25.1, which has three columns and seven rows.

1. Point to the Table button in the toolbar (the twelfth one from the left) and hold down the left mouse button. You will see a miniature grid, which represents the rows and columns of a table, as shown in Figure 25.2.

2. Drag the mouse slightly down.

As you drag the mouse, some of the squares in the grid become black to show they are selected. This is how you indicate the size of the table you want to create. The indicator beneath the grid shows the number of rows and columns currently selected. By dragging the mouse

Regional Sales Territory	1993	1994
North	1,474,186.00	1,663,383.00
South	1,623,983.00	1,730,792.00
East	1,541,862.00	1,693,827.00
West	1,687,151.00	1,759,217.00
Total	$6,327,182.00	$6,847,219.00
Average	$1,581,795.50	$1,711,804.75

FIGURE 25.1:

Sample table

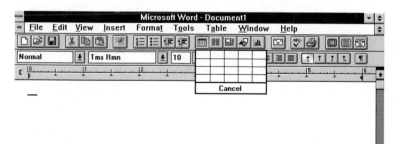

FIGURE 25.2:

Miniature grid representing table

down and to the right, you can expand the grid to create a table with as many as 30 rows and 13 columns.

3. Continue dragging the mouse past the last row in the grid. The grid will expand to reveal additional rows.

4. Move the mouse down until the indicator below the grid says 7 x 1 Table, then to the right two columns until it says 7 x 3 Table.

5. Release the mouse button.

A blank table appears at the top of the screen, and the ruler will change to table scale, as shown in Figure 25.3. In this scale, the ruler indicates the width of the columns, not tab settings. Each T symbol marks a column boundary. However, if you move the insertion point outside the table, the ruler will change to show indent scale.

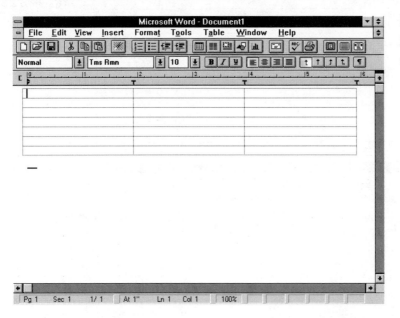

FIGURE 25.3:

Blank table on the screen

Each *cell* in the table is referenced by its row and column numbers. The top-left cell is R1C1. The first four rows are referenced like this:

	A	B	C
1	R1C1	R1C2	R1C3
2	R2C1	R2C2	R2C3
3	R3C1	R3C2	R3C3
4	R4C1	R4C2	R4C3

The dotted lines that outline the cells help you visualize the whole table and the width of each cell. These lines do not print with the table, but you can format the table with lines that will print, as you will learn shortly.

Creating a Table with the Keyboard

With the keyboard, you create and work with tables by using the options on the Table menu. Follow these steps to create the sample table (Figure 25.1):

1. Pull down the Table menu, and you will notice that most of the options are dimmed. They will become available after you create a table.

2. Select Insert Table to see the dialog box shown in Figure 25.4.

3. Type 3 in the Number of Columns text box.

4. Type 7 in the Number of Rows text box. The blank table will appear on the screen (Figure 25.3).

When Auto is selected for the Column Width option, Word will divide the page width evenly among all the columns, so the table spans the width of the page from the left to right margin. If you want the table

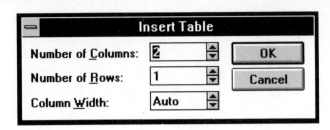

FIGURE 25.4:

The Insert Table dialog box

to be narrower, type the column width in the text box, or click on the arrows to change the setting. For example, entering 1" for Column Width will produce a table that is 3 inches wide.

5. Select OK in the Insert Table dialog box.

Entering Data in a Table

With the table structure established, all you need to do is type the data you want to appear in each cell. To place the insertion point in a cell, click on the cell with the mouse. Using the keyboard, press Tab, Shift-Tab, or the arrow keys to move from cell to cell.

The cell height will adjust automatically to the amount of text you type. If you press ↵ within a cell, the cell height will increase by one line.

Now you will fill in the table on your screen, but you will not type data in all the cells. In the next section, you will have Word calculate and insert the remaining entries.

1. The insertion point is in cell R1C1. Type **Regional Sales Territory**.

Depending on the font you are using, the word *Territory* may wrap to the next line, automatically expanding the height of the first row. If the word does not wrap and is not fully displayed in the cell, you should change fonts or turn off the Line Breaks and Fonts as Printed option in the Options dialog box (pull down the Tools menu and select **O**ptions).

2. Press ↓ to reach cell R2C1 and type **North**.

3. Press ↓ to reach cell R3C1 and type **South**.

4. Press ↓ to reach cell R4C1 and type **East**.

5. Press ↓ to reach cell R5C1 and type **West**.

6. Press ↓ to reach cell R6C1 and type **Total**.

7. Press ↓ to reach cell R7C1 and type **Average**.

8. Use the mouse, arrow keys, or the Tab key to reach cell R1C2, the first cell in the second column, and type **1993**.

9. Press ↓ to reach cell R2C2 and type **1,474,186.00**.

10. Complete the next three cells in that column with the following data.

CELL	ENTRY
R3C2	1,623,983.00
R4C2	1,541,862.00
R5C2	1,687,151.00

11. Use the mouse, arrow keys, or Tab key to reach cell R1C3 and type **1994**.

12. Complete the next four cells in that column with these figures.

CELL	ENTRY
R2C3	1,663,383.00
R3C3	1,730,792.00

CELL	ENTRY
R4C3	1,693,827.00
R5C3	1,759,217.00

Using Fields for Calculations

The last two rows in our table are for totals and averages of the figures we entered. Not only can Word calculate these figures, but it will update the results whenever you change a value used in the calculation.

Let's start by inserting the total of the cells in the second column.

1. Place the insertion point in cell R6C2.

2. Pull down the Insert menu and select Field to display the dialog box shown in Figure 25.5.

The Insert Field Type list box, on the left, contains all the field commands. The expression field type, which is the one we will use to

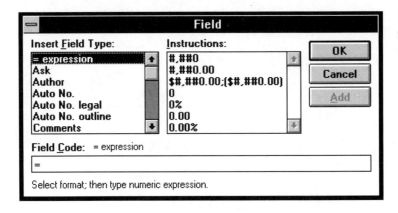

FIGURE 25.5:

The Field dialog box

insert formulas in the table, is already selected. The Instructions list box on the right contains options that allow you to customize the way each field operates. You will learn more about fields in Lesson 26.

3. Click in the Field Code text box. With the keyboard, press Alt-C, then →. Be careful not to delete the equal sign (=).

4. Type **sum([R2C2:R5C2])**. Check your typing carefully. If you make a mistake, Word will not be able to perform the calculations. The R and C can be either uppercase or lowercase.

The sum function computes the total of a range of cells. In this case, the range includes all cells defined by the rectangular area from cell R2C2 to cell R5C2. To define a range, type the cells in the upper-left and lower-right corner of the rectangular area, separated by a colon. The other mathematical functions are listed in Table 25.1.

You can format the results of the calculation using the options in the Instructions box. We want the totals to automatically appear with a dollar sign and two decimal places, which is the third instruction in the list box. This instruction also places negative numbers in parentheses.

5. Click on the instruction $#,##0.00;($#,##0.00). With the keyboard, press Alt-I, then press ↓ three times.

6. Select **Add** to place the instruction in the Field Code text box, next to the formula.

7. Select OK. Word calculates the total, $6,327,182.00, and inserts it in the cell.

Now we need to place a similar formula in cell R6C3 and format it by using the same instruction.

8. Place the insertion point in cell R6C3, pull down the Insert menu and select Field.

FUNCTION	RESULT
Average()	Calculates the average of the range.
Count()	Displays the number of items in the range.
Max()	Displays the largest number in the range.
Min()	Displays the smallest number in the range.
Sum()	Calculates the total of the range.
Product()	Multiplies the items in the range.
Int(x)	Calculates the integer value of the number.
Mod(x,y)	Returns the remainder of x divided by y.
Round(x,y)	Rounds number x to y positions.
True	Returns the value 1.
False	Returns the value 0.
Abs(x)	Returns the absolute value of the argument, which is the number regardless of its sign.
And(x,y)	Returns 1 if all the arguments are true. Returns 0 if one or more of the arguments are false.
Defined(x)	Returns 1 if the argument is evaluated without an error (if the bookmark exists or the calculation does not divide by zero). Returns 0 if an error is detected.
If(x,y,z)	If argument x is true, the function performs operation y. If argument x is false, the function performs operation z. For example, the field code ={If(1=1, 3+3, 4+4) displays the value 6.
Not(x)	Returns the reverse of the argurment: 0 if the argument is true; 1 if the argument is false.
Or(x,y)	Returns 1 if any of the arguments are true. Returns 0 if all the arguments are false.
Sign(x)	Returns 1 if the argument is positive, −1 if the argument is negative, or 0 if the argument is zero.

TABLE 25.1:

Word's Mathematical Functions

9. Click in the Field Code box (or press Alt-C then →) and type **sum([R2C3:R5C3])**.

10. Select the third instruction, then **Add**, and then **OK**.

Instead of using the Field dialog box to calculate the averages for the last row of the table, you will type the formulas directly in the cells. You could use the Average function (see Table 25.1), but in this example, you will divide the totals by four. This will demonstrate how to reference a single cell in a table calculation.

11. Place the insertion point in cell R7C2 and press Ctrl-F9 to display the opening and closing brackets, { }, Word's codes for a field.

12. The insertion point is between the brackets. Type **=sum([R6C2])/4**.

13. Press F9, the Update key.

Word replaces the formula with the results, displayed in the same format as the cells referenced in the formula. If you see an error message on the screen, or hear a beep, press Shift-F9 to redisplay the formula, correct your mistake, and then press F9 again.

14. In the same manner, in cell R7C3, enter and calculate the formula **=sum([R6C3])/4**.

You cannot reference a single cell by itself in a calculation. Word would report an error if you tried entering [R6C3]/4. You must use the sum function in the formula to convert the single cell reference to its numeric value.

WORKING WITH TABLES THAT CONTAIN FIELDS

When working with your table, you might want to see the field codes rather than the results of the calculations. To display the field codes, pull down the View menu and select Field Codes to turn it on. When you want to see the result, select the option again to toggle it off. You'll learn how to print the table showing field codes rather than results in Lesson 33.

To display the field codes in a single cell, place the insertion point on the displayed results in the cell, and then press Shift-F9. Press Shift-F9 again to redisplay the results. In page layout view, pressing Shift-F9 toggles between the results and codes display for the entire table. Also, pressing Ctrl-F9 in page layout view to enter a field code automatically displays the field codes in the entire table.

If you change any of the numbers used in a calculation, the field will not change automatically on the screen. To display the new figures, print the table or position the insertion point in a cell you want to update and press F9.

Formatting Tables

You can enhance your tables by adding character styles, changing the alignment, and including lines (or rules) that will print. You format table entries in the same way that you format regular text. Lines are added through the Border Table dialog box (accessed through the Border option on the Format menu). You can quickly select an entire row or column or the whole table by using the Select options on the Table menu.

Now we will boldface and center the column headings in our table, right align the numbers under the year columns, and add lines around the cells.

1. Place the insertion point in the first row, pull down the Table menu and choose Select Row.

2. Select the Bold button in the ribbon (Ctrl-B).

3. Select the Center button in the ribbon (Ctrl-E).

4. Click the mouse, or press an arrow key, to deselect the cells.

5. Select cells R2C2 to R7C3 (drag the mouse or insertion point to select cells), and then select the Right button in the ribbon (Ctrl-R).

6. Click the mouse or press an arrow key to deselect the cells.

7. Make sure the insertion point is in the table, then pull down the Table menu and select Select Table. With the keyboard, press Alt-5, using the 5 key on the numeric keypad.

8. Pull down the Format menu and select Border to display the dialog box shown in Figure 25.6.

The options in the Border Table dialog box let you set the type of line to use for the table border (the **Box** option) or grid lines (the **Grid** option). You can also select individual border or grid lines in the Border box, which contains a facsimile of the page. The **Shading** button displays a dialog box with options for background and foreground colors and background shading in cells.

9. Select **Grid** in the Preset section at the bottom of the Border Table dialog box. The thick line in the Line section will be selected.

10. Select OK to set a grid with that line style. The dotted lines in the table will be replaced by solid lines (as in Figure 25.1).

11. Click the mouse or press an arrow key to deselect the table.

12. Click on the Print button in the toolbar to print the document. With the keyboard, pull down the File menu and select Print (Ctrl-Shift-F12), then OK.

13. Click on the Save button in the toolbar. With the keyboard, pull down the File menu and select Save (Shift-F12).

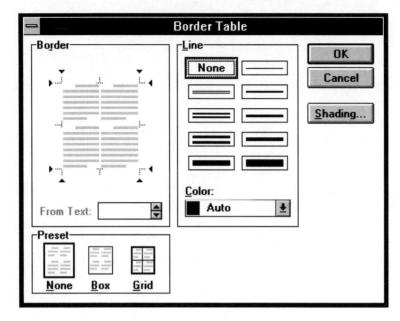

14. Type **Sales**, and then select OK twice.

15. Pull down the File menu and select Exit (Alt-F4) to exit Word.

CHANGING COLUMN WIDTHS

With the mouse, you can make columns wider or narrower by dragging either the column-boundary markers (the T symbols) on the ruler, or the dotted column borders in the table. When you point to a column border in the table, the mouse pointer changes to a double-vertical line with left- and right- pointing arrows. Unless you select the rows you want to affect before dragging a marker or boundary, the column width for all the rows in the table will be changed.

To change the column width with the keyboard, place the insertion point in any cell in the column, and then pull down the Table menu and select Column Width. In the dialog box, enter the new width for the column.

Moving and Copying Tables

You can move or copy a table, or selected cells, in the same way that you move or copy text. Select the table, and then use any of the techniques that you learned in Lesson 9, including *drop and drag*. If you cut or copy selected cells in the table, the Edit menu will show Paste Cells in place of Paste.

In this lesson, we inserted the table at the start of a blank page. However, if there is already text in the document, Word will insert the table at the location of the insertion point. This means that you can place a table anywhere in the document by positioning the insertion point where you want the table, and then adding the table using the Table button on the toolbar or the Insert Table option in the Table menu.

Performing Calculations in Text

You can use the expression field type to quickly perform math in text as well as in tables. For example, suppose you're typing the sentence

You ordered 25 units at $12.25 each, for a total of $

To insert the total of the order, press Ctrl-F9 to display the field brackets {}, then type

= 25 * 12.25

The sentence will appear on the screen as

You ordered 25 units at $12.25 each, for a total of ${= 25* 12.25}.

Place the insertion point inside the field code brackets and press F9. Word will calculate the total and replace the formula with that value.

Word gives precedence to multiplication and division. For example, it will calculate the formula

{= 90 + 95 + 85/3}

as 213.33 by first dividing 85 by 3, then adding 90 and 95 to the result. If you want the average of the three numbers, which is 90, enter the formula as

{=(90 + 95 + 85)/3}

Word will perform the calculations within parentheses first, and then divide the results by 3.

To add a column of numbers in a table without using a field code, highlight the numbers, and then pull down the Tools menu and select Calculate. Word will perform the calculation, then briefly display

The result of calculation is:

on the status bar, followed by the total. Word places the results of the calculation in the Clipboard. To insert the results in your document, pull down the Edit menu and select Paste (Ctrl-V).

You can also use the Calculate option in the Tools menu to quickly perform four-function math. For example, you could highlight the formula in the sentence

You now owe 500 + 234 - 250

and then select Calculate. Word will insert 484 in the Clipboard. Press Ctrl-V to replace the highlighted formula with the results. (If you are not in the default mode, in which typing replaces selection, first press Del to erase the formula, then press Ctrl-V.)

Using Fields

In Lesson 25, you learned that you can insert fields to perform calculations in tables and text. This lesson shows you how to use fields to have Word insert text, such as the date and time, in your documents.

Inserting Dates and Times

In the previous lessons, you entered the date manually. But you can also have Word supply the date or time for you.

Your computer has a built-in clock that maintains the current date and time. You can insert the date and time into your document by using a field, much like the expression field you used in Lesson 25. For example, you can press Ctrl-F9 to display the field brackets, type **date** or **time**, then press F9 to update the field. You can also press Alt-Shift-D to insert the date and Alt-Shift-T to insert the time. In both cases, the date appears in the format 11/17/93 and the time in the format 10:53 AM.

In page layout view, pressing Ctrl-F9 to insert a field automatically turns on the display of field codes. In this view, after updating a field with F9, press Shift-F9 to display the results.

SETTING THE DATE AND TIME FORMAT

If you want to insert the date and time in other formats, use the Date and Time dialog box (accessed by selecting Date and Time from the Insert menu). Here are the steps for using this dialog box:

1. Place the insertion point where you want to insert the date or time.

2. Pull down the Insert menu and select Date and Time to display the dialog box shown in Figure 26.1.

3. Select the format you want to use, and then select OK. The date and time will be inserted into the document in the selected format.

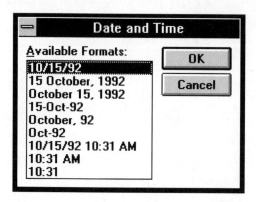

FIGURE 26.1:

The Date and Time dialog box

CUSTOMIZING THE DATE AND TIME FORMAT

If you do not like any of the available formats in the Date and Time dialog box, you can customize the format by using the Field dialog box. Follow these steps:

1. Pull down the Insert menu and select Field to display the Field dialog box.

2. Scroll through the Field Type list box until you see the name Date and select it. (Select Time to insert the time.)

   The Instructions list box now contains various formats in which you can have the date appear, as shown in Figure 26.2. The characters used in date and time formats are described in Table 26.1.

3. Select a format, or enter your own format in the Field Code text box after the field Date or Time. Enter \@ and type the format you want using the codes listed in Table 26.1, enclosing the format in quotation marks.

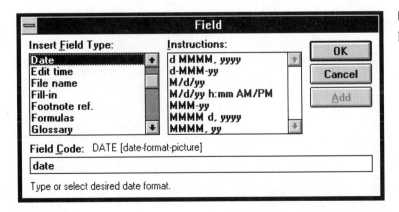

FIGURE 26.2:

Date instructions

FUNCTION	CHARACTER	FORMAT
Month	M	1–12, no leading zeros
	MM	01–12, leading zeros
	MMM	JAN–DEC
	MMMM	January–December
Day	d	1–31, no leading zeros
	dd	01–31, leading zeros
	ddd	Mon–Sun
	dddd	Monday–Sunday
Year	yy	00–99
	yyyy	1900–2040
Hours	h	1–12, no leading zeros
	hh	01–12, leading zeros
	H	0–23, no leading zeros
	HH	00–23, leading zeros
Minutes	m	0–59, no leading zeros
	mm	00–59, leading zeros
AM/PM	AM/PM	AM or PM
	am/pm	am or pm
	A/P	A or P
	a/p	a or p

TABLE 26.1:

Characters used for Date and Time Format Instructions

For example, if you want to combine the date and time like this:

05:12 PM   1991 Sunday December 22

your Field Code text box would appear like this:

date \@ "hh:mm AM/PM yyyy   dddd MMMM dd"

Remember to use an uppercase M for months, a lowercase m for minutes.

4. Select OK. The date will appear on the screen.

If you save the document and open it another day, the original date will appear. When you print the document, however, the date will automatically change. You can also update the field, or change it to the current date, by placing the insertion point on the date and pressing F9 twice (once to change the display to field codes and a second time to display the current date and time).

The following fields also display and print dates:

{date}	Inserts the current system date
{createdate}	Inserts the date the document was created
{printdate}	Inserts the date the document was last printed
{savedate}	Inserts the date the document was last saved
{time}	Inserts the current system time
{edittime}	Inserts the amount of time spent editing the document

FIXING THE DATE OR TIME

You may want to insert a date or time that will not change, such as the time a specific portion of text was added or edited. To make sure the date does not change, you have to unlink, or *fix*, it. This converts the displayed date or time to regular text, deleting the field code.

Follow these steps to fix the date or time entry:

1. Make sure the date or time, not the field code, is displayed on the screen. If necessary, select the field code then press F9, turn off the field codes display by selecting Field **C**odes from the **V**iew menu, or select the code and press Shift-F9.

2. Place the insertion point in the date or time, and then press Ctrl-Shift-F9 to display the date or time as highlighted text.

3. Deselect the text.

After you fix the date or time, it is regular text. It will not change when you print the document, and it cannot be updated with the F9 key.

Using Other Fields

Word for Windows provides many other fields that you can use to insert text. Some of the most useful ones are listed in Table 26.2.

CREATING A FAX COVER PAGE

One useful application of fields is to automatically generate a fax cover page for your documents.

Type in the following document to produce a sample fax cover page with information provided by Word. You can insert the fields by pressing Ctrl-F9 to display the field brackets and typing the field name, or by selecting Field from the Insert menu and selecting the field from the list box.

Title: {title}   Stored As: {filename}

Author: {author}   Created On: {createdate}

Editing Time: {edittime}

Size: {numpages} pages   {numchars} characters

Last Revision:

Number: {revnum}   Saved By: {lastsavedby}

Last Printed: {printdate}

FIELD	PRINTED OUTPUT
{author}	The author's name from the Summary Info dialog box. Unless you change it, this is the name you entered when you first started Word for Windows.
{comments}	The comments from the Summary Info dialog box.
{filename}	The file name of the document.
{keywords}	The keywords from the Summary Info dialog box.
{lastsavedby}	The name of the last person who saved the document.
{numchars}	The number of characters that were in the document the last time it was saved or when the Summary Info dialog box was last updated.
{numpages}	The number of pages that were in the document the last time it was saved or when the Summary Info dialog box was last updated.
{numwords}	The number of words that were in the document the last time it was saved or when the Summary Info dialog box was last updated.
{subject}	The subject of the document from the Summary Info dialog box.
{template}	The name of the template used with the document.
{title}	The document's title from the Summary Info dialog box.

TABLE 26.2:

Useful Field Codes for Headers, Footers, and Text

If you use the Fields dialog box, you will notice that in the Fields list box, fields are spelled out, as in No. of Pages and Print Date. However, when selected, the fields will appear as codes, such as {numpages} and {printdate}.

27 L E S S O N

FEATURING

Dividing a
document into
panes

Editing panes

Seeing different
views in panes

▼

Using Panes to Work with Long Documents

As your document grows longer, you will find yourself scrolling back and forth through its pages to copy or move text, or to refer to information on another page. With Word, however, you can split the document into *panes* to view and edit different areas of the same document.

In this lesson, you will create a document longer than one screen. You will then divide the screen into two panes, or parts, to streamline editing.

Dividing the Window into Panes

When you have a document that is two or more screens long, you may want to divide it into panes so different sections are visible. To create panes, you use the *split box*, which is the black rectangle just above the arrow on top of the scroll bar. With the keyboard, you use the Split option on the Control menu.

Our sample document will consist of a memo, followed by a list of items on the next page. Follow these steps to create the document and divide it into panes:

1. Start Word and type the following letter. Enter the date field, {date}, by pressing Ctrl-F9 then typing **date**. Press End to move the insertion point outside the field brackets.

To:	Marie Melnickie, Purchasing
From:	Thadius Martin, Research and Development
Subject:	Laboratory Supplies
Date:	{date}

Because of the time constraints imposed by the funding agency, we must accelerate our efforts in the super-conductivity study. Enclosed is a list of items which we need as soon as possible and which should receive priority handling. These items are needed within two weeks if we are to fulfill our commitments.

Due to the unusual rush with this order, please contact the following vendors who have an excellent delivery history:

Margate Chemical Supplies, Margate, NJ
Morris Scientific Supply Corp., Philadelphia, PA
Chesin Laboratory, Inc., New Hope, PA

Please contact me if you anticipate any delays.

2. Press Ctrl-↵ to insert a page break after the memorandum and before the list of supplies you are about to add.

3. Type the following list.

QUANTITY	ITEM	REFERENCE NUMBER
2	Coulter Counter	5623A43
1	Centrifuge	6ACT45209-8
5	Spectrophotometer	SPTR-U6543
100	Test Tubes - #3	654f58
5	Microscope - Oil Immersion	7655
145	Beakers - 1 Lt.	82341L
145	Beakers - .5 Lt.	8235.5L
1 gallon	Oxalic acid	HCO-45
1 gallon	Ethanol	CHOH-56
2 gallons	Magnesium	MgCO33

Now that you have created a two-page document, you can divide it into panes.

4. Place the pointer on the split box, and the pointer will change to a double horizontal line with up- and down-pointing arrows. With the keyboard, press Alt-hyphen to pull down the Control menu, and then select Split. A line appears across the screen with a double-pointed arrow.

5. Drag the split box to the center of the scroll bar. With the keyboard, press ↑ or ↓ to position the line where you want the split to appear and press ↵ (press Esc to cancel the split).

The window is now divided into two panes, each with its own scroll bar, as shown in Figure 27.1. The bottom pane is active because it contains the insertion point.

6. Scroll the text in the bottom pane to see the beginning of the document.

The text in the top pane does not scroll. Scrolling is performed independently in both panes, even though they contain the same document.

7. To select the top pane, click anywhere in it. With the keyboard, press F6 to switch panes.

8. Scroll the text in the top pane to see the start of the document.

If you have a mouse, you can quickly divide the window into two equal-size panes by double-clicking on the split box.

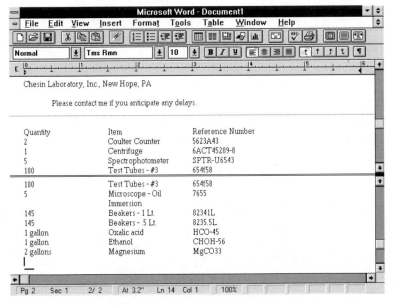

FIGURE 27.1:

Document displayed in two panes

Editing with Panes

Now that you have the same area of the document appearing in two panes, let's see what happens when you edit text.

1. Place the insertion point in front of the first line, and then press ↵ to insert a line at the top of the memo.

Notice that the text in both panes moves down, even though only the top pane is active. Editing in one pane is duplicated in the other.

2. Press ↑, click on the Center button in the ribbon or press Ctrl-E, and type **Memorandum**. Every keystroke in the top pane is echoed in the bottom one.

3. Place the insertion point at the end of the first paragraph. Again, the bottom pane did not scroll.

Now suppose that you want to add a line to the first page of the document and you need to refer to some stock numbers on the second page. Without panes, you would have to scroll to the bottom to see the numbers, then scroll back to the first paragraph to insert them. Let's see how using panes makes this task easier.

4. Select the bottom pane by clicking in it or pressing F6.

5. Scroll to display the last items in the document.

6. Select the top pane.

7. With the reference numbers displayed in the bottom pane, add the following sentence to the end of the first paragraph.

We are particularly concerned with items HCO-45, CHOH-56, and MgCO33.

Now we will use panes to copy text from one area of the document to another.

8. Scroll to display the list of suggested vendors.

9. Select the list, and then pull down the Edit menu and select Copy (Ctrl-C).

10. Select the bottom pane.

11. Place the insertion point at the end of the document, then type **Possible Vendors**.

12. Press ↵ twice, and then pull down the Edit menu and select Paste (Ctrl-V). The list of suggested vendors will appear at the end of the text.

13. Select the top pane, and then scroll to reach the bottom of the document. You will see that the text you just inserted in the bottom pane also appears in the top pane, as shown in Figure 27.2.

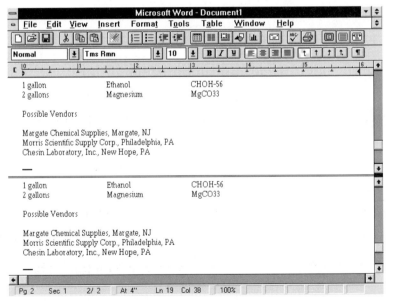

FIGURE 27.2:

The same text in both panes

14. To close one pane, double-click on the split box, or drag the split box back to the top of the scroll bar. With the keyboard, press Alt-Shift-C. The bottom pane will close, or disappear, and the top pane will fill the screen.

15. Click on the Save button in the toolbar. With the keyboard, pull down the File menu and select Save (Shift-F12).

16. Type **Order**, and then select OK twice.

17. Pull down the File menu and select Exit (Alt-F4) to exit Word.

As you have seen, editing occurs simultaneously in panes, but they are independent in most other ways.

Seeing Different Views of the Same Document

One of the advantages of panes is that they can appear in different views. For example, when you are working with a table, you might want to view the codes in one pane and the results in another, as shown in the example in Figure 27.3. This way you can quickly refer to each view without switching back and forth using the menu or keyboard commands.

If you want to see more than two views of the same document, or want to see two views side by side, you have to open separate windows, as you will learn in the next lesson.

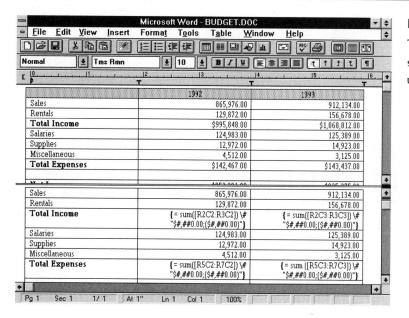

FIGURE 27.3:

Two views of the same document using panes

FEATURING

Opening windows

Resizing and positioning windows

Saving all open documents

▼

Using Windows with Multiple Documents

P anes can be used to show two different segments or views of the same document. You use windows to edit more than one document at a time, as well as to show different views or sections of a single document. When you have different documents in each window, editing performed in one window has no effect on the text in the other windows.

For example, if you're typing a report and you have to refer back to a document you typed last week, you can open both documents at the same time and divide the screen into two text windows. With both documents on the screen, you can switch back and forth and even copy text from one to the other. In fact, you can divide the screen into as many as nine windows at one time, moving from window to window using the mouse or keyboard.

Opening Document Windows

Suppose that you have to write a document and need to refer to another one already stored on the disk. While you're working, however, a few items come to mind that you want to quickly jot down. Here's where dividing the screen into windows can save you time and effort.

In the following steps, you will divide the screen into three windows: one with the document you are just writing, another with an existing document you need for reference, and a third as a notepad area to write down ideas.

1. Start Word and type the following text.

Thadius:

I've ordered the items you requested. They should arrive within the week so check with the supply office for the following:

2. Press ↵ twice.

To include the correct items, you have to refer to the ORDER document. Instead of pulling a copy of the memo from the filing cabinet, you will display that document in its own window.

3. Open the ORDER document.

The newly opened document will appear on the screen. The document you just typed is in its own window underneath the active one containing the ORDER document. Word provides several ways to switch back and forth between the windows: use the Windows menu, which shows a numbered list of all the currently open documents; press

Ctrl-F6; or select Next Window from the Control pull-down menu (press Alt-hyphen then N).

4. To switch back to the original document, pull down the Window menu and select Document1, or press 1.

The note that you typed as Document1 appears on the screen; the ORDER window is now underneath. Now let's open a third window for notes.

5. Click on the New Document button in the toolbar. With the keyboard, pull down the File menu and select New, then OK.

Now you have a new document window, which Word placed in the foreground.

6. Type the following notes.

Check supplies for Thadius
Call Margate Supplies on Tuesday

Now you will insert several lines in the ORDER document into your memo in Document1. Rather than switch back and forth between the windows, you can display all three documents on the screen at the same time.

7. Pull down the Window menu and select Arrange All.

The screen splits into three separate text windows, as shown in Figure 28.1. The active window, the one with the insertion point, has a scroll bar. The scroll bar area is blank in the inactive windows.

Notice that each document window has its own ruler and title bar, separate from the Word title bar without a document name. That's because there is a separate application window containing the Word for Windows screen beneath the others. The Word application window contains the Word title bar, menu bar, toolbar, and the status bar. The

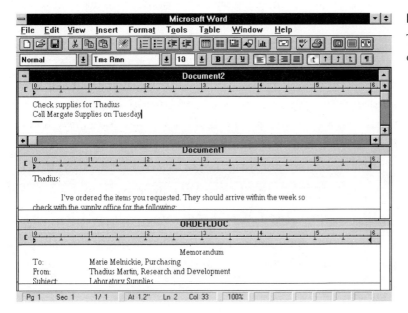

FIGURE 28.1:

Three windows on the screen

information in the status bar and icons on the ribbon will reflect the settings and status of the active window.

8. Select the ORDER document by clicking in the ORDER window or by pressing Ctrl-F6 twice.

9. Scroll until you display the last three items in the list of items, and then select them.

10. Pull down the Edit menu and select Copy (Ctrl-C) to copy the selected text.

11. Select Document1.

12. Position the insertion point at the end of the document, pull down the Edit menu and select Paste (Ctrl-V) to paste the text.

As you've seen, it's very easy to switch back and forth between document windows. You can use this to your advantage if you are working on confidential material. To safeguard your document from prying eyes while you are working on it, open a new document to display a blank document window. Select your document window and continue working. When someone who should not see your work approaches, press Ctrl-F6 to display the blank window. You can quickly return to your document by pressing Ctrl-F6.

OPENING ANOTHER WINDOW FOR A SINGLE DOCUMENT

If you want to open another window that contains the active document, pull down the Window menu and select the New Window option. The title bar of the window Word opens will contain the title of the document followed by the number of this window. For example, if you create a new window for the ORDER document, one window will show ORDER:1 in the title bar, the other ORDER:2. When you close one window, the other closes as well.

Opening two windows on the same document is much like splitting a window into panes. However, using windows, you can display more than two views of the same document and place them side by side.

Maximizing Windows

When you want to continue working on one of the documents displayed in a window, you can quickly return it to full size, or *maximize* it, by clicking on its maximize box or by pressing Ctrl-F10. Now we will complete the sample letter in the window for Document1. But because there are two other windows on the screen, that window is too small to display much text. Rather than save the other documents and close the windows at this point, follow these steps to maximize the window:

1. Click on the maximize box (the up-pointing triangle on the right side) in the Document1 title bar. With the keyboard, press Ctrl-F10.

The other windows move behind, and Document1 fills the entire screen. The Word and document title bars are now combined.

2. Complete the note with the following sentence.

Please let me know if they have not arrived by Wednesday.

3. To close the ORDER document, pull down the Window menu and choose ORDER.DOC, and then pull down the File menu and select Close.

Repositioning and Resizing Windows with the Mouse

If you have a mouse, you can adjust the size and placement of each window by dragging it. Let's adjust the two windows that are still on your screen.

1. Pull down the Window menu and select Arrange All to display both windows on the screen.

2. Move the mouse pointer to the bottom-right corner of the top window, and the pointer will become a diagonal, double-pointed arrow.

3. Drag the pointer down to the bottom of the screen and to the left, about halfway across the screen. As you drag the pointer, an outline of the window will move with it. Release the mouse button. The window will fill half of the screen, as shown in Figure 28.2.

4. Select the other document window.

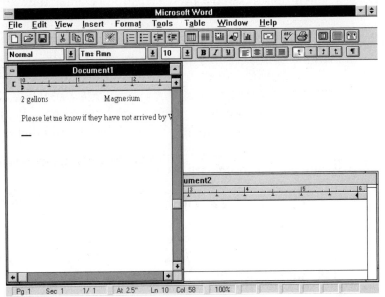

FIGURE 28.2:

Window reduced
by dragging the
right border

5. Move the mouse pointer to the top-left corner of the window, and the pointer will become a diagonal, double-pointed arrow.

6. Drag the pointer up to the top of the screen and to the right to position the windows side by side. Your screen should look similar to the one shown in Figure 28.3.

By selecting and dragging one of the corners, you can change both the height and width of a window at one time. To change just the height, place the pointer on the window's top or bottom border. When the pointer changes to a vertical double-pointed arrow, drag the border to the desired position. To change the width of a window, place the pointer on the window's left or right border. When the pointer becomes a horizontal double-pointed arrow, drag the border to make the window wider or narrower.

To move a window without changing its size, point to the title bar and drag the mouse. As you move the mouse, an outline of the window

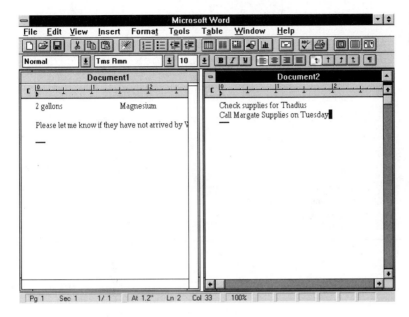

FIGURE 28.3:

Side-by-side windows

moves along with it. When the outline is positioned where you want the window to appear, release the mouse button.

Changing the Size of Windows with the Keyboard

Follow these steps to resize the windows displayed on your screen if you are using the keyboard instead of a mouse:

1. Press Alt-W, then A to display both windows on the screen.

2. Press Alt-hyphen to pull down the Control menu of the top, active, window.

3. Press S to resize the windows. A four-pointed arrow appears in the window. Your next keystroke determines which of the four window borders you want to move.

4. Press → to select the right border.

If you now press either the → or ← key, the right border of the window will change. However, you want to move the window's lower-right corner.

5. Press ↓. The pointer moves to the corner and changes to a diagonal arrow.

6. Use the ↓ and ← keys to position the right border about halfway across the screen.

7. Press ↵ to exit resize mode.

8. Press Ctrl-F6 to select the other window.

9. Press Alt-hyphen to pull down the Control menu.

10. Press S to select resize.

11. Press ↑, then ← to select the top-left corner of the window.

12. Use the ↑ and → keys to position the left border about halfway across the screen, so the windows are side by side, and then press ↵.

Saving Multiple Documents

When you have two or more windows open, Word gives you the chance to save each one. Now we will save the letter and notes.

1. Pull down the **File** menu and select Save All. A dialog box will appear asking if you want to save the changes to Document2.

2. Select Yes, type **Remind**, and then select OK twice. A dialog box will appears asking if you want to save the changes to Document1.

3. Select Yes, type **Thadius**, and select OK twice.

If you exit Word now, the next time you start Word, it will be in the arrange all mode, with the text window separate from the Word window. Since there will be two separate title bars (one for Word and one for the document) and extra window borders, you will see fewer lines of text on the screen. Unless you are working with multiple windows, you probably will not want to remain in arrange all mode.

4. To turn off arrange all mode, click on the Maximize button in the title bar of the active document. With the keyboard, press Ctrl-F10 to maximize the document window.

5. Pull down the File menu and select Exit (Alt-F4) to exit Word.

FEATURING

Inserting a header or footer

Formatting headers and footers

Printing page numbers

▼

Creating Headers and Footers

Have you ever come across a page of an unidentified document that has somehow become separated from the rest of the pages, and you now have no idea where it belongs? This can easily happen to your long documents. After all, a staple or paper clip can become dislodged, scattering your document to the winds.

This lesson will show you how to identify every page of your documents with headers, footers, and page numbers in your documents. Then you will always know where a page belongs, even if it goes far astray.

Adding Headers and Footers

Headers are standard lines of text that print on the top of each page; *footers* print on the bottom.

Using a header, for example, you could print the title at the top of each report page, or the date and the recipient's name on every page of a letter. The footer could include messages such as *Please turn the page* or *Continued*, indicating to the reader that more pages follow. Headers and footers can also include page numbers. Then if all 50 pages of your report get separated, the reader can easily put them back in order.

In the following steps, you will add another page to the beginning of the COMPUTER document, and then create headers and a footer to print on each page. The header for the first page will include the seminar name; the header for the following pages will contain the name plus the date. The footer, for the page number, will print on all pages except the first one.

1. Start Word and open COMPUTER.

2. Press Ctrl-↵ to insert a page break above the existing text, place the insertion point on the page break line, and press ↵.

3. Place the insertion point in the top line of the screen and select the Left button in the ribbon (Ctrl-L).

If you do not explicitly select left alignment, the text you type will be centered, the format of the first line in the COMPUTER document.

4. Type the following text for the new page.

To All Seminar Participants:
The enclosed materials will be discussed during the seminar. Please bring them with you to every session.
During the seminar, you will be provided with several large collections of documents and a folder to store your papers.

These reference materials are yours to keep when the seminar is over. They are a valuable source of information and have been provided as a courtesy to seminar participants.

5. Pull down the File menu and select Save As (F12), type **Reports**, then select OK twice.

6. To begin creating the headers and footers, pull down the View menu and select Header/Footer. You will see the dialog box shown in Figure 29.1.

If you wanted the same header and footer to appear on every page, you could select Header or Footer from the list box. But in this case, we don't want the footer to appear on the first page, and we want a different header on the first and subsequent pages.

7. Select Different First Page. The list box will now contain the options Header, Footer, First Header, and First Footer.

Selecting Different First Page affects both the headers and footers. So if you wanted a different footer but the same header on all pages, you

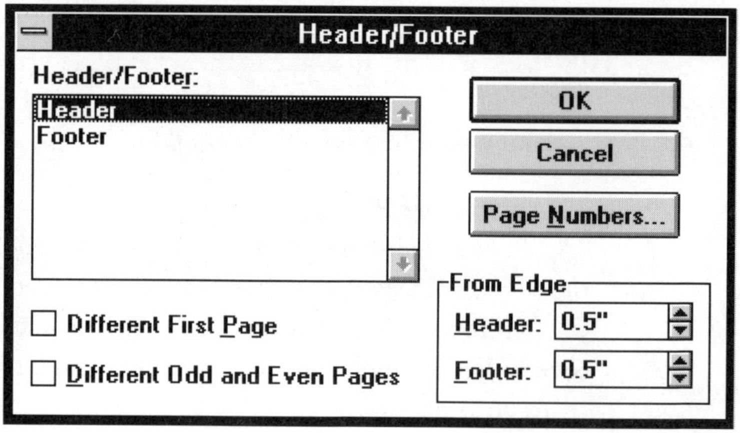

FIGURE 29.1:

The Header/Footer dialog box

would have to enter the same header twice: once for the first page and again for subsequent pages.

8. Select First Header, then OK. A separate pane, called the *header pane*, appears on the bottom of the screen, as shown in Figure 29.2.

In the header pane, you create, format, and edit the text of the header. Its menu bar includes three icons and the commands Link to Previous and Close. Its title, First Header (S1), indicates that it is the header for the first page in section 1. You'll learn how to use the icons and commands shortly.

By default, header and footer panes are formatted with a centered tab at 3 inches and a right tab at 6 inches.

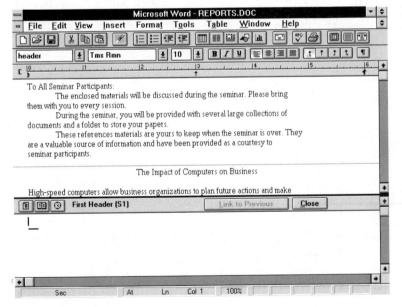

FIGURE 29.2:

The header pane

9. Press Tab to reach the centered tab, and then type the text of the header for the first page: **1993 Computer Seminar**.

10. Click on Close button at the top of the header pane. With the keyboard, press Shift-F10 to activate the menu bar, and then select Close.

11. Pull down the View menu and select Header/Footer to enter the text of the headers for the remaining pages. The Header option is already selected.

12. Select OK to display the header pane.

13. Type **1993 Computer Seminar**.

14. Press Tab twice, type **Prepared on**, and then press the spacebar.

15. Select the date icon in the header pane's menu bar (the second one on the left). With the keyboard, press Alt-Shift-D.

If you chose to display the field codes (see Lesson 26), the {date} code will appear. If not, you'll see the date. When the document is printed, the date will appear in the header.

16. Close the header pane.

17. To create the footer, pull down the View menu and select Header/Footer again, then Footer, then OK. You will see the footer pane, which looks similar to the header pane.

18. Press Tab to reach the centered tab at 3 inches, type **Page**, and then press the spacebar.

19. Select the page number icon in the footer pane's menu bar (the first one on the left). With the keyboard, press Alt-Shift-P.

Depending on your display setting, either the page number or {page} field code will appear. When the document is printed, each footer will contain the number of the page.

20. Close the header pane.

21. Pull down the File menu and select Print Preview, then Two Pages to see how the headers and footers will look. Your preview should look like the screen shown in Figure 29.3.

22. Select Cancel or press Esc to exit preview mode.

In page layout view, instead of working with your header or footer in a separate pane, you type and edit it within its area of the page. When you select to create or edit a header or footer, the insertion point will jump directly to the header or footer area of the page. After you are finished working with the header or footer, you can scroll back to the document.

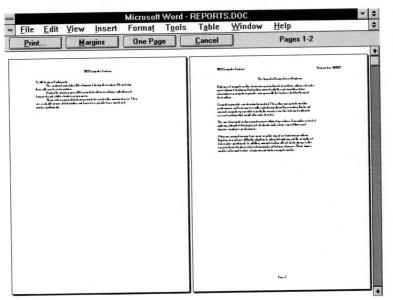

FIGURE 29.3:

Preview of headers and footers

Editing and Formatting Headers and Footers

You edit and format characters in headers and footers in the same way that you work with any other text in a document. Pull down the View menu and select Header/Footer, then the specific header or footer (such as Different First Page, then First Header) to display the existing text in the pane. Edit or format the text, and then close the pane.

You can also format headers and footers to appear differently on alternate pages. For example, in published books, the even-numbered pages are always on the left and the odd-numbered ones are on the right. Select Different Odd and Even Pages and make sure Different First Page is not selected. You can then create an even footer, odd footer, even header, and odd header. In the header or footer pane, type the text for the even pages at the left margin, and the text for odd pages at the right margin using the right-aligned tab stop.

Positioning Headers and Footers

The default position of headers and footers from the top and bottom margins depends on your printer. To change the top or bottom margin, change the settings in the From Edge section of the Header/Footer dialog box.

Pull down the View menu, select Header/Footer and then select Header or Footer in the bottom-right corner of the dialog box. Enter the distance you want the header or footer to print from the edge of the page, but be careful not to set the position so that headers and footers print in your text area. If you do, Word will print the headers and footers where you specified and print the text in the remaining space.

The Page Numbers button in the Header/Footer dialog box lets you change the format of the page numbers and restart numbering for different sections. You will learn more about these formatting options in the next lesson.

Printing Page Numbers

If you want to print only a page number on the top or bottom of the page, you do not have to use a header or footer. An easy way to set up page numbers, without any text, is through the Page Numbers dialog box (accessed by selecting Page Numbers from the Insert menu). This dialog box provides various numbering scheme options, as well as selections for formatting the page number.

In most cases, you will want the pages of your document numbered consecutively from number 1. But for some documents, you will want to set up special numbering schemes. For example, you may not want to number the first page of the document if it is a cover page or title sheet. For a long report that includes a title page and table of contents, you might like to number the table of contents using lowercase roman numerals (i, ii, iii, and so on) and start the actual report as page 1.

Let's see how this works by changing the page numbering on the REPORTS document, which begins with a cover letter.

1. Pull down the Insert menu and select Page Numbers. You will see the Page Numbers dialog box, with the bottom option already selected, as shown in Figure 29.4.

2. Select **C**enter in the Alignment section at the bottom of the dialog box to center the page number between the margins.

3. Select the Format button on the right side of the dialog box to display the dialog box shown in Figure 29.5.

4. Pull down the Number Format list box to display the numbering options.

5. Select the fourth format for small roman numerals.

6. Select OK to return to the Page Number dialog box.

7. Select OK to return to the document.

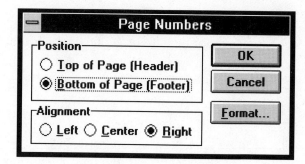

FIGURE 29.4:

The Page Numbers dialog box

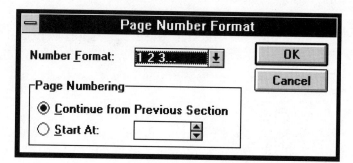

FIGURE 29.5:

The Page Number Format dialog box

Since you already have a footer that contains a page number, you will see a dialog box with the message

Do you want to replace the existing header/footer with page numbers?

8. Select Yes to remove the existing footer.

Now we'll format the page numbers to appear on every page.

9. Pull down the View menu and select Header/Footer. You will see that the Different First Page option is selected.

When you insert a page number, Word automatically selects the Different First Page option so the number does not appear on the first page. Having the page number appear only on the second and subsequent pages is a common format for documents. However, for this document, we do want a page number to appear on the first page.

10. Select Different First Page to turn off the option. The page number will now print on every page of the document.

11. Select OK to display the header pane, and then close the pane.

12. Pull down the File menu and select Exit (Alt-F4), then choose Yes to leave Word and save your changes.

With these settings, the page number will appear on every page of the document in small roman numerals, so you have to change the format for the second and subsequent pages. You will do this in the next lesson.

Inserting page numbers may affect the placement of any existing headers and footers. For example, since it automatically turns on the Different First Page option, any existing header or footer will not appear on the first page unless you have already designated a specific First Header or First Footer. After inserting a page number, preview the document to make sure the headers and footers appear as you intended. If necessary, pull down the View menu, select Header/Footer, and add a First Header or First Footer.

Remember, before printing your documents, preview them with the Print Preview command. This is particularly useful if you have headers, footers, and page numbers that don't appear on the screen in the normal window. By previewing your document, you'll know exactly how it will look on the printed page—no surprises. You can also see how the finished document will appear by switching to page layout view (and turning off the display of field codes if necessary). In this view, you will see the actual text of headers, footers, and page numbers.

30 LESSON

Working with Sections

FEATURING

Starting a new section

Using different page numbers, headers, and footers

Formatting sections

▼

Dividing a document into sections allows you to use different page formats within the same document. For example, when you insert an envelope into a document, Word places it in its own section, with the proper formatting for envelope-sized paper. In this lesson, you will learn how to define sections, so that you can format certain pages differently than the rest of the document.

Dividing a Document into Sections

If you want to include different margins or page sizes, or vary the page format within a document in another way, start a new section where you want the format change to begin. After you have created the new section, you can select the new margins, paper size, or other formatting.

You mark the beginning of a section by using the Break option on the Insert menu. In the last lesson, you added page numbers to the REPORTS document and formatted them as small roman numerals. Now we will divide that document into sections so that only the first page has the roman numeral. The next and subsequent page numbers will be in arabic numerals, beginning with 1.

1. Start Word and open REPORTS.

2. Place the insertion point at the beginning of the second page and delete the page break.

3. Pull down the Insert menu and select Break to display the dialog box shown in Figure 30.1.

The Section Break choices are at the bottom of the Break dialog box. The Next Page option inserts a page break and begins a new section at the position of the insertion point. When you select the Continuous option, a section-break indicator appears on the screen, but the

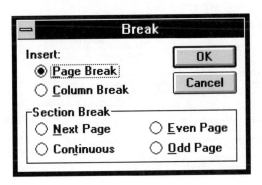

FIGURE 30.1:

The Break dialog box

different section formats will not begin until after the next actual page break. Choose the Even Page or Odd Page option to start the section formats on either the next even or odd page.

4. Select Next Page, then OK.

The section indicator on the status bar changes to Sec 2, and a double line appears across the screen at the section break, as shown in Figure 30.2.

5. Pull down the View menu and select Header/Footer.

6. Select Page Numbers to display the Page Number Format dialog box.

7. Enter 1 in the Start At text box.

8. Pull down the Number Format list box and select the 1 2 3 format.

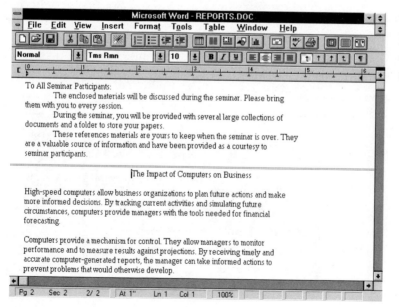

FIGURE 30.2:

Document divided into sections

9. Select OK to return to the Header/Footer dialog box, and then choose Close.

10. Click on the Print button in the toolbar to print the document. With the keyboard, pull down the File menu and select Print (Ctrl-Shift-F12), then OK.

11. Pull down the File menu and select Exit (Alt-F4), then No to exit Word.

The first section (the first page) remains as you formatted in the last lesson, with a lowercase roman numeral page number. The second section (the remaining pages) is formatted to print with arabic page numbers, starting with 1.

Using Different Headers and Footers

When you create a new section, the header and footer from the previous section are automatically copied to the next one. To create a different header or footer in each section, position the insertion point in a section, pull down the View menu, select Header/Footer, and then click on OK. Edit the text in the header or footer pane to change the headers or footers in the new section.

When you change the header or footer of a section, the Link to Previous option in the header or footer pane becomes available. Use this option if you later want to restore the original header or footer from the previous section. When you select Link to Previous, Word displays a dialog box with the message

Do you want to delete this header/footer and link to the header/footer in the previous section?

Select Yes to delete the section's header or footer and copy the text from the previous section.

Setting the Section Vertical Alignment

You can set other section formats through the Section Layout dialog box. Pull down the Format menu and choose Section Layout to see the dialog box shown in Figure 30.3. These options determine the number of columns, discussed in Lesson 44, the placement of line numbers down the left margin, and the alignment of the text vertically on the page.

The Vertical Alignment options (at the bottom of the Section Layout dialog box) are useful for formatting pages that are not filled:

- Top: Begins text at the top margin, with no extra spacing (the default alignment).

- Center: Centers all the text on the page between the top and bottom margins. Use it to quickly create a title page: type the text of the title page in its own section, then select Center as the Vertical Alignment.

- Justified: Expands the spaces between paragraphs in shorter pages so the text fills the page.

Figure 30.4 shows the same text in two different sections, one with centered alignment and the other with justified alignment.

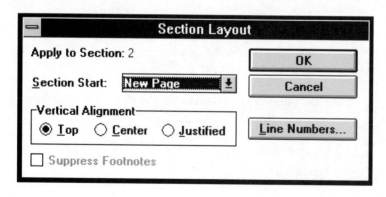

FIGURE 30.3:

The Section Layout dialog box

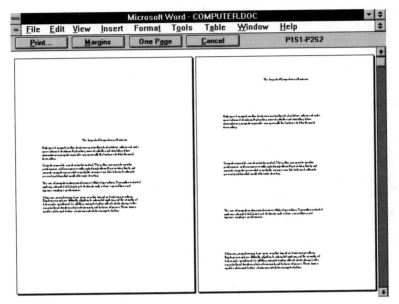

FIGURE 30.4:

Text with centered and justified vertical alignment

FEATURING

**Locating text
Setting
bookmarks**

▼

Searching for Text and Formats

Suppose that you have to find the exact place in a long report where you first introduce a subject or name. Rather than scrolling through the text, you can have Word find it for you. In this lesson, you will learn how to use two of Word's features that take you to a specific place in your document: the search function and bookmarks.

Finding Text

By using the Find option on the Edit menu, you can search either backward or forward through the document, placing the insertion point directly on a specific word or phrase.

In the following steps, you will search for specific text in the COMPUTER document.

1. Start Word and open COMPUTER.

2. Pull down the Edit menu and select Find to display the dialog box shown in Figure 31.1.

3. Type **compute** in the Find What text box.

4. Select Find Next (in the upper-right corner of the Find dialog box).

The insertion point moves to the word *Computers* in the title, and the first seven letters will be selected. Since you did not choose Match Whole Word, the program found the first occurrence of the characters *c o m p u t e* in the text, even though they are part of another word. When you select Match Whole Word, the text located must be a whole word. Word recognizes a whole word as the characters in the Find What text box surrounded by spaces or punctuation marks, but no other characters.

5. Select Find Next again to continue the search, and the insertion point will move to the next occurrence of the characters.

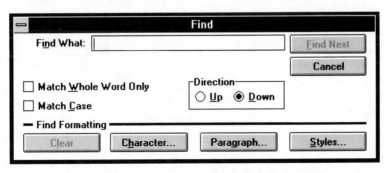

FIGURE 31.1:

The Find dialog box

6. Double click in the Find What text box. With the keyboard, press Alt-N.

7. Type **IMPACT** (all uppercase) and select Find Next. The insertion point will go to the word *impact* in the last paragraph.

Although you typed the word in all uppercase letters, Word found the lowercase characters because you did not select the Match Case option in the Find dialog box. When you choose Match Case, the characters located in the document must be in the same case as those you entered in the Find What text box. Otherwise, any combination of uppercase and lowercase letters will be considered a match.

8. Select Find Next. You will see a box with the message

Word has reached the end of document. Do you want to continue searching at the beginning?

Word has searched from the position of the insertion point down to the end of the document, because the Down option was selected in the Find dialog box. Since the insertion point was not at the start of the document when you began the search for the word *impact*, Word wants to know if you want to look through the remainder of the document. If you had selected the Up option, which searches from the insertion-point position to the start of the document, when Word reached the beginning of document, it would ask if you want to continue searching at the end.

9. Select Yes. The word *impact* in the title will be selected.

10. Select Find Next again. Word moves again to the word *impact* in the last paragraph.

11. Select Find Next, and a dialog box will appear with the message

Word reached the end of the document

12. Select OK.

13. Select Cancel to close the Find dialog box.

14. Pull down the File menu and select Exit (Alt-F4) to exit Word.

If Word cannot find the characters in the Find What text box in the document, it will display a message to let you know.

Searching for Formats

You can also search for a place where you used a particular format, such as italic characters or justified text. Perhaps you want to quickly move to a heading in 14-point Times Roman or a long quotation that's centered between the margins.

To locate a specific format, use the options in the Find Formatting section of the Find dialog box. For example, suppose you want to find the italic text *Journal*. Pull down the Edit menu and select Find. Type the word *journal* in the Find What text box, and then select the Character button. The Find Character dialog box, which has the same options as the Character dialog box (see Figure 2.3), will appear. Select Italic, then OK to return to the Find dialog box. The message

Format: Italic

will appear under the Find What text box to indicate the format included in the search. Select Find Next to begin the search.

Use the Paragraph button to search for paragraph formats and the Styles button to find specific styles (which you will learn about in Lesson 40). To cancel the format specification, select the Clear button in the Find Formatting section of the Find dialog box.

Using Bookmarks

Another way to quickly move the insertion point to a specific location is to set a bookmark in the text. Suppose you have a long document with many references to personal computers. You now want to quickly find the main section about them. You could use the Find option to look for the characters *personal computers;* however, Word will stop at each occurrence, not go directly to the main section in the document.

A more efficient method is to use the Bookmark option in the Insert menu to name the place to which you want to return. Then you can use the Go To option in the Edit menu to select and move the insertion point to that bookmark.

SETTING BOOKMARKS

To set a bookmark, place the insertion point at the location in the text, pull down the Insert menu and select Bookmark (Ctrl-Shift-F5). You will see the dialog box shown in Figure 31.2, which lists any existing bookmarks and allows you to name a new one.

Type a name you want to associate with the bookmark, and then select OK. Bookmarks names must begin with a letter and can be up to 20 characters long, without any spaces or punctuation marks except the underline (_) character. If you enter the name of an existing bookmark or select a bookmark name from the list box, you will redefine the bookmark so that it is associated with the new position or selected text.

Set bookmarks at strategic locations to which you might have to return. For example, you may edit a document in a number of different

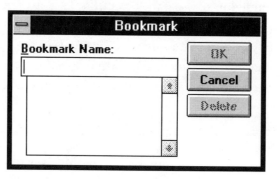

FIGURE 31.2:

The Bookmark dialog box

sessions. When you're finished with one session, place the insertion point at the beginning of the unedited section and mark it with a bookmark name such as *here*. When you start a new session, you can quickly jump to that bookmark.

MOVING TO A BOOKMARK

To move to a bookmark, pull down the Edit menu and select Go To. The Go To dialog box appears, as shown in Figure 31.3. Type the name of the book mark in the Go To text box or select the bookmark from the list box, and then select OK. The insertion point will move to that location. You can also move to a specific page by entering the page number in the Go To dialog box and selecting OK.

You can also move to a bookmark by pressing F5. The message

Go to:

will appear in the status bar. Type the name of the bookmark and press ↵ to move the insertion point there.

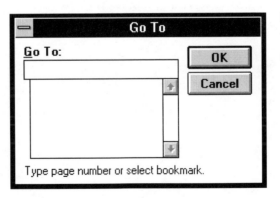

FIGURE 31.3:

The Go To dialog box

REMOVING BOOKMARKS

To remove the bookmark but not the text associated with it, pull down the Insert menu and select Bookmark. Highlight the bookmark in the list box, and then select Delete. Select Close to return to the document.

32 LESSON

Replacing Text and Formats

Have you ever misspelled the same word several times in the same document or realized that you entered the wrong information in several places? Or do you have a document that could easily be modified for another use if certain text were changed several times? For example, perhaps a proposal could be used again if you changed each occurrence of the client's name. As you will learn in this lesson, these situations can easily be handled with Word's replace feature.

Replacing Text Automatically

The Replace option in the Edit menu allows you to automatically locate any text and replace it with something else, no matter how many times it appears. By using Replace, you can correct mistakes with just a few keystrokes.

You will now use Replace to make some changes in a document. First, you will create a short document, and then you will find and correct errors.

1. Type the following letter.

> Miss Drew Landing
> Provo Software, Inc.
> 24 University Avenue
> Provo, UT
>
> Dear Miss Landing:
> I am sorry that I missed your telephone call on Thursday. I hope Miss Robinson was able to answer your questions about our 1992 FullTax software.
> I have taken the liberty of sending you a complete catalog of our accounting and tax preparation software, as well as a demonstration disk of 1992 FullTax.
> If I can be of any additional help, Miss Landing, please call at any time.
>
> Sincerely,
>
> Robert P. Sheppard
> Vice President for Marketing

After typing the letter, you see that you made a mistake: you meant to mention the 1993, not the 1992, product. This error can easily be corrected by using the Replace option.

2. Place the insertion point at the start of the document.

3. Pull down the Edit menu and select Replace to display the Replace dialog box, shown in Figure 32.1.

Like the Find dialog box, the Replace dialog box has a Find What text box. It also has a Replace With text box, in which you type the text you wish to substitute for the found text. The Match Whole Word Only and Match Case options work in the same way as they do in the Find dialog box: if you select Match Whole Word Only, the program will not replace characters that are parts of other words; if you select Match Case, Word will replace only text that matches the case of the characters you entered in the Find What box.

4. Type 1992, the text you wish to replace, in the Find What box.

5. Select Replace With and type 1993.

Since you know that you want to replace *every* occurrence of 1992 with 1993, you can make the changes quickly with the Replace All option.

6. Select the Replace All button (on the right side of the dialog box). Both occurrences of 1992 will be changed to 1993.

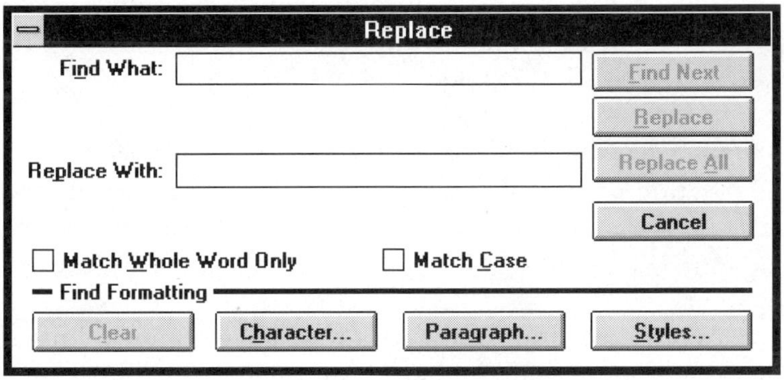

FIGURE 32.1:

The Replace dialog box

7. Select Close to close the Replace dialog box.

After you finish with the replacement operation, the insertion point remains at its original position.

Confirming Replacements

Suppose that your secretary just informed you that Drew Landing is a man, not a woman. Now you must correct the serious mistake of addressing him as Miss instead of Mr. Can you use automatic replacement here as well?

Take a look at the letter. If you select unconfirmed replacement but use the other defaults, the word *missed* in the second paragraph would be changed to *Mr.ed!* Definitely not the way to impress a new client.

In this case, you have several choices. You could match for case only, locating *Miss* but not *miss*, or you could specify a whole word search. Instead of these methods, we'll confirm each replacement.

1. Place the insertion point at the beginning of the document.

2. Pull down the Edit menu and select Replace.

3. In the Find What text box, type **Miss**.

4. Select Replace With and enter **Mr.**

5. Select Find Next to locate the first occurrence of the text. The insertion point will move to the word *Miss* in the address, and it will be highlighted.

6. Select the Replace button to make the replacement. The insertion point will move to the next occurrence of the word.

7. Select Replace again.

Word now stops at the *Miss* for Miss Robinson. Miss Robinson is indeed a female, so you do not want to make the replacement.

8. Select Find Next to locate the next occurrence of the text without making the replacement.

9. Select Replace to substitute *Mr.* for the last occurrence of *Miss*.

10. Select Close to close the dialog box.

11. Pull down the File menu and select Exit, then No to exit Word.

In this example, you saw that automatic replacement is a powerful tool, but it can also result in unwanted and unexpected results. Use unconfirmed replacement with caution.

Replacing Formats

At first glance, the capability to search for and replace formats may not seem as useful as replacing text. But suppose, thanks to a rich uncle or a raise in pay, you just purchased a laser printer capable of printing different type styles and sizes. Wouldn't you like to change every underlined heading in your report to 18-point Times Roman, or change the underlined bibliographic references to italic? These changes can be quickly accomplished through the Find Formatting options in the Replace dialog box.

To replace formats, pull down the Edit menu and select Replace to display the Replace dialog box. With the insertion point in the Find What text box, select Character, Paragraphs, or Styles, and then select the formats you want to change. Place the insertion point in the Replace With text box and select the formats you want to insert. Set the other options as necessary, and then proceed with the replacement.

You can search for and replace combinations of text and formats, such as a specific underlined word. To do so, enter the text in the Find What and Replace With text box, and select the formats for each.

When you want to cancel the formats, place the insertion point in each text box and select Clear (in the lower-left corner of the dialog box).

33 LESSON

FEATURING

Printing selected pages and items

Setting printing options

Using Print Manager

▼

Using Advanced Printing Features

So far, you've been printing documents using all of Word's default printing options, which generate one copy of every page of the document, excluding the information in the Summary Info dialog box. However, as you will learn in this lesson, Word provides many options that allow you to control the printing process.

As you learned in Lesson 4, before printing for the first time, you should select your printer in the Printer Setup dialog box. Appendix A describes how to install and set up your printer when you install Word or Windows itself. If you have printer problems while working with

Word, you will have to use Windows' Print Manager, as described at the end of this lesson.

Selecting What to Print

To select what to print, pull down the File menu and select Print. This displays the Print dialog box, which does not appear when you select the Print button on the toolbar.

To print elements associated with the document, pull down the Print list box to see the following choices:

- Document: Prints the document in the active window (the default).

- Summary Info: Prints the Summary Info dialog box information.

- Annotations: Prints annotations (reviewer's comments that can be inserted into documents).

- Styles: Prints a copy of the style sheet (a template containing collections of paragraph-formatting commands).

- Glossary: Prints a copy of the glossary.

- Key Assignments: Prints the key combination assigned to macros (stored sequences of keystrokes).

Specifying Quantity and Pages to Print

In the Copies text box in the Print dialog box, type the number of copies that you want printed. If you select more than one copy, Word will print each page of the entire document first, then start over from the beginning.

The Range options determine how much of your document will print: every page, selected text, or specific pages. In many cases, you will use the default setting, **All**, which prints every page of the document. But suppose you find and correct a small mistake on one page of the document. Rather than reprint the whole thing, you can choose to print specific pages. You can even print individual sections of text.

Choose Current Page to print the page in which the insertion point is located. This option changes to Selection if you highlight text before selecting Print from the File menu. Choose Selection to print just the highlighted text.

To print specific pages, select From and type the number of the first page you want to print. Then select To and enter the number of the last page. To print a single page, type its number in both text boxes. If you want to print from a specific page to the end of the document, enter the starting page number in the From text box and leave the To box blank.

If your document has more than one section, you can specify the section number following the page. For example, to print the first page of the second section, you would enter 1S2.

When printing specific pages, however, be sure to check that editing has not changed the final pagination. For example, after printing a document, suppose you make a minor change on the second page. Before printing a copy of just the second page, make sure your change did not push some existing text onto the third page. If it did, it would be a mistake to reprint only page 2 and then insert it into the original printout. The text that moved to page 3 would not appear at all.

Using Other Printing Controls

The Print to File option at the bottom of the Print dialog box records the printed output in a disk file rather than sending it directly to the printer. Once the output is in a disk file, you can print the document using the DOS PRINT command. Select Print to File and then choose OK to see the dialog box shown in Figure 33.1. Type a name for the file and select OK.

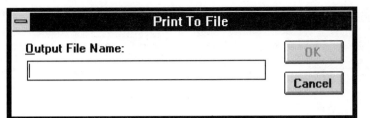

FIGURE 33.1:

The Print To File
dialog box

The Collate Copies option determines how copies of multiple page documents are printed. With Collate Copies selected (the default setting), the first entire copy is printed, the second whole copy, and so on. If you turn off this option, Word will print all copies of the first page, then all copies of the second page, and so on.

Use the Setup button if you need to select a different printer or change a printer's setup. It displays the same dialog box that appears when you select Print Setup from the File menu.

Adjusting Printing Settings

The Options button in the Print dialog box displays the dialog box shown in Figure 33.2. In this dialog box, you can choose printing options, select what will be included on the printout, set up for an envelope feeder, and turn on and off widow and orphan control for the current document.

CHOOSING PRINTING OPTIONS

In the Printing Options section of the Options dialog box, select from the following choices:

■ Draft Output: Prints your document without character formats. Select it to make quick review copies, especially on slower printers.

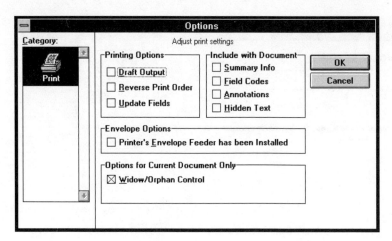

FIGURE 33.2:

The Options
dialog box for the
Print category

■ Reverse Print Order: Prints your document in reverse order, starting with the last page and finishing with the first. This is useful with laser printers that eject pages face up as they are printed, so the first page is on the bottom, the last page on top. Selecting this option prints the pages so they are in the proper order in the output tray.

■ Update Fields: Updates all fields, including those that are not normally updated when the document is printed. Note that certain fields, such as {date} and {time}, are updated during printing regardless of how this option is set.

SELECTING WHAT TO INCLUDE WITH THE DOCUMENT

The Include with Document options in the Options dialog box allow you to choose items to print in addition to the document:

■ Summary Info: Prints the information in the Summary Info dialog box on a separate page after the document. This option is available only when the Print selection is Document.

- Field Codes: Prints the field codes, not the results of the codes, even when the results appear on the screen. Select this option to print a reference copy of the document. Then, if you accidentally erase the document, you will have a record of the fields and equations you entered.

- Annotations: Prints the annotations on a separate sheet of paper following the document. This option is available when the Print selection is Document.

- Hidden Text: Prints text that would not normally appear on the screen or in the printout. (You will learn more about hidden text in Lesson 36.)

CHOOSING ENVELOPE OPTIONS

The Envelope Options section of the Options dialog box has one option. Select Printer's Envelope Feeder has been installed if you have an automatic envelope feeder attached to your printer. This option is used when you print an envelope inserted with the Envelope option (with either the Envelope button on the toolbar or the Create Envelope option on the Tools menu).

CONTROLLING WIDOWS AND ORPHANS

Select Widow/Orphan Control to prevent Word from printing widows or orphans. A *widow* is a single line that appears at the top of a page. An *orphan* is a line that appears by itself at the bottom of a page.

Handling Printing Problems with Print Manager

When you print a document, Word passes control of the process to Print Manager, a Windows program that handles all communications between your computer and printer. In most cases, your printing jobs will go smoothly, and you will not have to be concerned with Print Manager. However, if a problem halts the printing process while you are working with Word, you will need to run and use Print Manager.

Print Manager places all your printer requests in a waiting line in which Windows stores all the documents that you want to print, called a *queue*. Each job in the queue is printed in turn. As long as nothing goes wrong with your printer, your document will be printed when its turn comes up in the queue. But things do go wrong: ribbons break, toner needs replenishing, or the printer runs out of paper. When a printer error occurs, Print Manager will stop printing documents until you correct the problem and tell it to resume printing.

If your nonlaser printer is set for manual feed, Print Manager will wait until you insert a sheet of paper and instruct it to begin printing. You have to run Print Manager and give the command to begin printing after you load each sheet of paper.

In the following steps, you will handle a sample printing problem:

1. Open any of your documents and turn your printer *off*.

2. Click on the Print button in the toolbar to attempt to print the document. With the keyboard, pull down the File menu and select Print (Ctrl-Shift-F12), then choose OK. You will see the dialog box shown in Figure 33.3.

3. Select OK.

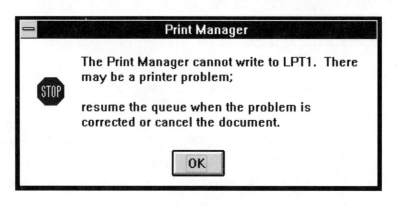

FIGURE 33.3:

Warning that the job cannot be printed

Word continues to send your entire document to Print Manager, although it is not able to print it. Let's access Print Manager without saving your document or exiting Word.

4. Click on the Control menu in the title bar and select Switch To. With the keyboard, press Ctrl-Esc. You will see the Task List dialog box, which lists all the currently running applications, as shown in Figure 33.4.

5. Select Print Manager, then Switch To. The Print Manager window will overlap the Word window, as shown in Figure 33.5.

6. Turn on your printer to correct the problem.

7. Select the **R**esume button (beneath the Print Manager menu bar).

8. To leave Print Manager and return to Word, click anywhere in the part of the Word window that you can still see. With the keyboard, press Alt-Tab. The Word window will reappear (Print Manager is still active but in the background, underneath the Word window).

9. To return to Print Manager, press Alt-Tab.

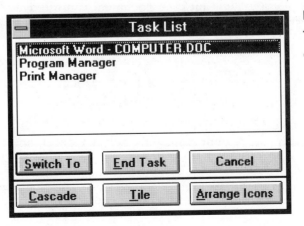

FIGURE 33.4:

The Task List dialog box

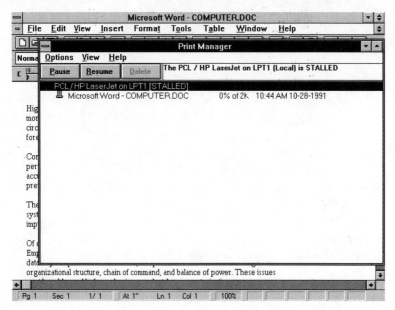

FIGURE 33.5:

Print Manager
window over
Word window

With both Word and Print Manager running, you can switch back and forth between the two programs by pressing Alt-Tab. You can also press Ctrl-Esc and select another program from the dialog box.

10. Wait until the document is printed, and then close Print Manager by pulling down the Control menu and selecting Close (Alt-F4). The Word screen will reappear.

If you try to close Print Manager while it still has documents to print, you will see a dialog box with a message informing you that closing Print Manager will cancel all pending print jobs. If you don't want to cancel your print jobs, select Cancel, and then switch back to the Word screen.

11. Pull down the File menu and select Exit (Alt-F4) to exit Word.

To cancel a print job, select the document from the Print Manager window, choose the Delete button beneath the Print Manager's menu bar, and then select OK to confirm that you want to terminate the job. Select the Resume button and return to Word (or switch to another application).

In this lesson, we opened both Word and Print Manager as windows, then switched back and forth between the two. This is particularly convenient if you are using a nonlaser printer with manually fed paper, because you can switch to Print Manager to instruct it to begin printing without exiting Word.

You can also reduce Word to an icon (or minimize it) before accessing Print Manager, which allows you to quickly return to Word to continue working. Select the Minimize box in the Word title bar (the second one on the right). With the keyboard, press Alt-spacebar, then N. To return to Word, double-click on its icon on the bottom of the screen, or press Ctrl-Esc and then select Microsoft Word in the dialog box.

34 LESSON

FEATURING

Creating
letterhead,
formatting, and
editing macros

Running macros
in a document

▼

Recording and Using Macros

Macros provide a way to store and reuse keystrokes. For example, you might use the same formatting or editing commands in many different documents. A macro can store text as well as commands. Every time you have to perform the task saved in the macro, you just run the macro to repeat the keystrokes. You can even link macros with the key combinations, or insert them into Word's pull-down menus, making them instantly accessible.

In this lesson, you will create several useful macros. The first will contain text and formatting commands to produce a letterhead. The other macros will contain formatting and editing commands that will save you from repeating often-used keystrokes.

Creating Macros

By using the Record Macro option on the Tools menu, you can easily create macros. As you type, Word will store the keystrokes in the computer's memory.

When you are recording a macro, the mouse can be used only to select menu and dialog box options. You must use the cursor-movement and text-selection keys to move the insertion point and select text.

RECORDING A LETTERHEAD MACRO

The first macro you will record will contain the keystrokes to create a letterhead. Follow these steps:

1. Start Word, pull down the Tools menu and select Record Macro to display the dialog box shown in Figure 34.1.

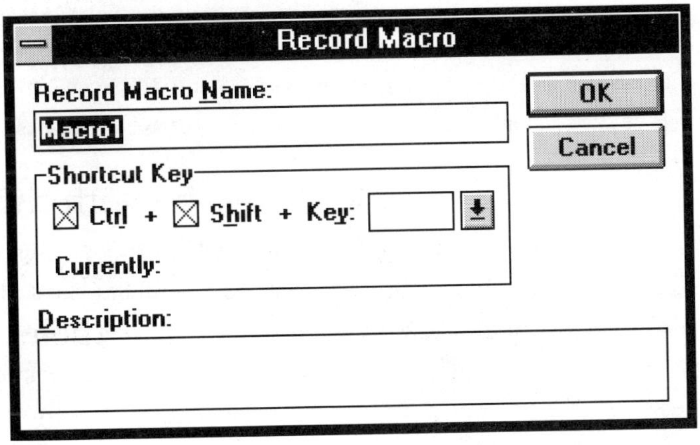

FIGURE 34.1:

The Record Macro dialog box

Macro1 appears as the macro name. You can accept that name and have Word continue to number your macros consecutively (Macro2, Macro3, and so on), or you can enter your own macro name.

2. Type **Letterhead** as the macro name.

You can enter the purpose of the macro in the **Description** text box. You can later use the description to make sure you are running the correct macro. The Shortcut Key options let you assign your macro to a key combination using either Ctrl, Shift, or both. Choose combinations that are not already used by Word. Don't use just the Shift key with a letter or number key, or you won't be able to type the uppercase letter or normal character generated by the Shift-number combination.

3. Select Key and type L (uppercase) to select the Ctrl-Shift-L combination. You will see the message

Currently: [unassigned]

This indicates that the key combination is not being used. When the key combination is already assigned, the name of the macro it is associated with will appear.

4. Select OK, and Word will begin recording the keystrokes.

If another macro with this name already exists, Word will display a message asking if you want to replace the existing macro. You can select **Yes** to replace the macro, or choose **No** or **Cancel** and enter another name.

If you are using a template other then NORMAL.DOT, you will see the dialog box shown in Figure 34.2 after selecting OK from the Record Macro dialog box. Select As **G**lobal to add the macro to the global glossary and template, or choose In **T**emplate to add the macro to your custom glossary and template. By using the **T**emplate option in the **F**ile menu, you can change the template where the macros are stored and specify that you should not be prompted, as explained in Lesson 24.

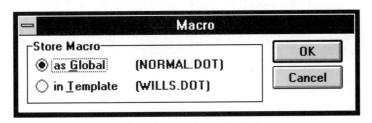

FIGURE 34.2:

The dialog box for adding a macro to the global or template glossary

5. To begin the letterhead, select the Center button in the ribbon (Ctrl-E) to center the insertion point.

6. Type your name and press ↵.

If you make a typing error, just correct it as usual. Word records the results of your macros; the keystrokes you used to change the text will not be included when you run the macro.

7. Type your street address and press ↵.

8. Type your city, state, and zip code, press ↵ twice, and select the Left button on the ribbon (Ctrl-L).

9. Pull down the Tools menu and select Stop Recorder (which replaced Record Macro in the menu) to end keystroke recording.

RECORDING A TRIPLE-SPACING MACRO

The next macro you will record will format text as triple-spaced. Follow these steps:

1. Pull down the Tools menu and select Record Macro.

2. Type **Triple** as the name of the macro.

3. Select Key, type **3**, and then select OK.

4. Pull down the Format menu and select Paragraph.

5. Select Line Spacing, then choose Exactly.

6. Select At, type **3**, and then select OK.

7. Pull down the Tools menu and select Stop Recorder to end the macro recording.

RECORDING AN EDITING MACRO

Your final macro will switch the position of two paragraphs. Follow these steps to create it:

1. Press Ctrl-1 to return to single-spacing.

2. Type **This is paragraph 1** and press ↵.

3. Type **This is paragraph 2** and press ↵.

4. Place the insertion point within the second sentence, which represents the paragraph you want to swap with the one above.

5. Pull down the Tools menu, select Record Macro, and type **Swap**.

6. Select Key, type **S** (uppercase), and then select OK.

7. Press F8 four times, pull down the Edit menu, and select Cut (Ctrl-X) to select and cut the paragraph.

8. Press Ctrl-↑ to place the insertion point in front of the first paragraph.

9. Pull down the Edit menu and select Paste (Ctrl-V) to insert the deleted paragraph from the Clipboard. The two paragraphs will now be reversed.

10. Pull down the Tools menu and select Stop Recorder to end the macro definition.

11. Pull down the File menu and select Close (Alt-F4), then No to clear the document window without saving the text.

12. Click on the New Document button on the toolbar. With the keyboard, pull down the File menu and select New, then OK.

You have now created three macros and assigned them to key combinations.

Running Macros

Word offers several ways to activate, or *run*, a macro:

■ Any macro can be run from the Macro dialog box.

■ If you assigned a key combination to the macro, you can run it by pressing those keys.

■ You can add a button for your macro to the toolbar.

■ You can include your macro on a Word pull-down menu.

In the following steps, you will use the first two methods. You will learn how to add macros to the toolbar or a menu in Lesson 35.

Macros are stored in the document's glossary, so in order to run a macro, you must be using the template attached to the document when you created the macro. If you saved the glossary in a template other than NORMAL.DOT, use the New option on the File menu and select the template for a new document. To use the macro with a document already on the screen, use the Template option on the File menu to change templates.

Follow these steps to use the macros you created:

1. Pull down the Tools menu and select Macro to display the dialog box shown in Figure 34.3.

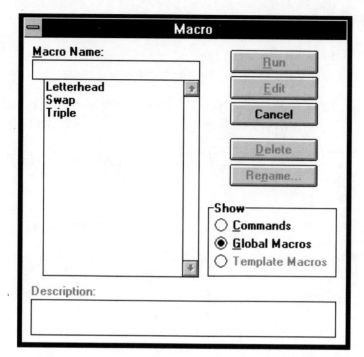

FIGURE 34.3:

The Macro
dialog box

2. Select Letterhead.

When you select a macro that you gave a description (in the the Record Macro dialog box), the description will appear in the Description box at the bottom of the dialog box.

3. Choose the Run button (in the upper-right corner of the dialog box).

Your address appears on the screen, character by character, just as you typed it. Now we'll try using the Swap macro, which is linked to the Ctrl-Shift-S key combination.

4. Type **I want this to be the second paragraph** and press ↵.

5. Type **I want this to be the first paragraph** and press ↵.

6. Place the insertion point in the second paragraph and press Ctrl-Shift-S.

The Swap macro is recalled from the glossary and run, switching the two words. You could also have run the macro by selecting it in the Macro dialog box.

After you create a number of macros, you may begin to forget their key assignments. As a guide, print their assignments as explained in Lesson 33: pull down the File menu, select Print, select Key Assignments from the Print drop-down list box, and then choose OK. Word will print a list of your custom key assignments, including the macro's name and description. Keep the list near your computer as a reference.

Saving Macros

Your new macros have been added to the NORMAL.DOT template but not yet saved on the disk. Save them now as you exit Word.

1. Pull down the File menu and select Exit (Alt-F4), then **No** to exit Word without saving the document. A dialog box will appear with the message

Do you want to save the global glossary and command changes?

2. Select Yes to save the template with the macros.

Using Other Macro Options

The other options in the Macro dialog box allow you to delete, edit, and rename macros. To delete a macro, select it in the Macro Name list box, then select the Delete command button.

To change the name of a macro, select it in the list box, and then select the Rename command button. Type the new name in the dialog box that appears, and then select OK. The OK button will remain dimmed if you enter the name of an existing macro.

EDITING MACROS

Editing a macro allows you to correct any mistakes you made when recording the macro without repeating the entire procedure. To edit a macro, highlight its name in the Macro dialog box and select the Edit button. The text of the macro will appear in a special editing window, as shown in Figure 34.4.

The functions and commands in the displayed macro are in a language called WordBASIC. This is an extensive programming language that can be used to write complete applications built around Word for Windows. If you are interested in using WordBASIC to edit and write macros, order the *Technical Reference* manual from Microsoft.

The Letterhead macro contains the following functions and commands:

Sub MAIN	Designates the start of the macro.
CenterPara	Centers the insertion point, performing the Center (Ctrl-E) command.
Insert	Inserts the text following it (enclosed in quotation marks) into the document.
InsertPara	Inserts a carriage return (like pressing ↵).
LeftPara	Moves the insertion point to the left margin, performing the Left Align command (Ctrl-L) command.
End Sub	Ends the macro.

If you want to change the text the Letterhead macro generates, edit any of the text within the quotation marks. Add InsertPara commands when you want to end lines and insert carriage returns, and Insert

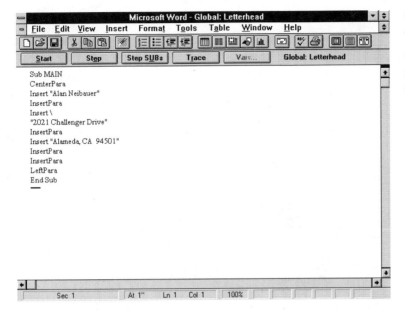

FIGURE 34.4:

Text of macro displayed in macro editing window

commands to include more text. For example, to add a telephone number to the Letterhead macro, after this line:

Insert"Alameda, CA 94501"

add these two lines:

Insert"555-1234"
InsertPara

After editing the macro, pull down the File menu and select Close. (You cannot save the macro with the Save button on the toolbar.) You will see a dialog box asking if you want to keep the changes you made to the macro. Select Yes to save the edited macro or No to retain the original version.

Customizing the Toolbar and Menus

During your work with Word, you will find that there are some commands and macros that you use often. You might, for example, frequently use the command to change orientation or page size, or run a macro to create a complex paragraph format. You can make your own macros or Word commands instantly accessible by adding them to the toolbar or to one of Word's pull-down menus, as you will learn in this lesson.

Changes you make to the toolbar and menus are stored with the document template. If you want your customized toolbar and menus to apply to every document, make sure you are using the NORMAL.DOT template when you make the changes.

Adding a Button to the Toolbar

You can replace an existing button in the toolbar with another command or macro, or retain all the existing toolbar buttons and add a new button in one of the spaces on the toolbar. As an example of customizing the toolbar, we will add a button for the Letterhead macro we created in Lesson 34. Follow these steps:

1. Start Word, pull down the Tools menu, and select Options.

2. In the Options dialog box, select Category, then Toolbar. You will see the options for modifying the toolbar, as shown in Figure 35.1.

In this dialog box, you select the button you want to change or the space you want to hold the new button, the command or macro you want to add, and the icon that you want to appear in the button.

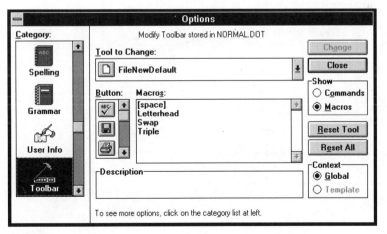

FIGURE 35.1:

The Options dialog box for the Toolbar category

3. Select Tool to Change to see a list of the buttons in the toolbar, as shown in Figure 35.2.

The Tool to Change list shows the icon and command assigned to
each button. Spaces between buttons are indicated by the [space]
markers. You can select a space to insert the new button there, or choose
an existing button to be replaced with the new one.

4. Scroll through the list to highlight the [space] marker following ToolsCreateEnvelope (the Envelope button).

5. Select Macros, and then choose the Letterhead macro in the
Macros list box.

The Macros list box shows the macros that are stored with the
template. When you want to add one of Word's built-in commands to

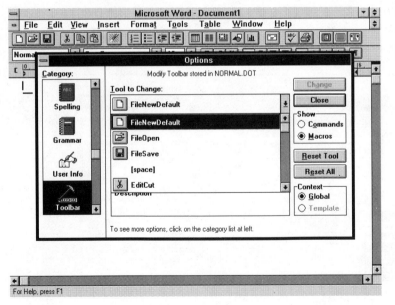

FIGURE 35.2:

Tool to Change
list

the toolbar, select the Commands button in the Show section (on the right side of the dialog box). The Macros list box changes to the Commands list box, and it includes all of Word's functions.

6. Select Button, and then scroll through the list to see the icons that are available to represent the macro.

You can select from graphic icons, as well as buttons containing numbers and letters. Word allows you to use an icon that is already on the toolbar, but you will have to remember which button performs which command.

7. Select the button that contains the letter *L* to represent the Letterhead macro.

If you are using a template other than NORMAL.DOT, you can select either **Global** or **Template** in the Context section (in the lower-right corner of the dialog box) to indicate where you want to store the modified toolbar. However, since you are using NORMAL.DOT, these options are not available.

8. Select Change (in the upper-right corner of the dialog box). The toolbar in the background window will change to include the new macro, as shown in Figure 35.3.

9. Select Close.

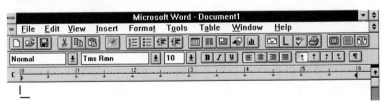

FIGURE 35.3:

The toolbar with the Letterhead macro button

To insert your letterhead in a document, just click on the new Letterhead button on the toolbar.

Removing a Button from the Toolbar

If you decide you no longer need a particular button on the toolbar, you can delete it through the Options dialog box for the Toolbar category. Follow these steps to remove the Letterhead button:

1. Pull down the Tools menu and select **O**ptions.

2. Select Tool to Change and highlight Letterhead.

3. Select the Reset Tool button, and then choose Close. The Letterhead button will disappear from the toolbar.

You can also delete a button by inserting a [space] marker in its place. To reset the entire toolbar to its default setting, select the Reset All button (on the lower-right side of the dialog box).

4. Pull down the File menu and select Exit (Alt-F4) to exit Word. You will be asked if you want to save the glossary and command changes.

5. Select No. (Since you restored the toolbar to its original condition, it actually doesn't matter if you select Yes or No).

If you change the toolbar for a template other than NORMAL.DOT, you will be asked if you want to save the changes to the template. When you modify the toolbar for your own work, select Yes to save the changes, either in NORMAL.DOT or a template.

Customizing the Menus

In addition to changing the toolbar, you can add new commands and your own macros to the pull-down menus. This is particularly useful if you do not have a mouse or have used up all the space in the toolbar.

Let's add the Swap macro to the Edit pull-down menu. This will enable you to change the position of paragraphs by selecting the option from the menu.

1. Start Word, pull down the Tools menu, and select **O**ptions.

2. Select **C**ategory, then Menus to display the options for modifying menus, as shown in Figure 35.4.

In this dialog box, you select the menu you want to change, the command or macro you want to add, and the text that you want to appear for that item on the menu.

3. Select **M**enu to see a list of the options in the menu bar. In the names, an ampersand (&) appears before the character that is underlined in the menu bar.

4. Highlight &Edit to select the Edit pull-down menu.

5. Select Macros, and then choose the Swap macro.

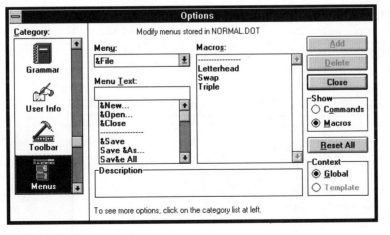

FIGURE 35.4:

The Options dialog box for the Menus category

6. Select Menu **T**ext. The name of the macro will appear in the text box, highlighted and preceded by the & symbol.

7. Change the text in the box to **&Swap two paragraphs**.

If you are using a template other then NORMAL.DOT, you can select either **G**lobal or **T**emplate (in the lower-right corner of the dialog box) to indicate where you want to store the modified menu. However, since you are using NORMAL.DOT, these options are not available.

8. Select **A**dd to make the changes to the Edit menu.

9. Select Close.

10. Pull down the Edit menu, and you will see the new command, followed by its key combination, as shown in Figure 35.5.

11. Press Esc.

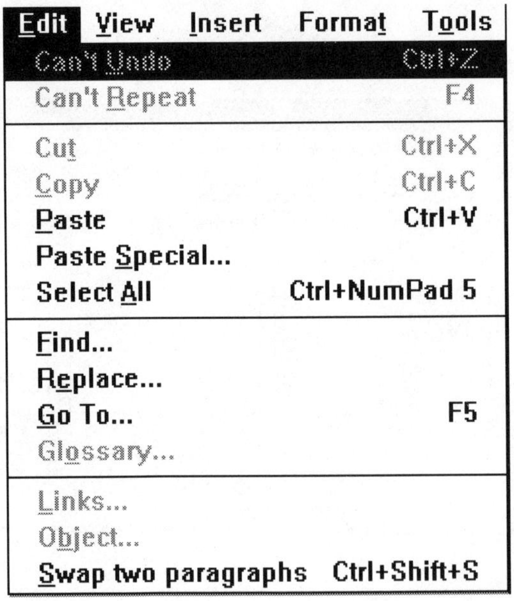

Edit **V**iew **I**nsert For**m**at **T**ools	
Can't **U**ndo	Ctrl+Z
Can't **R**epeat	F4
Cu**t**	Ctrl+X
Copy	Ctrl+C
Paste	**Ctrl+V**
Paste **S**pecial...	
Select **A**ll	**Ctrl+NumPad 5**
Find...	
Replace...	
Go To...	F5
Gl**o**ssary...	
Links...	
Ob**j**ect...	
Swap two paragraphs	**Ctrl+Shift+S**

FIGURE 35.5:

The Edit menu with the new option

To swap two paragraphs, you can either press Ctrl-Shift-S or select the option from the Edit menu.

Resetting the Menus

Through the Options dialog box for the Menus category, you can reset all the menus to their default condition, or delete specific items. Follow these steps to remove the Swap macro from the Edit menu:

1. Pull down the Tools menu and select **O**ptions.

2. Select **R**eset All, and then choose Close.

To delete a specific item from a menu, select the menu name in the Menu list box, and then choose the macro or command from the Macros or Commands list box. Select **D**elete, then Close.

3. Pull down the File menu and select Exit (Alt-F4) to exit Word. You will be asked if you want to save the glossary and command changes.

4. Select No. (Since you restored the menus to their original condition, it doesn't matter if you select Yes or No.)

When you modify the menus for your own work, select Yes to record the changes on your disk before leaving Word.

36 LESSON

FEATURING

Hiding text

Turning on and off the display of hidden text

Printing hidden text

▼

Using Hidden Text

This may sound like something from a spy novel, but you can enter hidden text—text that you make visible or invisible—into your documents. You can use this feature as a scratch pad, recording informal reminders and messages to yourself that you do not want to print, or to record other information that should not be available to everyone who sees the document.

For example, a teacher might use this feature when writing exams. After each question, the answer can be entered as hidden text. The hidden text won't appear in each student's copy of the test, but it can be displayed and printed in the teacher's copy.

Hiding Text

You designate characters as hidden by using the Ctrl-H key combination or by selecting the Hidden option in the Character dialog box (accessed by selecting Character from the Format menu). You can hide text before or after you type it, and enter it whether or not hidden text is displayed.

HIDING TEXT AS YOU TYPE

As an example, we will create a sample student exam and add some hidden text to it. Follow these steps:

1. Start Word and type the following text.

1. Parts of a computer include:
   a. input devices
   b. output devices
   c. printers
   d. all of the above
   e. none of the above

2. Word processing features include:
   a. word wrap
   b. justification
   c. pagination
   d. all of the above

2. Place the insertion point in the blank line after the first question.

3. Pull down the Tools menu and select **O**ptions. Choose the View category if it is not already displayed.

4. Select Hidden Text, and then choose OK.

5. Press Ctrl-H to format the next characters you type as hidden text, and then type the following answer.

E none of the above. While these are examples of parts of a computer system, they are actually peripheral devices attached to the computer itself.

The text appears on the screen, underlined by a row of dots, as shown in Figure 36.1. These indicate that the displayed text is hidden. Now let's see what happens when you turn off the display of hidden text.

6. Pull down the Tools menu, select **O**ptions, choose Hidden Text, and then select OK.

The hidden text disappears from the screen. Note that if you turn on the display of codes (by using the Show All button on the ribbon or by selecting All in the View category of the Options dialog box), hidden text will appear no matter how you set the Hidden Text option.

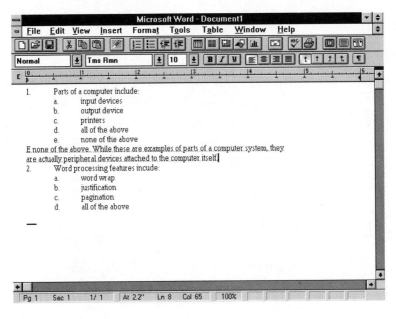

FIGURE 36.1:

The dotted underline indicates that displayed text is hidden

Now that the display of hidden text is turned off, let's type some invisible text.

7. Place the insertion point at the end of the second question, press Ctrl-H, and type the following.

> **D All of the above are features found on word processing systems.**

As you typed, the insertion point stayed in the original position, and the hidden text did not appear on the screen. However, it was entered into the document, as you shall see in a moment. Pressing Ctrl-H formats text as hidden, but it has no effect on the display.

8. Select Hidden Text from the Options dialog box again to turn the display of hidden text back on. The text you just typed will now appear on the screen.

HIDING EXISTING TEXT

You can also enter text as normal, then convert it to hidden text by selecting it and pressing Ctrl-H or by choosing Hidden in the Character dialog box. Let's try this now.

1. Place the insertion point at the top of the document, press ↵, and then press ↑ to insert a blank line at the top.

2. Type the following sentence.

> **Do not grade this test on a curve.**

3. Select the line, and then pull down the Format menu and select Character.

4. In the Character dialog box, choose Hidden, and then select OK.

The selected text is now underlined with a row of dots, designating it as hidden.

Printing Hidden Text

You select whether or not to *display* hidden text through the Options dialog box, but you select whether or not to *print* it through the Print dialog box. Even if the hidden text is visible on the screen, it will be printed only if you select Hidden Text in the Print Options dialog box. This also means that you can print hidden text whether or not it is displayed on the screen.

Now we will print the document twice: once without the hidden text and once with it. Follow these steps:

1. Click on the Print button on the toolbar to print the document. With the keyboard, pull down the File menu and select Print (Ctrl-Shift-F12), then OK. The document will print without the hidden text, even though it is displayed on the screen.

2. Pull down the File menu, select Print, and then choose **O**ptions.

3. Select Hidden Text, and then select OK twice. The hidden text will be printed.

4. Pull down the File menu and select Exit (Alt-F4), then No to exit Word without saving the text.

Converting Hidden Text to Normal Text

You can convert hidden text to normal text, so that it is always displayed and printed. Turn on the display of hidden text and select the hidden text you want to convert. Then press Ctrl-H or select Hidden in the Character dialog box.

Selecting hidden text and pressing Ctrl-spacebar also changes hidden text to normal text. However, it will cancel all other character formats, including font and point size selections, as well.

Creating a Data File for Form Documents

I f you work in a business office, you already know the importance of form letters. You can send personalized letters to as many people as you want after typing the letter just once. But what if you don't use Word for business? Should you skip the lessons about form documents?

Think about it for a moment. Aren't there repetitive letters or other documents that you need? How about responses to classified ads, requests for information, or letters of complaint? Perhaps you are sending notes, thank-you letters, or invitations to family members or friends. These are also examples of form letters. In each case, you have a basic document that you want to send to everyone on your list. Except for some personalized text, such as the name and address, each letter has the same words.

The first task in creating a form letter is to create the data file, as you will do in this lesson. In the following lessons, you will learn how to create the main form document and generate the finished documents.

Structuring a Data File

A *data file* contains all the pertinent information about a group of items. It could be the name, address, and other information about clients or employees. It could be the company's inventory or price list.

Picture the data file as an electronic version of an index card file. Every card, called a *record*, contains all the data about one item. Each record has several pieces of information, such as the name of the item, quantity on hand, supplier, and price. Each piece of information is called a *field*.

To create a data file, you first need to determine which fields are needed and give each a name. Field names can contain up to 20 characters but must start with a letter and be a single word (without spaces). They can include numbers, letters, and the underscore (_) character.

In this and the following lessons, you will create and produce a form letter to request product information from a number of companies. The data file will contain the company names and addresses and the names of products. Here are the fields that you will use for the sample data file:

INFORMATION IN FIELD	FIELD NAME
Company name	Company
Company address	Address
Additional address information	Location
Company city	City
Company state	State

INFORMATION IN FIELD	FIELD NAME
Company zip code	Zip
Product of interest	Product

Now that you have the structure, you can create the data file.

Using Print Merge

There are several ways to create a Word data file. In this book, you will use the Print Merge option in the File menu. This option guides you through the process of creating the data file as a Word table and creating the main form document.

Follow these steps to create the sample data file:

1. Start Word, pull down the File menu, and select Print Merge to see the dialog box shown in Figure 37.1.

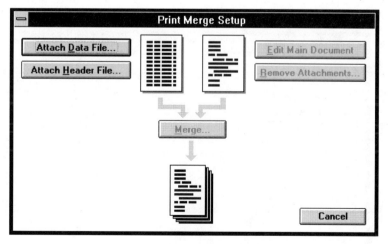

FIGURE 37.1:

The Print Merge Setup dialog box

You use the options on the left side of the dialog box to work with the data file. The options on the right side of the dialog box apply to the main form document. The Attach Header File option allows you to save the names of your fields in a file separate from the actual data, and then add the names to the data at another time.

2. Select Attach **D**ata File. You will see a dialog box that resembles the Open dialog box, with the addition of the Create Data File option.

3. Select **C**reate Data File to see the dialog box shown in Figure 37.2.

In the Create Data File dialog box, you enter each of the field names. Word will automatically add them to the data file in the proper format.

4. In the Field Name box, type **Company**, the first field name.

5. Select Add or press ↵.

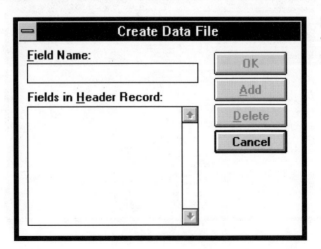

FIGURE 37.2:

The Create Data File dialog box

6. Continue to add each field name by typing its name in the Field Name box and selecting **Add** or pressing ↵: **Address**, **Location**, **City**, **State**, **Zip**, and **Product**.

7. Select OK, and the Save As dialog box will appear.

8. Type **Vendors**, and then select OK.

A table appears with the field names as column titles, although several columns scroll off the right side of the screen, as shown in Figure 37.3. This first row in the data file table is called the *header record*. Notice that the toolbar now includes several new buttons labeled with letters. These are used to perform advanced functions for managing your data file, as explained in Table 37.1.

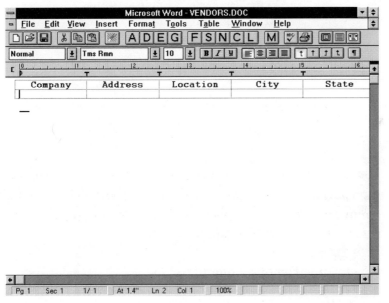

FIGURE 37.3:

The data file appears as a table with field names as column labels

BUTTON	NAME	FUNCTION
A	Add Record	Adds a new record (row) to the table
D	Delete Record	Deletes a record from the table
E	Edit Record	Edits a record (prompts you with a series of dialog boxes)
G	Go To Record	Goes to a specified record
F	Add Field	Adds a new field (column) to the end of the table
S	Sort Records	Sorts the records in the table on up to three keys in ascending or descending order
N	Number Records	Numbers the records by adding a new column, with consecutive numbers in each cell, at the start of the table
C	Clean Up Data File	Checks the data file for improper spacing and a valid header record
L	Link Data File	Links the data file to an Excel database
M	Main Document	Switches to the main document window

TABLE 37.1:

Toolbar Buttons for Managing Data File Tables

Adding Information to the Data File Table

You enter the *variable* information (the information that is different in each document) in the data file by typing the data for each field in a different cell of the table. Follow these steps to add the company information to the VENDORS data file.

1. Type **Famous Computers, Inc.**

2. Press Tab to reach the next column.

3. Type **Frankford and Grant Avenues** and press Tab.

4. Type **Suite 304** and press Tab.

5. Type **Abington** and press Tab.

6. Type **PA** and press Tab.

7. Type 19114 and press Tab.

8. Type **computers** and press Tab.

When you pressed Tab after entering data in the last column, Word automatically inserted a new row at the end of the table.

9. In the same manner, enter the information about the next company in the second row.

> **Williamson Peripherals**
> **Main and Ridge Streets**
> **Suite 102**
> **Camden**
> **NJ**
> 18087
> **monitors**

10. Enter the data for the last company. Do not press ↵ or Tab after the last column. Leave the Location field blank by pressing Tab in the cell.

> **Drexel, Inc.**
> **3001 Market Street**
>
> **New York**
> **NY**
> 10012
> **printers**

11. Click on the Save button on the toolbar. With the keyboard, pull down the File menu and select Save (Shift-F12).

12. When the Summary Info dialog box appears, select OK.

13. Pull down the File menu and select Close.

Word displays the window in which you can create the main form document, shown in Figure 37.4. The bar above the ruler is called the print merge bar. You will learn about this bar in Lesson 38.

You could type the main form document now, or *attach* (link) the data file to any main document. For our example, you will exit Word and then attach the VENDORS data file and create a main document in the next lesson.

14. Pull down the File menu and select Exit (Alt-F4) to exit Word.

Since the data file is a Word table, you can use all the editing commands to maintain the information. It's easy to search for specific records, edit the text, move and copy data between rows, and delete rows.

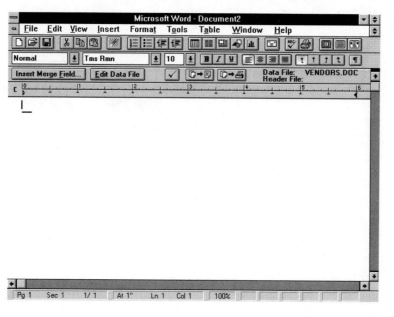

FIGURE 37.4:

Main document window for form documents

Other Methods for Creating Data Files

You can also create a data file as a table using the techniques you learned in Lesson 25. Set up a table with a column for each field and a row for each record. Type the field names in the first row and the information for each record in a different row. You can then attach the table to the main document, as explained in Lesson 38.

Another approach is to create the data file as a document rather than as a table. The document must be set up as follows:

- The first paragraph in the document contains the field names, separated by commas.

- Each record is entered in its own paragraph.

- Each field in the record is separated by a comma.

- To include a comma in a field, enclose the field in quotation marks.

- Blank fields are indicated by a comma.

Generally, it's easier to have Word create the data file table for you.

FEATURING

Attaching a data file

Adding fields

Creating an envelope form document

▼

Creating the Main Form Document

Now that you have a data file, you can attach it to a main document and create the form letter. Rather than typing in the field codes for the merge fields, you can have Word insert them for you. Then you don't have to worry about misspelling a field name or other errors. In this lesson, you will learn how to prepare for merging form documents.

Attaching the Data File

When you attach a data file to a form document, you are making its records available. You can attach a data file to as many form documents as you like. So, for example, you can use the same data file to produce letters, envelopes, and invoices for the same individuals.

Follow these steps to attach the VENDORS data file to a main form document:

1. Start Word, pull down the File menu and select Print Merge.

2. In the dialog box, select Attach Data File.

3. Select Vendors from the list box, and then choose OK.

Word displays the main document window (see Figure 37.4). Since you already created and attached the data file, your next task is to type the main form document.

To create and print merge documents, you will be using the print merge bar, which is just above the ruler in a main document window. Table 38.1 summarizes the functions of the buttons on the print merge bar.

BUTTON	FUNCTION
Insert Merge Field...	llows you to insert a merge variable into the main document by selecting from a list of fields in the data file
Edit Data File	Switches to the attached data file so you can add or edit records
✓	Checks the main document and attached data file for errors, such as undefined fields and spelling mistakes
⬚→🗎	Merges the document to a new document on the screen
⬚→🖨	Merges and print the documents immediately
Data File: Header File:	The name of the attached data file, and a separate file, if any, that contains the header record

TABLE 38.1:

Print Merge Bar Buttons

Setting Up the Main Document

The main form document contains the text that you want to appear on every letter and the print merge fields that represent the variable information in your data file. You insert the print merge fields in the main document by clicking on the Insert Merge Field button (Alt-Shift-F) and selecting from the list of fields.

In the following steps, you will create the main document, using the Letterhead macro (from Lesson 34) and date and time fields (covered in Lesson 26).

1. Press Ctrl-Shift-L to run the Letterhead macro and insert your letterhead in the document.

2. Select the Center button in the ribbon (Ctrl-E) to center the insertion point.

3. Pull down the Insert menu and select Date and Time.

4. Select the third date format in the list box, and then choose OK.

5. Press ↵ twice and select the Left button in the ribbon (Ctrl-L).

6. Click on the Insert Merge Field button (Alt-Shift-F) to see the Insert Merge Field dialog box, shown in Figure 38.1.

This dialog box shows the fields in the attached data file in the Print Merge Fields list box and Word's fields in the other box. You can

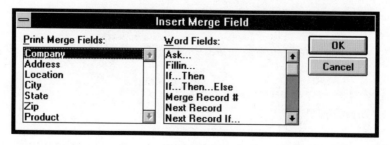

FIGURE 38.1:

The Insert Merge Field dialog box

use Word's fields to perform advanced merge functions, such as requesting data as each record is merged or for conditional merging based on the values of fields.

The first field in the data file, Company, is already selected.

7. Select OK to accept the selected Company field. The code <<Company>> will appear in the document.

8. Press ↵.

9. Click on the Insert Merge Field button (Alt-Shift-F), select Address, select OK, and press ↵.

10. Click on the Insert Merge Field button (Alt-Shift-F), select Location, select OK, and press ↵.

11. Click on the Insert Merge Field button (Alt-Shift-F), select City, and select OK.

12. Type a comma (,), and then press the spacebar.

13. Click on the Insert Merge Field button (Alt-Shift-F), select State, and select OK.

14. Press the spacebar twice.

15. Click on the Insert Merge Field button (Alt-Shift-F), select Zip, and select OK.

16. Press ↵ twice after the address.

17. Type the salutation and start the first paragraph of the letter as follows.

Dear Sir:

We are upgrading our computer system and are interested in receiving product specifications from

18. Insert a space after the word *from*, click on the Insert Merge Field button (Alt-Shift-F), and select OK to insert the Company field again.

19. Type a period (.) to end the sentence, and then press ↵.

20. Type the beginning of the next paragraph.

> **Please send specifications and product information on your**

21. Press the spacebar to insert a space after the word *your*.

22. Click on the Insert Merge Field button (Alt-Shift-F), select Product, and select OK.

23. Press the period to end the sentence, and then press ↵ twice.

24. Type the closing.

> **Sincerely,**
>
> **Alvin A. Aardvark**

Your screen should look like the one shown in Figure 38.2.

25. Click on the Save button on the toolbar. With the keyboard, pull down the File menu and select Save (Shift-F12).

26. Type **Requests** and select OK twice.

After you prepare the main document, you can merge and print the form letters, as you will learn in the next lesson.

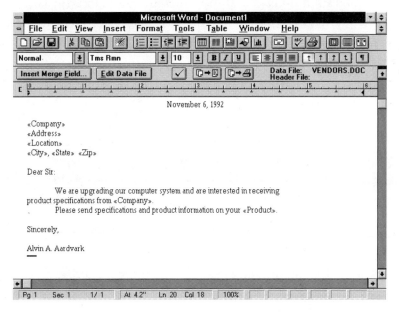

FIGURE 38.2:

Completed form letter with variables

Creating a Form Document for Envelopes

A data file can be used with any main document that contains its field names. In our example, you can use the VENDORS data file with any document containing the field names Company, Address, Location, City, State, Zip, and Product. This is handy for printing envelopes.

You could create a separate document to merge and print envelopes. However, when Word merges the envelope with the data file, it will insert an extra page break after each envelope, so that your printer will eject a blank sheet of paper after every envelope.

If you delete the envelope's page break before merging, the envelope's page formatting will be lost. On a laser printer, for example, the envelopes will print in portrait orientation or whatever paper is loaded into the tray.

The solution is to add the envelope to the letter's main document. This way, you will print the envelope and letter at the same time and save yourself the trouble of matching the letters to their envelopes later.

In the following steps, you will add an envelope to the main document and then save the document under a different name.

1. Click on the Envelope button on the toolbar. With the keyboard, pull down the Tools menu and select Create Envelope. The Create Envelope dialog box will appear with the letter's inside address—the series of merge codes—in the Address To text box.

2. Select Add to Document to insert the envelope in the document, as shown in Figure 38.3.

3. Pull down the File menu and select Save As. Type **Envelope**, and select OK twice.

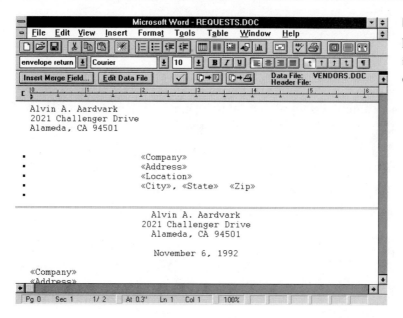

FIGURE 38.3:

Envelope inserted into the form document

4. Pull down the File menu and select **Close**.

5. Click on the New Document button on the toolbar. With the keyboard, pull down the File menu, select **New**, then **OK**.

Merging Labels and Data Files

In Lesson 22, you used the MAILLABL template to format labels that you typed in. Now you will merge the data file onto the labels automatically. Follow these steps:

1. Pull down the File menu and select **New**.

2. Select the MAILLABL template, then **OK**. The dialog box of labels will appear.

3. Select 5160 Address, then **OK**.

Word automatically sets up a table in the document, and then displays the dialog box giving you a choice between single or multiple labels.

4. Select Multiple Labels. A dialog box will appear with the question

> **Are the merge names and data contained in two separate files, a header file and a data file?**

5. Select No. The Attach Data File dialog box will appear.

6. Select Vendors, then **OK**. Word will display the Layout Mailing Labels dialog box, shown in Figure 38.4.

You use this dialog box to insert and layout the merge codes by selecting codes from the Field Names list box, and spaces and punctuation marks from the Special Characters list box.

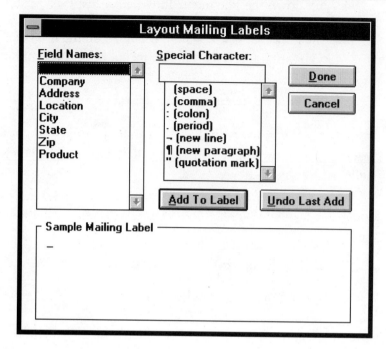

FIGURE 38.4:

The Layout Mailing Labels dialog box

7. Select Company from the Field Names list box, and then select new paragraph in the Special Characters list box. (You need to insert the new paragraph mark so the next line of the label will appear on a new line.)

8. Select Add to Label. The company field, followed by a paragraph mark will be inserted in the Sample Mailing Label box.

9. Select Address from the Field Names list box, new paragraph in the Special Characters list box, and then Add to Label.

10. Select Location from the Field Names list box, new paragraph in the Special Characters list box, and Add to Label.

11. Select City from the Field Names list box, a comma (,) in the Special Characters list box, and Add to Label.

12. Select a space in the Special Characters list box, and then choose Add to Label.

13. Select State from the Field Names list box, a space in the Special Characters list box, and Add to Label.

14. Select Zip from the Field Names list box, new paragraph in the Special Characters list box, and Add to Label.

15. Select Done.

Word adds the field codes to each of the cells in the table in the document, and then displays a dialog box saying that the main document has been set up.

16. Select OK. Figure 38.5 shows how the labels will appear.

17. Click on the Save button on the toolbar. With the keyboard, pull down the File menu and select Save.

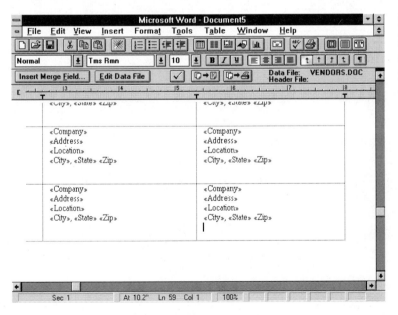

FIGURE 38.5:

Labels filled in as a main document for merging

18. Type **Labels**, and then select OK twice.

19. Pull down the File menu and select Exit (Alt-F4).

Editing and Changing Data Files

From the main document window, you can return to the attached data file by selecting Edit Data File (Alt-Shift-E). Edit the data file as necessary, and then pull down the File menu and select Close to return to the main document.

Word will use the data file attached to the main document when you produce the form letters. However, you may want to change the data file from time to time. For example, you might have two lists of vendors from which you desire information. To attach a new data file to the document, open the main document, pull down the File menu, select Print Merge, and then choose Attach Data File. Select the data file from the list that appears in the dialog box, and then select OK.

To remove an attachment, pull down the File menu, select Print Merge, and choose Remove Attachments. When you are asked to confirm the action, select OK.

39 LESSON

Merging and Printing Form Documents

Once you have prepared your main form document and attached a data file to it, you can generate the individual copies of the form letters. As you will learn in this lesson, using the Print Merge option on the File menu, you can either merge and print the letters immediately or save the merged form letters as a new document for printing later.

Merging Form Documents to the Printer

With a mouse, you can quickly print form documents by clicking on the Merge to Printer button, which is the last button on the right side of the print merge bar. (Using the Print button on the toolbar merely prints a single copy of the main document without inserting variable information from the data file.) With the keyboard, use the Print Merge dialog box to generate the documents. This dialog box also contains merging options, which are not offered when you use the print merge bar button.

In the following steps, you will use the Print Merge dialog box to merge the REQUEST document with the VENDORS data file and print the resulting documents.

1. Start Word and open the REQUESTS document.

2. Pull down the File menu, select Print Merge, and then select Merge. You will see the dialog box shown in Figure 39.1.

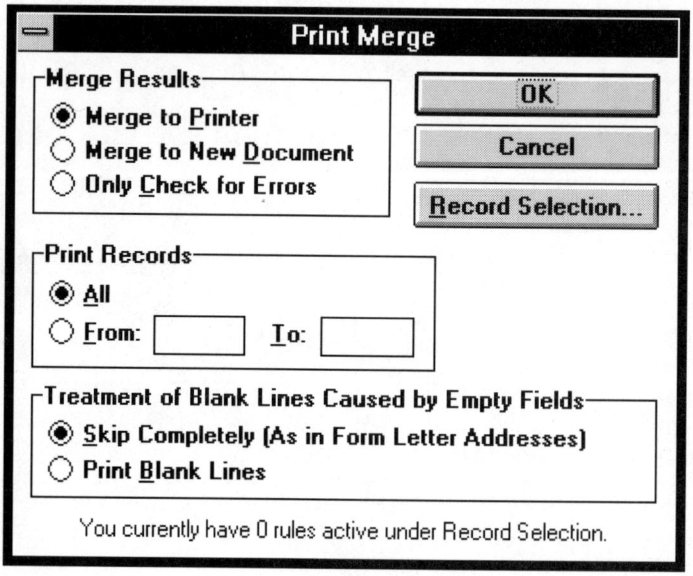

FIGURE 39.1:

The Print Merge dialog box

The Merge to Printer button is already selected. This option merges and prints the form documents. The Merge to New Document option in the Merge Results section lets you merge the document to a new document on the screen. The Only Check for Errors option just checks the file for any errors, such as undefined fields. You can also check a document from the main document window by clicking on the button with the check mark on the print merge bar, or by pressing Alt-Shift-K.

If you don't want to merge every record in the data file, select a range of records in the Print Records section of the dialog box. To merge just the first two records, for example, type 1 in the From text box and 2 in the To text box.

The other options in the dialog box give you a choice of how to treat blank lines caused by empty fields. Not every record in the data file contains information in each field. In our VENDORS data file, for example, one company does not have an entry in the Location field. The Skip Completely option (the default) omits blank fields, so that Word will not print any blank lines. If you select Print Blank Lines, empty fields will appear as blank lines in the printout.

3. Select OK to merge and print the letters using the default options. The Print dialog box will appear.

4. Select OK.

When the first letter is printed, the appropriate variable information is inserted wherever its field name is in merge codes. For example, *Famous Computers, Inc.* is printed at every occurrence of <<Company>> in the first letter.

After the first letter is printed, Word determines if another record is in the data file. If there is another record, its data is assigned to the field names and a second letter is printed. This procedure continues until there are no records left in the data file. You can have 3, 30, or even 300 records. Word will continue merging the variable items into the letters as long as records exist.

Merging Form Documents on the Screen

Now let's merge the letters again. This time you will merge the letters with their envelopes, and instead of printing them immediately, you will merge them to a new document. This way, you can save the merged documents to a disk file and print them later. First, clear the document window and open the ENVELOPE document.

1. Pull down the File menu and select Close.

2. Click on the Open button on the toolbar. With the keyboard, pull down the File menu and select **O**pen.

3. Select Envelope, and then choose OK.

4. Click on the Merge to New Document button (the second button on the right side of the print merge bar). With the keyboard, pull down the File menu, select Print Merge, then Merge, then Merge to New Document, then OK.

Word merges the documents and displays the results on the screen as a document titled Form Letters1. Each of the letters and envelopes are separated by page breaks.

5. Pull down the File menu and select Close, then No. The ENVELOPE document appears.

6. Pull down the File menu and select Close.

Selecting Records to Merge

In the steps above, you merged all the records in the database with the form document. If you want to print a range of records, you can specify them in the Print Records section of the Print Merge dialog box, as explained in the previous section. However, you might want to select records based on the contents of the fields. For example, you could print form documents for just the customers in certain states or only the vendors who sell particular products.

You can merge records selectively by setting specifications in the Record Selection dialog box (displayed by the Record Selection button in the Print Merge dialog box). As an example, you will print labels for companies in Pennsylvania.

1. Click on the Open button on the toolbar. With the keyboard, pull down the File menu and select **O**pen.

2. Select Labels, then OK. The mailing labels will appear in a main document window.

3. Pull down the File menu, select Print **M**erge, then Merge.

4. Select Record Selection to see the dialog box shown in Figure 39.2.

The options in the Record Selection dialog box allow you to select records based on up to five different rules, or criteria. In this example, we are performing a selection based only on the value of the State field.

5. In the Field Name list box, select State. With the keyboard, press Alt-F, then select the State field.

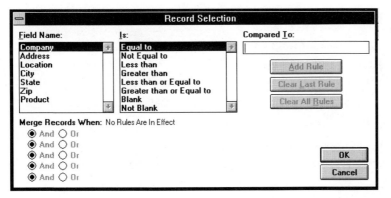

FIGURE 39.2:

The Record Selection dialog box

Since we are looking for a specific state, we will leave the Is list box set to the default Equal To.

6. Select Compared To and type **PA**.

7. Select Add Rule.

8. Select OK to display the Print Merge dialog box.

9. Select Merge to New Document, and then choose OK twice.

Word merges the label main document with the data file, but only fills out labels for companies with PA in the State field.

10. Pull down the File menu, select Exit (Alt-F4), then No to exit Word.

The selections in the Is list box can be used to specify other comparisons for merging records, such as if the field is not equal to the value, less than the value, or greater than the value. For example, suppose our mailing list contained vendors from ten different states and we want labels to every customer except those in Pennsylvania. We would select Not Equal To so the rule would appear as

State is Not Equal To PA

Labels would be printed for every customer that has a value other than PA in the State field.

By combining selections in the Is list box with the And and Or options shown at the bottom of the dialog box, you can specify complex criteria for your form document using up to five rules. For example, if you are printing invoices using a data file of customers, you could select only those customers who owe over $1000 or who have placed an order since 10/11/91. The Record Selection dialog box settings for these criteria are shown in Figure 39.3.

If you will want to merge records selectively for your work, you should experiment with various selection rules to see their results. However, use Merge to New Document so you don't waste paper, envelopes, or labels while you are experimenting.

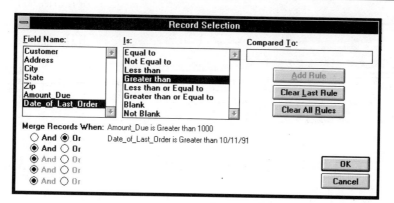

FIGURE 39.3:

Record selection using multiple rules

40 L E S S O N

Using Automatic Styles

style is a set of formatting instructions that is stored on disk. When you want to use that format, you just apply the style instead of selecting the individual formatting options. Word provides 34 automatic styles that you can use to quickly format text. In fact, throughout this book you've been using a style called Normal, which formats text as flush left in your printer's default font.

Unless you select another style or manually format text, Word will use the Normal style for your text. In this lesson, you will learn how to apply Word's automatic styles.

Taking Advantage of Styles

The real power of styles is their ability to affect all existing text in a document. For example, suppose you added 20 headings to a document, manually formatting each as 14-point bold. If you wanted to change the headings to another point size or font, you would have to select and reformat each one. However, if you used a 14-point bold heading style, you could change all 20 headings by simply changing the style. All the headings would change automatically.

You have used automatic styles in previous lessons. You saw that headers and footers automatically include a centered tab at the 3-inch position and a right tab at the 6-inch position. This is the format of the Footer and Header styles supplied with Word.

Most of the automatic styles are based on the Normal style. For example, the Heading 1 style (in Windows 3.0) is defined as

Normal + Font: Helv 12pt, Bold Underline, Space Before 1 li

This means that it starts using the formats of the Normal style, then changes to the Helv font in 12 points, turns on bold and underlining, and inserts a blank line before each heading. (Helv is similar to the Helvetica font.)

If you wanted to format a headline in this way, you could select all the individual formats from the ribbon or Format dialog boxes, or you could simply apply the Heading 1 style in one step.

Creating a Document with Styles

You can apply automatic styles in three ways: using the Style box on the ribbon, the Ctrl-S key combination, or the Style dialog box. In the following steps, you will use all of these methods to create a document that has several formats.

1. Start Word and make sure the ruler and ribbon are displayed. If not, select Ruler and Ribbon from the View menu to turn them on.

The word *Normal* in the Style box on the ribbon shows that the Normal style is in effect. Although you don't need to display the ribbon to change styles, seeing it will help you understand the effects of selecting styles. Now let's change the style to enter a heading.

2. Pull down the Style list box to display a list of four automatic styles, as shown in Figure 40.1. With the keyboard, press Ctrl-S to select the Style text box, and then press ↓ to pull down the list box.

All the 34 automatic styles can be used with any document, but their names will not appear in the list box until you use them.

3. Select Heading 1.

Now notice the changes to the ribbon. Heading 1 appears in the Styles box, the font and point size boxes show Helv and 12, and the Bold and Underline buttons are selected.

4. Type **Principles of Business Management**. The text will be formatted according to the Heading 1 style, as shown in Figure 40.2.

5. Press ↵, and the ribbon will indicate that text will now appear in the default Normal style.

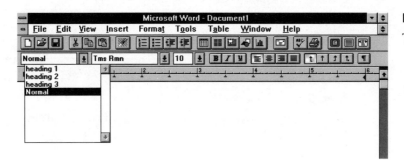

FIGURE 40.1:

The Style list box

6. Type the following sentence.

Management involves the planning, organizing, initiating, and controlling of activities to accomplish objectives.

7. Press ↵ twice after the paragraph.

Now let's turn off the ribbon and use the keyboard to format a subheading.

8. Pull down the View menu and select Ribbon to turn off the ribbon.

9. Press Ctrl-S. The status bar reads

Which style?

10. Type **Heading 1** and press ↵.

If you forget the name of the style you want to apply, you can press Ctrl-S a second time to display the Style dialog box. You will use this dialog box shortly.

11. Type **The History of Management**, and then press ↵.

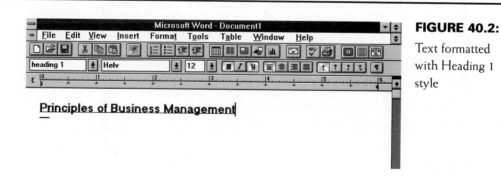

FIGURE 40.2:

Text formatted with Heading 1 style

12. Type the following text under the second heading.

The practice of management changed dramatically with the Industrial Revolution.

13. Press ↵ twice.

14. Pull down the **V**iew menu and select Ribbon to turn the ribbon back on.

Now you will apply one more style. This time, you will use the Style dialog box, which allows you to see the formats each style includes.

15. Pull down the Forma**t** menu and select Style to display the dialog box shown in Figure 40.3. With the keyboard, press Ctrl-S twice.

16. Pull down the Style Name list box. Only the four basic styles will be listed.

17. Press Ctrl-Y to display all the automatic styles. As you highlight each style, its definition will appear at the bottom of the dialog box.

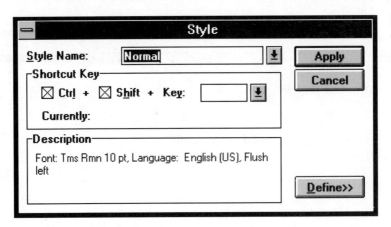

FIGURE 40.3:

The Style dialog box

18. Scroll down and select Normal Indent.

19. Select Apply in the Style dialog box.

20. Type the following text.

> **Charles Babbage was the first to use scientific methods to improve productivity. He applied the principles of work measurement and cost determination to the industrial area.**

21. Press ⏎. Unlike the Heading styles, which are followed by normal paragraphs, the Normal Indent style will not change when you press ⏎.

22. Pull down the Style list box and select Normal.

23. Click on the Print button on the toolbar to print the document. With the keyboard, pull down the File menu and select Print (Ctrl-Shift-F12), then choose OK.

To apply a style to existing paragraphs, select the text and then choose the style through the Style list box, using Ctrl-S, or through the Style dialog box. The text will conform to the selected style. As you will learn in the next lesson, you can assign key combinations to styles to apply them in a single step.

Displaying the Style Name Area

As your documents become more sophisticated, you might find yourself using a greater number of styles for formatting. If you forget which style you applied to a paragraph, place the insertion point in the paragraph and look at the Style text box on the ribbon.

You can also display a style name area along the left side of the screen. This is a vertical pane that shows the name of the style used for each paragraph. Follow these steps to display the style name area:

1. Pull down the Tools menu, select Options, and then choose the View category.

2. Select Style Area Width. To see the style name area, you must enter a measurement greater than 0.

3. Type 1, and then select OK. The style name area appears on the screen, as shown in Figure 40.4.

To adjust the size of the style name area, place the mouse pointer on the line separating the area from the text. The pointer will change to a double vertical line, with arrows pointing to the left and right. Drag the

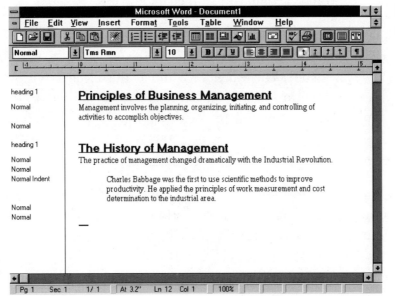

FIGURE 40.4:

Style name area

style name area split line with the mouse. To change the size of the style name area with the keyboard, enter a new measurement for Style Area Width in the View category of the Options dialog box.

4. To close the style name area, drag the split line to the left edge of the screen. With the keyboard, pull down the Tools menu, select Options, choose the View category, and enter 0 for Style Area Width.

5. Click on the Save button on the toolbar. With the keyboard, pull down the File menu and select Save (Shift-F12).

6. Type **Styles**, and then select OK twice.

7. Pull down the File menu and select Exit to exit Word.

In the next lesson, you will learn how to modify Word's built-in styles and create your own styles.

41 L E S S O N

FEATURING

Modifying automatic styles

Assigning shortcut keys to styles

Defining custom styles

▼

Changing and Creating Styles

W ord's built-in styles determine the default values used to format characters and paragraphs, headers, footers, footnotes, and other standard document elements. If these styles are not suitable for your work, you can modify them as necessary and save your changes to use with other documents. As you will learn in this lesson, you can change any of the 34 automatic styles, or even create your own styles for formats that you use often.

Changing Built-In Styles

The Normal style in NORMAL.DOT formats character styles, paragraph spacing, and tab stops. This means that you can change the Normal style to use other page formats, such as to double space lines or automatically indent the first line of every paragraph. You can even save the changed Normal style in NORMAL.DOT, so each new document that uses the Normal template will conform to your new default formats. Since many of the other built-in styles are based on the Normal style, when you change that style, you change those styles as well.

In the following steps, you will change the Heading 1 and Normal styles. By modifying these two styles, you will actually be changing 33 of the 34 built-in styles.

1. Start Word and open the STYLES document.

2. Pull down the Format menu, select Style, and then choose **D**efine. The Style dialog box will expand, as shown in Figure 41.1.

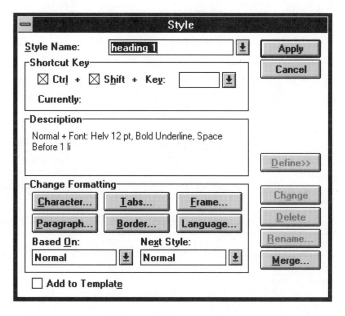

FIGURE 41.1:

The Style dialog box for defining a style

You use these options to change an existing style or create your own. The Heading 1 style is already selected.

If you use a style often, you may want to assign a key combination to it. Select Ctrl, Shift, or both, and then choose one of the options in the Key list box. This is the same as assigning key combinations to macros, as described in Lesson 34. You can assign key combinations to Word's built-in styles, modified styles, and your own styles.

3. Select Character to display the Character dialog box.

4. Select All Caps (Alt-A) to turn on that format.

5. Select OK to return to the Style dialog box.

Changing a style modifies it only for the current document. It does not add the new format to NORMAL.DOT or the document template. This way, you can change a style to make it easier to format a specific document without affecting Word's default styles.

Saving and Applying the Style

To add the edited style for all new documents or one particular document, you have to explicitly tell Word you want to save the style along with the global or document template. Follow these steps to save and apply your new style:

1. Select Add to Template (at the bottom of the Style dialog box) to save the style.

2. Select Apply, and you will see a dialog box with the message

Do you want to change the properties of the standard style?

3. Select Yes.

All the text formatted with the Heading 1 style automatically changes to the new style, all capitals. If you select another style to change before closing the Style dialog box, you will be asked if you want to save the changes to Heading 1. Select Yes to save the changes for the current document.

Creating a Style by Example

Now let's change the Normal paragraph formats. This time, you will modify a style by using a technique called *style by example*. In the following steps, you will format a paragraph, select it, and tell Word to redefine the Normal style to use this paragraph's format.

1. Place the insertion point in the first paragraph of text.

2. Drag the first-line indent marker in the ruler to the $\frac{1}{2}$-inch position. With the keyboard, press Ctrl-Shift-F10, place the ruler cursor at the $\frac{1}{2}$-inch position, press F, and then press ↵.

3. Pull down the Style list box and select Normal. You will see a dialog box with the message

> **Do you want to redefine the style "Normal" based on the selection?**

4. Select Yes to change the style.

Now that you changed the Normal style, every other style based on it will format text with the first line at the $\frac{1}{2}$-inch position. Note that the headings, which are also based on the Normal style, are now indented $\frac{1}{2}$ inch. Let's change that style again so that the headings are at the left margin.

5. Place the insertion point in any of the headings.

6. Drag the first-line indent marker on the ruler to the 0 position.

7. Pull down the Style list box and select Heading 1.

8. Select Yes to change the style.

In order to save styles changed by example, you must use the Style Define dialog box to add them to a template.

9. Place the insertion point in any of the paragraphs.

10. Pull down the Format menu, select Style, and then choose Define. Normal will appear in the Style Name text box.

11. Select Add to Template.

12. Select Change, then Close.

13. Pull down the File menu, select Exit (Alt-F4), then No to exit Word without saving the document. You will see the prompt

Do you want to save the global glossary and command changes?

14. Select Yes if you want to save the changes, or No to retain the original default values.

You can also change styles by example by using the Ctrl-S key combination or the Style dialog box. Select text formatted in the style you want to change, and then modify the formats by using the ribbon, ruler, or Format dialog boxes. If the ribbon is not on the screen, press Ctrl-S to see the prompt

Which style?

Type the name of the style you want to change, and then press ↵.

Creating Custom Styles

Rather than modifying a built-in style, you can define your own from scratch. Styles can be created through the Style Define dialog box (accessed by selecting Style from the Format menu, then Define) or by example.

In the following steps, you will add a new style that formats paragraphs with 1-inch left and right indentations, for use with long quotations. You will add the style to the NORMAL.DOT template so it is available with all documents.

1. Start Word, pull down the Format menu, select Style, and then choose **Define**.

2. Type **Indent**, and then select Paragraph to display the Paragraph dialog box.

3. Enter 1 in the From Left text box.

4. Select From **Right**, and then enter 1.

5. Select OK to return to the Style dialog box.

6. Select Add to Template.

7. Select Add, then Close.

8. Pull down the File menu, select Exit (Alt-F4), then Yes to save the template with the Indent style.

To create your own styles by example, format and select the text, and then select the Style text box on the ribbon. Type the name of the new style and press ↵. Remember to save the style by selecting it in the Style Define dialog box, selecting Add to Template, and then choosing Add. You can also create a style by example by using Ctrl-S or the Style dialog box.

Using Other Style Options

The other options in the Style Define dialog box let you delete and further customize your own styles. To delete a style, select its name in the Style Name list box, then select Delete. You will see the message

Do you want to delete style <style name>?

with the options Yes, No, and Help. Select Yes to delete the style, then OK to return to the document. You can delete only your own styles, not any of Word's original 34 automatic styles.

You can also choose to rename one of your styles, merge styles with other templates, base a style on an existing one, and assign a next style value. The Language option lets you select an alternate language to use for the spelling and grammar checker. You will learn about the Border and Frame options in later lessons.

The Based On option determines the starting point for a style. If you want to create a style that uses the default paragraph and character formats, set Based On to Normal.

The Next Style option determines what happens when you press ↵ after entering text in the style. For example, the Heading styles use Normal as the Next Style setting. When you type the heading and press ↵, the Normal style will automatically be selected. If you want to be able to enter several lines using the same format, enter the style itself at the Next Style option. That style will be applied until you select another style.

To print a list of your styles, select Styles from the Print list box in the Print dialog box (see Lesson 33 for details).

Restoring the Standard Default Styles

If you change your mind about changes you have made to the Normal template, you can delete your custom styles. Select each style in the Style Define dialog box, then select Delete.

To return the default styles to their original format, select each one, and then change the character, paragraph, and other styles to their original values.

You can quickly restore the original Normal template by deleting the file NORMAL.DOT in the Winword directory on your disk. However, this will also delete any macros that you might have created and saved.

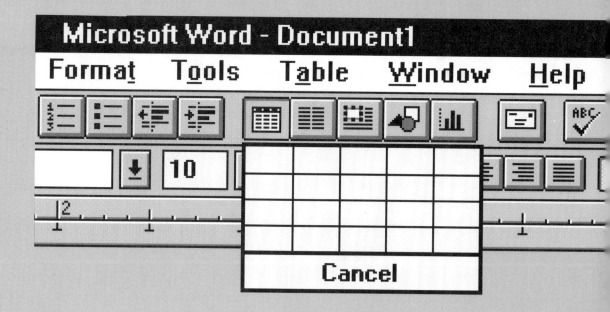

PART 5

Desktop Publishing

42 L E S S O N

FEATURING

Adding rules to paragraphs

Enclosing text in boxes

Creating ruled forms

Adding a page border

▼

Adding Rules and Boxes

You may want to add horizontal and vertical rules to your documents to separate text on the page or simply to add some visual interest. Surrounding text with a box calls attention to it and can draw the reader's eye to important points. As you will learn in this lesson, by using the Border option in the Format menu, you can draw rules above and below text or along the margins, and place boxes around paragraphs. The rules and boxes will appear on the screen and when the document is printed.

Drawing Horizontal and Vertical Rules

Rules are paragraph oriented. That is, they are linked, or associated, with the paragraph containing the insertion point when you selected the Border option.

In the following steps, you will add a horizontal rule to the COLLECT document to separate the letter from the list of unpaid invoices.

1. Start Word and open the COLLECT document.

2. Place the insertion point in the blank line before the title *Unpaid Invoices.*

The rule you will add in these steps will be linked with the empty paragraph where you just placed the insertion point. To add a rule beneath a paragraph, place the insertion point anywhere in the paragraph itself.

3. Pull down the Format menu and select Border to display the Border Paragraphs dialog box, shown in Figure 42.1.

You specify the position of the rule by selecting the appropriate portion of the diagram in the Border box, as illustrated in Figure 42.2. For example, to place the rule on top of the paragraph or highlighted section of text, select the top border of the diagram. To draw rules both above and below the text, select both the top and bottom of the diagram (hold down the Shift key and select each border). Click within the Border box but outside the diagram to draw rules on all four sides.

4. To select the bottom side of the diagram in the Borders box, click just below the last "line of text" in the diagram. With the keyboard, press Alt-R to select Borders, then press ↓ four times, until triangles appear just at the bottom of the diagram.

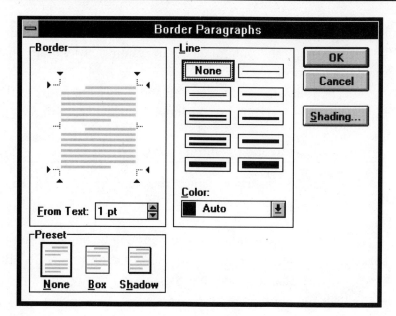

FIGURE 42.1:

The Border Paragraphs dialog box

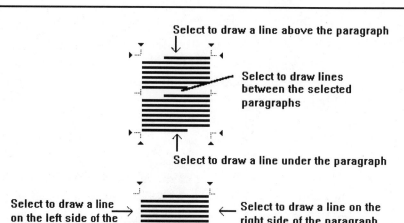

FIGURE 42.2:

Selecting where to draw horizontal and vertical rules

The available line styles appear in the Line box. If you are selecting a line with the keyboard, each option is identified by its position. Press Alt-1 to select None, Alt-2 to select the single line to its right, Alt-3 to select the next line, and so on.

5. For the line style, select the double line just below the None option in the Line section. With the keyboard, press Alt-3.

6. Select OK. A double-horizontal rule will appear on the screen.

7. Click on the Print button on the toolbar to print the document. With the keyboard, pull down the File menu, select Print (Ctrl-Shift-F12), and then choose OK.

DELETING RULES

If you delete the paragraph associated with a rule, the rule will also be deleted. Let's see what happens when you remove the blank line between the two paragraphs.

1. Place the insertion point on the double rule you just inserted, and then press the Del key to delete the carriage return between the two paragraphs. The rule will disappear along with the blank line.

2. Press ↵ to reinsert the blank line.

To delete just a graphic rule itself, place the insertion point in the associated paragraph, pull down the Format menu, select Border, and select None as the line style in the Border Paragraphs dialog box.

ADDING TEXT BELOW A RULE

If you draw a rule at the end of the document (by placing the insertion point in the last paragraph and selecting the bottom border in the Border Paragraphs dialog box), you will not be able to move the insertion point below the rule to enter text.

If you want to be able to add text below a rule at the end of a document, before you add the rule, press ↵ to insert a blank line. Then draw the rule at the top of the blank line paragraph by selecting the top border. The rule will appear above the insertion point, and you can add text below it.

ADDING A VERTICAL RULE TO A PAGE

Since rules are paragraph oriented, they appear with the paragraph in which the insertion point is located. To add a vertical rule down the left or right side of the page, you must first select the entire document.

Select the document, and then select either the left or right border of the diagram in the Border Paragraphs dialog box. Select the line style in the Line box and choose OK. To delete the rule, select the entire document, and then choose None for the line style in the Border Paragraphs dialog box.

Enclosing Text in a Box

You use the Preset options at the bottom of the Border Paragraphs dialog box to draw boxes around paragraphs. You can enclose any amount of text in a box, but like rules, boxes are paragraph oriented. To box more than one paragraph, you must first select all the paragraphs. Rules will be drawn around the perimeter of the paragraphs but not between them. If you want to box a single paragraph, place the insertion point anywhere in the paragraph (it does not have to be selected first).

Follow these steps to place a box around the list of unpaid invoices:

1. Select all the text, from the title *Unpaid Invoices* to the end of the document.

2. Pull down the Format menu and select Border.

3. Select the Shadow option in the Preset section of the dialog box.

4. Select OK, and then deselect the text.

A shadow box has thicker lines along the right and bottom borders to give a three-dimensional effect, as shown in Figure 42.3. The lines in the box created by the Box option are all of equal thickness.

5. Pull down the File menu, select Close, then No to clear the document window without saving the text.

6. Click on the New Document button on the toolbar. With the keyboard, pull down the File menu, select New, then choose OK.

You can customize the border lines by selecting individual borders and various line styles. The Preset options provide a quick way to insert a box using default values.

To quickly draw boxes, create a style using a border format. When you want to insert the box, just select the style from the ribbon.

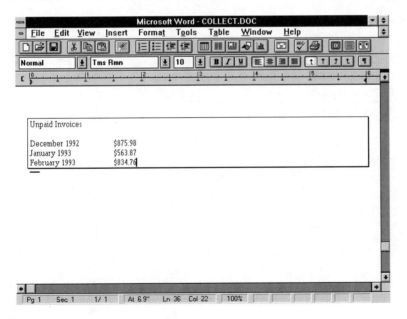

FIGURE 42.3:

Shadow box added to text

CHANGING THE SIZE OF A BOX

Word boxes are dynamic; that is, they will expand and contract to accommodate the text within them. If you type text in a box, the box will expand when word wrap takes effect or when you press ↵.

The height of the box changes automatically to accommodate the text in the box, but the width is fixed to remain as wide as the margins. Notice that the box you created around the unpaid invoices extends across the width of the page, even though the lines of text are quite short.

To create narrower boxes, you must change the paragraph's margins. Figure 42.4 shows two wide boxes and two narrow boxes. The top boxes were formed around paragraphs with the default left and right margins, so they extend the full width of the page. For the third box, the right margin was moved to the 1¼-inch position. Both margins were moved to create the last, smaller box around a centered title.

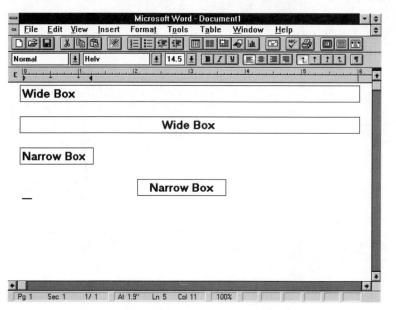

FIGURE 42.4:

Effects of margins on boxes

Creating Ruled Forms

If you want to draw a rule between selected paragraphs as well as a box around all of them, select the center border in the Border diagram in addition to the Box or Shadow option in the Border Paragraphs dialog box.

Using this technique, you can quickly create ruled forms. As an example, we will create the form shown in Figure 42.5.

1. Select the Center button on the ribbon (Ctrl-E) and type **Williams Company.** Do not press ↵.

2. Press Shift-↵ to insert a line break.

As you learned in Lesson 15 (when you created a tabular list), pressing Shift-↵ ends the line but not the paragraph, so both lines will be included in the same box in the form.

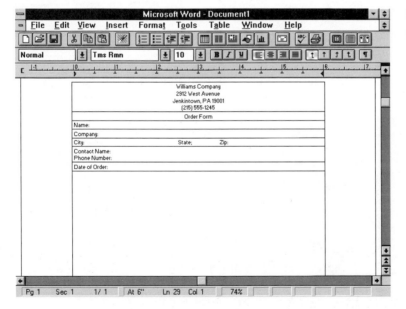

FIGURE 42.5:

Sample ruled form

3. Type the rest of the address, pressing Shift-↵ at the end of each line except the last. Press ↵ after the phone number.

> **2912 West Avenue**
> **Jenkintown, PA 19001**
> **(215) 555-1245**

4. Type **Order Form** and press ↵.

5. Select the Left button on the ribbon (Ctrl-L) to cancel the centering.

6. Type the following, pressing ↵ after each line.

> **Name:**
> **Company:**
> **Address:**
> **City:**   **State:**   **Zip:**

7. Type **Contact Name**: and press Shift-↵.

8. Type **Phone Number**: and press ↵.

9. Type **Date of Order**: and press ↵.

10. Press Shift-↵ 29 times to create the large box for the details of the order, and then press ↵.

11. Select the entire document, pull down the Format menu, and select Border.

12. Select Box in the Preset section.

13. Select the center border in the diagram. With the keyboard, press Alt-R, then ↓ twice, then Alt-2.

14. Select OK, and then deselect the text.

15. Click on the Print button on the toolbar to print the document. With the keyboard, pull down the File menu, select Print (Ctrl-Shift-F12), and then choose OK.

16. Pull down the File menu, select Exit, then No.

The form is printed with boxes around each paragraph or group of lines ending with Shift-↵.

FILLING OUT RULED FORMS

When you are filling out a ruled form on the screen, don't press ↵ after entering information in each box. If you press ↵, Word will expand the height of the box, changing the overall length of the form. With long forms, this may push the bottom cells onto the next page.

Type the information in the box, and then use the mouse or arrow keys to move the insertion point to the next box. If you find that some boxes are too small, redesign the form to handle the information required.

Creating Page Borders

To place a border around the entire page, create a header that contains one large box. First you must adjust the top margins so the border and text do not overlap.

Follow these steps when you want to create a border for letter-size paper:

1. Pull down the Format menu, select Page Setup and select the Margins button.

2. Enter a minus sign in front of the top margin setting, such as −1", and then select OK.

3. Pull down the View menu, select Header\Footer, choose Header, and then select OK to display the header pane.

4. Pull down the Format menu, select **Border**, and then choose the Box or Shadow option in the Preset section.

5. Select OK.

6. Pull down the Format menu, select Paragraph, and set the From Left and From Right options to **−.5**.

7. Set the Line Spacing At option to **60**. This provides a 10-inch border around the page. (If the resulting border is too large for the page, reduce this setting.)

8. Select OK, and then close the header pane.

9. Type your document.

As with all headers, you won't see the border in normal view, but it will appear in page layout view and preview mode, as well as when you print the document.

43 LESSON

FEATURING

Inserting graphic files

Enclosing images in boxes

Cropping and scaling pictures

▼

Adding Graphics to Your Documents

You can enhance your Word documents with drawings, charts, and pictures. For example, you can include a chart created with Lotus 1-2-3, a drawing made with Paintbrush, or a photograph you just digitized with your scanner. After you bring a graphic file into Word, the image can be modified in several ways. In this lesson, you will learn how to insert graphic files into documents and crop and scale the images. In the next lesson, you will learn other ways to manipulate graphics with Word.

Using Compatible Formats and Filters

You can use the techniques discussed in this lesson to insert a graphic created in any of the formats compatible with Word:

- AutoCAD (.PLT and .DXF)

- CompuGraphics Metafile (.CGM)

- Encapsulated PostScript (.EPS)

- Micrografx Draw! (.DRW)

- HP Graphic Language (.HGL)

- Lotus Graphics (.PIC)

- PC Paintbrush (.PCX)

- Tagged Image File Format (.TIF)

- Windows Bitmap (.BMP)

- Windows Metafile Format (.WMF)

- WordPerfect and DrawPerfect (.WPG)

You can always insert a Windows bit-map image into a Word document through the Clipboard. To insert a graphic file in any other format, you must have installed the appropriate graphic filters when you set up Word. These filters tell Word how to interpret the commands in the graphic file to display it on the screen and print it with the document.

If you performed a complete installation, all the graphic filters will be on your hard disk. However, if you performed a custom or minimal installation, the filters may not be available. If necessary, before continuing with this lesson, exit Word and run the Setup program, as explained in Appendix A. Select to perform a Custom Installation, and then choose the appropriate graphic filters for the files you want to be able to insert in your documents.

Inserting Pictures

You insert a picture into a Word document by using the Picture option on the Insert menu. This displays a dialog box listing the available graphic files.

As an example, we will add a drawing in the file called DISK35.WMF to the COMPUTER document. DISK35.WMF is one of several sample drawings in the Clipart directory provided with Word.

1. Start Word and open COMPUTER.

2. Place the insertion point in the blank line after the first paragraph.

3. Pull down the Insert menu and select Picture to display the dialog box shown in Figure 43.1.

4. Select the Clipart subdirectory in the Directories list box, and then choose OK. A list of graphic files with the WMF extension will appear in the File Name list box.

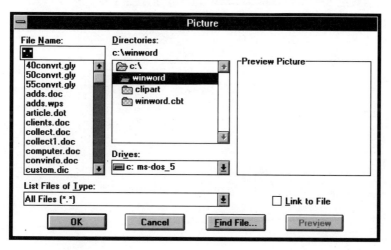

FIGURE 43.1:

The Insert Picture dialog box

5. Scroll through the list box and highlight the file DISK35.WMF.

6. Select Preview.

A picture of the file appears in the Preview Picture box. You can display any graphic file by selecting its name in the list box and selecting Preview.

7. Select OK.

The graphic image will appear on your screen, as shown in Figure 43.2. The blinking line on the right side of the graphic is the insertion point. The size of the image depends on how it was created or captured.

When you insert a picture, you store a complete copy of the graphic file in the document itself. If you later change the drawing,

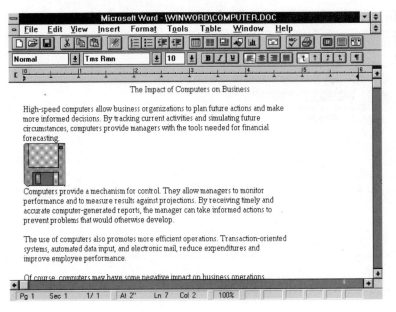

FIGURE 43.2:

Picture inserted in document

the original version will still print with the document. If you select Link to File in the Picture dialog box, however, you establish a dynamic link with the graphics disk file. When you change the graphic and then print the document, the new version will be printed.

Boxing Graphics

You can enclose a graphic in a box using the same techniques you used to box text in Lesson 42. Follow these steps to box the disk picture:

1. Select the graphic image by clicking anywhere in the picture. With the keyboard, hold down the Shift key and press ←.

As shown in Figure 43.3, the picture will be surrounded by a *selection box* with eight small squares, called *handles* (which are used to adjust the box, as you will learn shortly). The box is just there to show that the picture is selected; it is not a printable border.

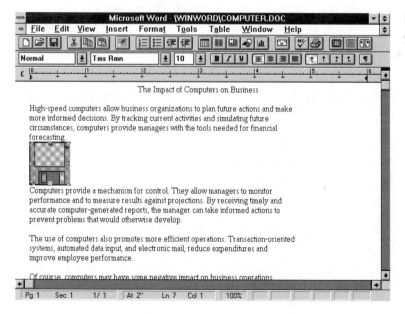

FIGURE 43.3:

Selected picture

2. Pull down the Format menu and select Border.

3. Select Box, then OK.

The box will be the same size as the selection box, so you won't see any changes on the screen. However, the box will remain when you deselect the picture.

4. Deselect the picture.

Adjusting Pictures

Within your document, a picture is contained in an invisible box. When you place a border around the graphic, you are drawing lines on the box. You can adjust the picture within the box by cropping or scaling it.

Cropping adjusts the size of the box in which the picture is located. When you crop a picture, you are changing the dimensions of the box, not the size of the picture. You can crop a picture to enlarge or reduce the amount of white space between the picture and the border, or to reduce the amount of the picture displayed and printed. *Scaling*, on the other hand, reduces the actual size of the picture. Cropping or scaling pictures is easier with a mouse.

CROPPING AND SCALING WITH THE MOUSE

In our document, the box is almost the same size as the picture of the disk, and the lines are too close to the graphic. To adjust the size of the box that surrounds the picture, you use the handles that appear when you select the box. You select a handle by moving the mouse pointer to the handle until the pointer changes to a double-pointed arrow.

In the following steps, you will crop the picture to provide more white space and then scale it to enlarge its size.

1. Select the picture.

2. Select the center handle on the right side.

3. Hold down the Shift key, and then press and hold down the left mouse button. The status bar will show

Cropping - .0" Right

You must press the Shift key before pressing the mouse button to crop the picture. If you press the mouse button first, Word will scale the picture, not crop it.

4. Slowly drag the pointer toward the right until the status bar shows

Cropping - .08" Right

5. Release the mouse button. The border will be more visible now because of the white space between it and the graphic.

6. To crop the left border, press the Shift key, select the center handle on the left, and drag it to the left until the status bar reads:

Cropping - .08" Left

7. In the same way, use the center handles on the top and bottom of the box to crop the top and bottom borders to −.08".

8. To scale the graphic, select the lower-right handle and drag the handle slightly down and to the right so the status bar reports the position as:

Scaling: 130% High 130% Wide

Depending on your mouse and how steady your hand is, you may have difficulty getting the exact measurements. So, just get as close as you can. To scale a picture to an exact size, you can use the Picture option in the Format menu, as explained in the next section.

9. Release the mouse button.

10. Deselect the picture.

11. Click on the Save button on the toolbar.

12. Pull down the File menu and select Exit to exit Word.

You can scale a picture by dragging any of the eight handles. Use the handles in the corners to reduce or enlarge the picture, changing both the height and width to keep it in its original proportions. Use the top, bottom, or side handles to change the size and proportions of the picture. Pictures usually look better when they are kept in their original proportions.

CROPPING AND SCALING WITH THE KEYBOARD

To scale or crop a picture without a mouse, you must use the Picture option in the Format menu. This displays the dialog box shown in Figure 43.4.

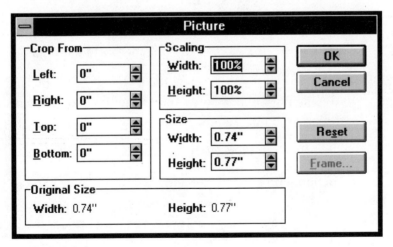

FIGURE 43.4:

The Format Picture dialog box

Follow these steps to crop the picture and then scale it to enlarge its size:

1. Pull down the Format menu and select Picture.

In the Picture dialog box, the insertion point is in the **W**idth text box under Scaling. To scale a picture, type the desired height and width percentages in the Scaling text boxes.

2. Type 130 in the **W**idth text box.

3. Press Tab to reach the **H**eight text box and type 130.

To crop a picture, enter measurements in inches in the text boxes under Crop From. To reduce the size of the graphic frame, enter positive measurements. For example, entering .5 in the Top text box crops $\frac{1}{2}$ inch off the top of the picture. Enlarge a box by entering negative numbers. For example, entering −1 in the Right text box will add 1 inch to the right side of the picture.

4. Press Alt-L to select the **L**eft text box and type −.08.

5. Press Tab to select the **R**ight text box and type −.08.

6. Press Tab to select the **T**op text box and type −.08.

7. Press Tab to select the **B**ottom text box and type −.08.

8. Press ↵ to return to the document.

9. Pull down the File menu and select Save (Shift-F12).

10. Pull down the File menu and select Exit to exit Word.

Working with Frames and Columns

After you have inserted a graphic file in your document, you can add a frame so that the text will flow around it. When a graphic is in a frame, you can position it anywhere on the page.

Another page layout that Word can set up for you is columns of text. As you will learn in this lesson, you can use Word's desktop publishing features to create professional-looking newsletters, reports, and other publications.

Positioning Graphics

To adjust the position of a graphic, you must insert it in a frame. A *frame* is a nonprintable border that allows the graphic to be positioned independently of the text on the page. Until you surround a graphic with a frame, the image is considered a separate paragraph. Once you add the frame, Word will wrap text around the graphic.

INSERTING A FRAME

You can use the Frame button on the toolbar or the Frame option on the Insert menu to add a frame. The frame is initially the same size as the invisible box that surrounds the graphic.

Follow these steps to insert a frame around the picture you added to the COMPUTERS document (in Lesson 43):

1. Start Word, open the COMPUTERS document, and select the picture of the disk.

2. Click on the Frame button on the toolbar (the ninth button from the right). With the keyboard, pull down the Insert menu and select Frame. If you are in normal view, you will see a dialog box asking if you want to change to page layout view.

3. Select Yes.

Word changes to page layout view and wraps the text around the frame, as shown in Figure 44.1.

DRAGGING THE GRAPHIC WITH THE MOUSE

In page layout view, you can change the position of the graphic by dragging it with the mouse. If you do not have a mouse, you can change the position of the graphic using the Frame dialog box, as described in the next section.

Follow these steps to use the mouse to change the position of the picture:

1. Place the mouse pointer in the picture. The pointer will change to a four-pointed arrow.

2. Drag the picture to the right side of the screen, and then release the mouse button.

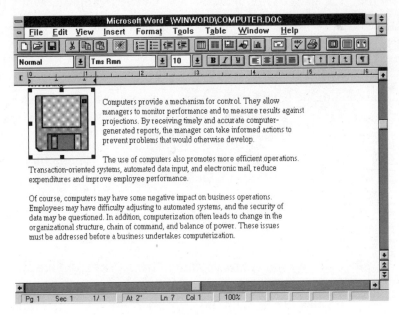

Text wraps around
the frame in page
layout view

By dragging the graphic with the mouse, you can place it anywhere on the page.

POSITIONING GRAPHICS WITH THE KEYBOARD

To set the frame position precisely, use the Frame option in the Format menu. This displays the dialog box shown in Figure 44.2. You can position the graphic relative to the column or page, or enter an exact horizontal and vertical position.

If you do not have a mouse, follow these steps to position the picture of the disk on the right side of the page:

1. Select the graphic, pull down the Format menu, and select Frame.

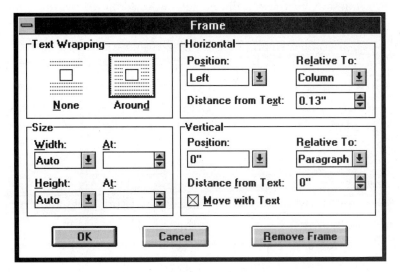

The Frame
dialog box

2. Press Alt-S to pull down the Position list box. The options are Left, Right, Center, Inside, and Outside.

3. Select Right, and then choose OK.

POSITIONING FRAMES ABSOLUTELY

Normally, your text flows freely on the page, moving down or up as you insert or delete text. However, you can tell Word to keep the frame in a specific position, no matter how much text you add or delete elsewhere on the page. This is called *absolute* positioning.

To designate a frame as absolute, pull down the Format menu and select Frame. In the Frame dialog box, turn off the Move with Text option (at the bottom of the Vertical section).

EDITING DOCUMENTS WITH FRAMES

You can edit documents with frames in normal, draft, or page view. In draft view, pictures will be represented by blank frames. In both draft and normal views, text will not flow around framed pictures, and the pictures may not appear in their actual position. In these views, the frame is indicated by a small black rectangle next to the graphic.

Switch to page layout view to see the document as it will appear when printed. Depending on your printer and monitor, some pictures will look distorted on the screen, and they may even appear to be missing segments. However, they will print correctly.

Adding Columns

You can format columnar documents by using the Column button on the toolbar or the Columns option on the Format menu. Your layouts can include single and multiple columns on the same page, as well as graphics within a column.

As an example, we will create a newsletter layout, with a headline and one paragraph in a single column across the page, followed by text in two columns. A graphic, enclosed in a box, will appear in the right column. First, you need to duplicate some of the text to make the COMPUTERS document long enough for two columns. Follow these steps:

1. Select the last three paragraphs in the document.

2. Pull down the Edit menu and select Copy (Ctrl-C).

3. Insert a blank line after the last paragraph, and then pull down the Edit menu and select Paste (Ctrl-V).

4. Insert another blank line after the last paragraph, and then pull down the Edit menu and select Paste (Ctrl-V) again.

5. Place the insertion point in the blank line following the first paragraph.

6. Click on the Column button on the toolbar (the one to the left of the Frame button). You will see a small diagram that represents four columns, as shown in Figure 44.3. (If you do not have a mouse, skip ahead to step 9.)

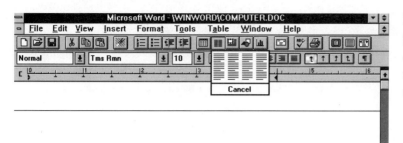

FIGURE 44.3:

Select the number of columns from the diagram on the toolbar

7. Click on the second column from the left in the diagram to select two columns.

Now all text in the document appears in two columns, not just the text from the insertion point down. You cannot have a different number of columns in a single section. If you want some one-column text and some two-column text on the same page, the page must contain two sections: one formatted as one column, the other as two columns. You could insert a section break, then change the number of columns. Instead, we will use the Columns dialog box to perform both functions. First, you need to change the document back to one column.

8. Click on the Column button on the toolbar, and select the first column in the diagram.

9. Pull down the Format menu and select Columns to display the dialog box shown in Figure 44.4.

10. Type 2 in the Number of Columns text box.

11. Select Apply To to display the options Whole Document and This Point Forward.

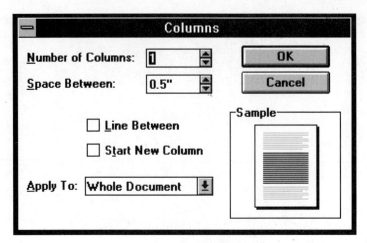

12. Select This Point Forward. This will insert a section break at the position of the insertion point and format the text in two columns.

13. Select OK.

Finally, you will adjust the position and size of the picture so it fits neatly in the second column.

14. Select the picture and enlarge it to almost the width of the column. With the keyboard, select the picture, then pull down the Format menu and select Picture. Press Alt-I to select Width and type **2.75**. Press Tab to select the Height, type **2.75**, and press ⏎. The picture will be centered in the right column, so you can skip ahead to step 16.

15. Drag the picture to the center of the column so it appears as shown in Figure 44.5.

16. Click on the Print button on the toolbar to print the document. With the keyboard, pull down the File menu, select Print (Ctrl-Shift-F12), and choose OK.

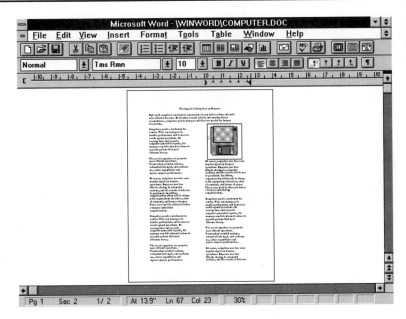

FIGURE 44.5:

Finished newsletter page in page layout view

17. Pull down the File menu, select Exit (Alt-F4), then No to exit Word.

Figure 44.6 illustrates some of the effects that you can create with Word. The line down the center of the page was created by selecting the Line Between option in the Columns dialog box. The graphic headline, including the curved word *Computers*, was formed using the Word-Art program (which you will learn about in Lesson 45). The three boxes in the text were created as frames. The large initial capital letter in the first paragraph and the box in the third paragraph use frames for text. To frame text, select the text and insert a frame by clicking on the Frame button in the toolbar or by choosing Frame from the Insert menu.

The only limitation to using graphics with Word is your imagination. Experiment with mixing text and graphics. Try using the dialog box options that were not discussed in detail in this chapter. Adding graphics to your documents can greatly enhance their impact and add a little fun to your word processing.

The Impact of Computers

High-speed computers allow business organizations to plan future actions and make more informed decisions. By tracking current activities and simulating future circumstances, computers provide managers with the tools needed for financial forecasting.

Computers provide a mechanism for control. They allow managers to monitor performance and to measure results against projections. By receiving timely and accurate computer-generated reports, the manager can take informed actions to prevent problems that would otherwise develop.

The use of computers also promotes more efficient operations. Transaction-oriented systems, automated data input, and electronic mail, reduce expenditures and improve employee performance.

Of course, computers may have some negative impact on business operations. Employees may have difficulty adjusting to automated systems, and the security of data may be questioned. In addition, computerization often leads to change in the organizational structure, chain of command, and balance of power. These issues must be addressed before a business undertakes computerization.

Read All About Computers!

Computers provide a mechanism for control. They allow managers to monitor performance and to measure results against projections. By receiving timely and accurate computer-generated reports, the manager can take informed actions to prevent problems that would otherwise develop.

The use of computers also promotes more efficient operations. Transaction-oriented systems, automated data input, and electronic mail, reduce expenditures and improve employee performance.

Of course, computers may have some negative impact on business operations. Employees may have difficulty adjusting to automated systems, and the security of data may be questioned. In addition, computerization often leads to change in the organizational structure, chain of command, and balance of power. These issues must be addressed before a business undertakes computerization.

Computers provide a mechanism for control. They allow managers to monitor performance and to measure

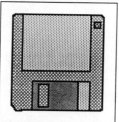

results against projections. By receiving timely and accurate computer-generated reports, the manager can take informed actions to prevent problems that would otherwise develop.

FIGURE 44.6:

First page of a newsletter using lines, graphics, and frames

FEATURING

Drawing with Microsoft Draw

Creating charts with Microsoft Graph

Creating special text effects with WordArt

▼

Creating Graphics and Charts

Word provides access to three Microsoft graphic programs: Draw, Graph, and WordArt. You can click on the button on the toolbar, create your drawing, chart, or text image, and then insert it in a Word document. In this lesson, you will learn some basic techniques for using these applications with Word.

You need a mouse to draw pictures using Microsoft Draw. If you do not have a mouse, skip ahead to the section about creating charts and graphs with Microsoft Graph.

Using the Drawing Tools

Microsoft Draw is a painting application, a simplified version of full-featured graphics programs such as Microsoft Paintbrush. You can use Draw to create drawings without leaving Word. The drawing tools are accessed through the Draw button on the toolbar.

In the following steps, you will create a simple drawing with Microsoft Draw. It will be a circle containing text, with a line through it.

1. Start Word and click on the Draw button on the toolbar (the button to the right of the Frame button). The Draw window will appear, as shown in Figure 45.1.

The icons along the left side of the window are the drawing tools. The functions of the tools are summarized in Table 45.1. Along the bottom of the screen are pallets for selecting the background and foreground colors of the images you create.

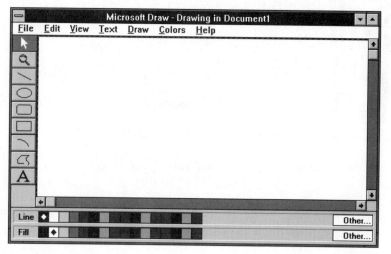

FIGURE 45.1:

Microsoft Draw window

TOOL ICON	NAME	FUNCTION
	Arrow tool	Selects images.
	Zoom In/Zoom Out tool	Zooms in and out to enlarge and reduce the displayed area.
	Line tool	Draws lines. As you drag, hold down Ctrl to draw a line from the centerpoint; hold down Shift to draw a straight line; hold down Ctrl and Shift to draw a straight line from the centerpoint.
	Ellipse/Circle tool	Draws circles and ellipses. As you drag, hold down Ctrl to draw a circle or ellipse from the centerpoint; hold down Shift to draw a circle; hold down Ctrl and Shift to draw a circle from the centerpoint.
	Rounded Rectangle/Square tool	Draws boxes with rounded corners. As you drag, hold down Shift to draw a square with rounded corners.
	Rectangle/Square tool	Draws boxes with square corners. As you drag, hold down Shift to draw a square with square corners.
	Arc tool	Draws arcs and curves. As you drag, hold down Shift to draw an arc that is part of a circle.
	Freeform tool	Draws free-hand shapes.
	Text tool	Adds text.

2. Click on the Ellipse/Circle tool. When you move the mouse into the drawing area, the pointer will change to crosshairs.

3. Place the crosshairs at the bottom of the drawing area, about ¾ of the way to the right side.

4. Drag the mouse up to the top of the window and to the left to draw a circle in the center of the window, and then release the mouse button. (To draw a perfect circle, hold down the Shift key before pressing the mouse button.)

5. Click on the Text tool, and then move the mouse to the drawing area. The pointer again changes to a crosshairs, but this time it has a smaller horizontal line.

In several of the next steps, you will be instructed to place the mouse pointer at specific locations on the circle. The locations will refer to clock positions, as if the circle were a clock. For example, the 12 o'clock position is at the top of the circle, and the 6 o'clock position is on the bottom.

6. Position the crosshairs just inside the circle, at the 9 o'clock position and click the mouse.

7. Type **Other Word Processing Software**.

8. To center the text, click on the Arrow tool. Four handles will appear around the text, as shown in Figure 45.2.

9. Point to the text, hold down the mouse button, and drag the text so it appears centered. As you drag, a dotted selection box will follow the mouse pointer.

10. Release the mouse button.

11. Click on the Line tool and position the crosshairs on the circle at the 10 o'clock position.

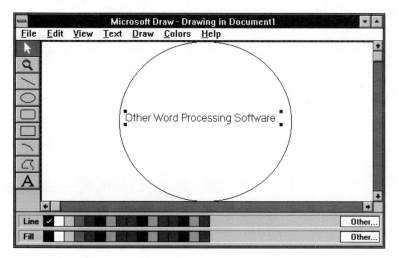

FIGURE 45.2:

Selected text in circle

12. Drag the mouse diagonally to the 4 o'clock position, and then release the button.

ADDING A DRAWING TO A DOCUMENT

You can easily add the drawing to a document when you leave the Microsoft Draw application. Follow these steps to insert your drawing into a new Word document:

1. Pull down the File menu and select Exit and Return to Document1. You will see a dialog box asking if you want to update Document1.

2. Select Yes.

The graphic appears in the Word window, as shown in Figure 45.3. You can now scale, crop, or move the graphic (see Lessons 43 and 44). To change the drawing, double-click on it. Microsoft Draw will start automatically with the image ready to be edited.

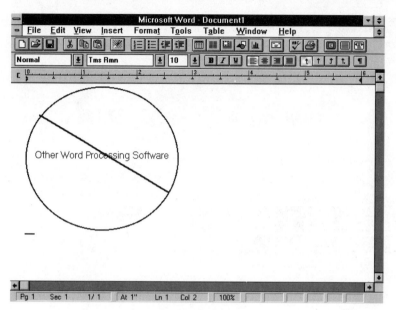

FIGURE 45.3:

Completed drawing in document

3. Pull down the File menu, select **Close**, then No to clear the document window without saving the text.

4. Click on the New Document button on the toolbar. With the keyboard, pull down the File menu, select **New**, and then choose OK.

Creating Charts and Graphs

Microsoft Graph will automatically create bar, line, and pie charts from data you enter into a table. You can also use Graph to import and edit charts created with Microsoft Excel. Let's use Graph now to create a three-dimensional graph.

1. Click on the Graph button on the toolbar (the one to the right of the Draw button). With the keyboard, pull down the

Insert menu and select **O**bject to see the dialog box shown in Figure 45.4, and then select Microsoft Graph. You will see the Graph window, which contains a sample table and chart, as shown in Figure 45.5.

2. Click on the Maximize button to enlarge the Graph window. With the keyboard, press Alt-spacebar, then X.

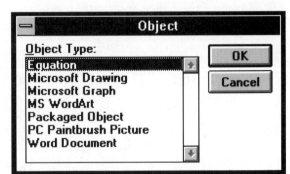

FIGURE 45.4:

The Object dialog box

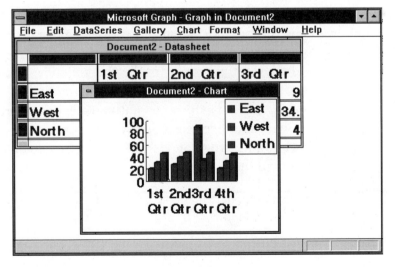

FIGURE 45.5:

Microsoft Graph window

3. Click on the table to bring it to the foreground. With the keyboard, press Ctrl-F6.

4. Pull down the Edit menu and select Select All (Ctrl-5 on number pad).

5. Pull down the Edit menu and select Cut (Ctrl-X).

6. Click the mouse or press an arrow key to deselect the table.

7. Enter the following table (see Lesson 25).

	1992	1993
Income	45000	56500
Expenses	25750	31900

Graph automatically aligns numbers on the right when you leave the cell or press ↵. As you enter the information in the table, the chart will appear in the background window.

8. Click on the chart to bring it to the foreground. With the keyboard, press Ctrl-F6.

The legend overlaps the chart, so let's enlarge the chart to make room.

9. Drag the lower-right corner of the chart window to make the chart about twice the width and 1½ times as high as the original size, as in Figure 45.6. With the keyboard, press Alt-hyphen, and then select Size. Press →, then ↓ to select the lower-right corner, press the → and ↓ keys to enlarge the window, and then press ↵.

10. Pull down the Chart menu and select Titles to see the dialog box shown in Figure 45.7.

11. Select OK to accept the Chart option. The word *Title*, surrounded by handles, will appear in the chart.

12. Type **Watson Company**, and then click the mouse in the chart. The text will not appear correctly until you click the mouse.

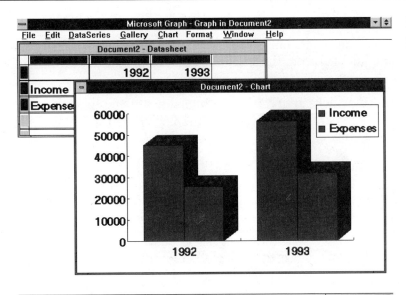

FIGURE 45.6:

Enlarged graph

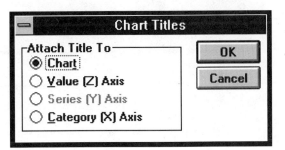

FIGURE 45.7:

The Chart Titles dialog box

CHANGING THE CHART TYPE

You can easily change the chart to another type by using the options on the Microsoft Graph Gallery menu. Let's see how our chart looks in another layout.

1. Pull down the **G**allery menu and select 3-D **C**olumn to display the dialog box shown in Figure 45.8.

This is the menu for selecting the type of three-dimensional column chart. Similar options are available for other types of charts.

2. Click on the second sample layout, and then click on OK. With the keyboard, press →, then ↵. You will see that the legend overlaps the chart lines again.

3. Click on the legend to select it, and then drag it to the top-right corner so it no longer overlaps. With the keyboard,

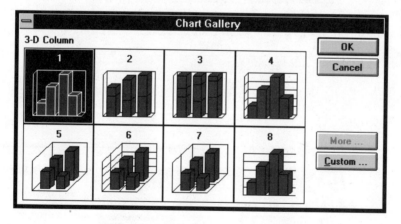

FIGURE 45.8:

The Chart Gallery menu

press → until the legend is selected. Pull down the Format menu and select Legend to display a dialog box of position options, select Corner, and then choose OK.

4. Pull down the File menu, select Exit and Return to Document2, and then choose Yes.

The chart appears in the document, as shown in Figure 45.9. To edit or change the chart, double-click on it to run Microsoft Graph.

5. Pull down the File menu, select Close, then No to clear the document window without saving the text.

6. Click on the New Document button on the toolbar. With the keyboard, pull down the File menu, select New, then OK.

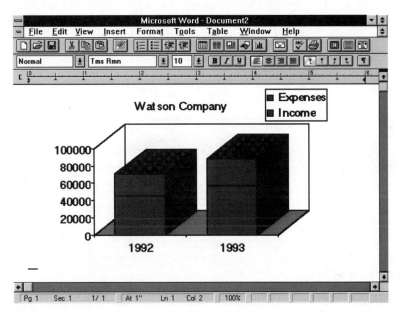

FIGURE 45.9:

Completed chart added to the Word document window

Creating Slanted, Curved, and Rotated Text

Microsoft WordArt is a unique program that lets you create slanted, curved, and rotated text, as well as other special text effects. For example, WordArt was used to create the large headline and curved text shown in the newsletter in Figure 44.6. You can use WordArt to create headlines larger than your largest available font or to rotate text to print portrait and landscape characters on the same page.

Follow these steps to see some of the special effects you can achieve with WordArt:

1. Pull down the Insert menu and select **O**bject.

2. Select MS WordArt, and then choose OK to display the WordArt dialog box, as shown Figure 45.10.

The options in this dialog box allow you to select effects for your text and preview them. The WordArt options are summarized in Table 45.2.

3. Type **Vote for** and press ↵.

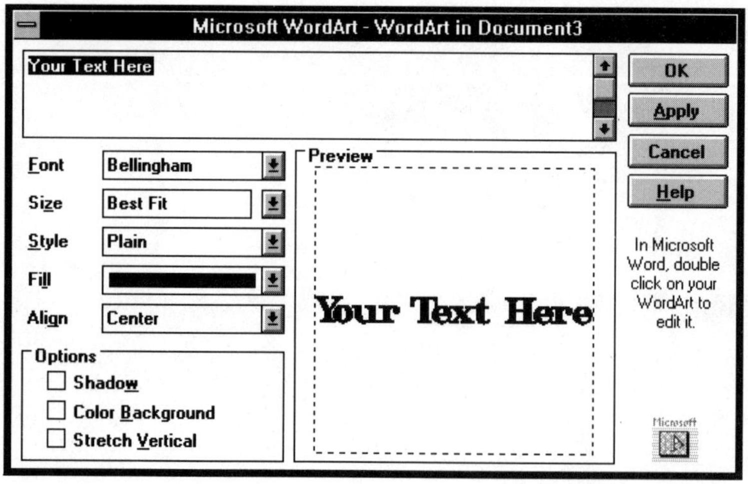

FIGURE 45.10:

The WordArt dialog box

OPTION	USE
Font	Select from 19 different graphic fonts.
Size	Select a point size. Select Best Fit to have Word select a size that best fits the frame.
Style	Select from top to bottom, bottom to top, plain, upside down, arch up, arch down, button, slant up (less), slant up (more), slant down (less) and slant down (more).
Fill	Select a color for the text. To print in reverse (light characters on a dark background), select White as the fill color, and then select the Color Background check box.
Align	Select the text alignment in the frame. The options are left, center, right, letter justify (space characters between the left and right sides), word justify (space words between the left and right sides) and fit horizontally (stretch the text to fit the frame).
Shadow	Switch between plain and shadow characters.
Color Background	Switch between normal and reverse printing.
Stretch Vertical	Select to stretch the text vertically to fill the frame from top to bottom.

TABLE 45.2:

WordArt Options

4. Type your name, press ↵, and type **State Senate**.

5. Pull down the Font list box. Your text will appear in the Preview box.

6. Select the Duvall font.

7. Pull down the Size list box and select 18.

8. Pull down the Style list box and select Button.

9. Select Shadow, and then select Color Background.

Figure 45.11 shows the formatted text. If you entered one line of text, it would appear in all three lines of the button.

10. Select Apply. Depending on your hardware, you may see the dialog box shown in Figure 45.12, which reports that the object is larger than the default object size. Select OK to adjust the size of the object.

11. Select OK to insert the graphic into the document and to return to the Word window.

EDITING A WORDART GRAPHIC

After the WordArt graphic is in a Word document, you can add a frame, crop, and scale it. To edit a WordArt graphic, double-click on it to run WordArt. Let's see how this works.

1. Double-click on the graphic. The WordArt window appears with the button inserted.

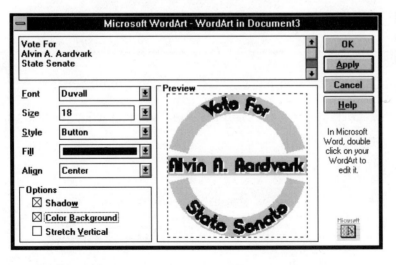

FIGURE 45.11:

Completed button graphic

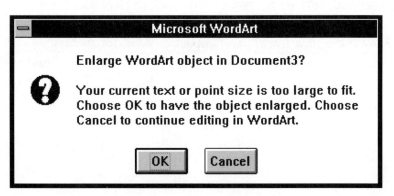

FIGURE 45.12:

The dialog box that appears when the WordArt graphic is larger than the default object size

2. Pull down the Style list box, and select Arch Up.

3. Select OK twice to return to the Word window and insert the edited picture, as shown in Figure 45.13.

4. Pull down the File menu, select Exit, then No.

Draw, Graph, and WordArt can be powerful tools for creating professional-looking documents. They can also be fun to use. When you have time, experiment with these programs, the sample WMF files

FIGURE 45.13:

Text formatted by the Arch Up option

supplied with Word, and with the picture, frame, and column functions described in this part of the book. As your skills with Word increase, so will the sophistication and impact of your documents.

I hope you've enjoyed learning about Microsoft Word and creating the sample documents throughout this book. You are now ready to apply the techniques that you have mastered to your own work. If you need to refresh your memory about any Word function, just return to the lesson and quickly review the instructions and figures.

APPENDICES

Installing Word for Windows

Now that you've purchased your copy of Word for Windows, you're no doubt ready to use it. But before you start your first document, it's a good idea to protect your investment by making backup copies. In this appendix, you will learn how to make a backup set of Word disks for your own safekeeping, run the Microsoft Setup program to install Word on your system, and make sure Windows is set up for your printer.

Making Backup Copies

Giving away copies of copyrighted software to your friends is called pirating. While it sounds exciting, it is unethical and illegal. However, you should make an extra set of disks for your own use; disks can wear out, and an extra set is simply a precaution against losing this valuable program.

To make the backup set, you'll need all your Word disks and an equal number of blank disks of the same size.

Before you start the backup procedure, protect your Word disks against accidental erasure. With 5¼-inch disks, place a write-protect tab over the small notch on the edge of each disk. (*Write-protect* tabs are the small rectangular stickers that are packaged with blank diskettes.) If you have 3½-inch disks, you protect the disk with the tab located on one side of it. You'll see a small square hole on both sides of the disk. One hole has a tab that can be used to cover the hole. If the hole is covered, the disk is unlocked and files can be erased. Lock the disk by pushing the tab so the hole is uncovered. Do not lock or write-protect the blank disks.

Now you're ready to back up your disks. The procedure you use depends on your computer system. If you have two identical floppy disk drives, follow the instructions for that type of setup. If you have two floppy disk drives that are different sizes or a single floppy disk drive, follow the steps for a system with one floppy disk drive.

BACKING UP WITH TWO IDENTICAL FLOPPY DISK DRIVES

You received two sets of disks with your Word for Windows package. One set is high-capacity 5¼-inch disks; the other is high-capacity 3¼-inch disks.

If your system has two of the same size and capacity drives (two high-capacity 5¼-inch drives or two high-capacity 3½-inch drives), you can make backup copies quickly from drive A to drive B.

Use this procedure even if you have two floppy disk drives and a hard disk. It is much easier to duplicate disks from floppy disk to floppy disk rather than use the procedure for only one floppy disk drive.

Your operating system directory contains a program called Diskcopy. You will use this program to make a duplicate set of your Word disks. In the following procedure, never place one of your original Word disks in drive B. If you do, and the disk is not protected or locked, you could destroy Word. Consult your operating system manual if you have any problems with this procedure.

1. Start your computer.

2. Make sure that the DISKCOPY.COM program is on the current directory. If not, log onto the appropriate subdirectory with the CD\ command, such as CD\DOS.

3. Type **Diskcopy A: B:**, and then press ↵. The screen will display

> **Insert SOURCE diskette in drive A:**
> **Insert TARGET diskette in drive B:**
> **Press any key to continue**...

4. Place one of your Word disks in drive A. This will be one of the original disks supplied with Word. You should have a write-protect tab on it, or it should be locked.

5. Place a blank disk in drive B and press any key. The copy procedure will run by itself. If the target disk is unformatted, DOS will format the disk as it makes the copy. When it is completed, you will see the message

> **Copy another diskette (Y/N)?**

6. Remove the disk from drive B and immediately label the copy accordingly. With 5¼-inch disks, write the name of the disk on the label before placing it on the disk (you can damage a disk by writing directly on it).

7. Remove the disk from drive A.

8. Press Y, then repeat this process until all the Word disks have been copied. Remember to always insert the original Word disk in drive A and a blank disk in drive B.

Place the original Word disks in a safe location. Use the copies when you run the Setup program.

BACKING UP WITH ONE FLOPPY DISK DRIVE

You will be making copies of your disks using only one disk drive. Use this procedure if you have one disk drive or two different types of disk drives.

During the process, you will be instructed to insert either the source diskette or the target diskette into drive A. The *source* diskette is the original Word disk that you will be copying. The *target* diskette is the blank disk that will hold the backup copy. Never insert the original Word disk when you are asked to insert the target disk or you could destroy your program. To be doubly safe, remember to write-protect or lock your Word disks.

1. Start your computer.

2. Make sure that the DISKCOPY.COM program is on the current directory. If not, log onto the appropriate subdirectory with the CD\ command, such as CD\DOS.

3. Type **Diskcopy A: A:**, and then press ↵. The screen will display

Insert SOURCE diskette in drive A:
Press any key to continue...

4. Place one of your Word disks in drive A. This will be one of the original disks supplied with Word.

5. Press any key. Soon you will see the message

> **Insert TARGET diskette in drive A:**
> **Press any key to continue**...

6. Remove the Word disk and insert a blank disk in drive A.

7. Press any key to begin copying.

You may be prompted several times to switch disks until all the information on the Word disk has been copied onto the blank disk. Be certain that the original Word disk is in the drive only when the screen requests the source diskette.

When the copy is completed, you will see the message

> **Copy another diskette (Y/N)?**

8. Remove the disks and immediately label the copy accordingly. With 5¼-inch disks, write the name of the disk on the label before placing it on the disk (you can damage a disk by writing directly on it).

9. Press Y, and then repeat this process for all your Word disks.

Place the original Word disks in a safe location and use the copies for running the Setup program, as described in the following section.

Running Word's Setup Program

Word's Setup program will copy the appropriate programs onto your hard disk so you can start using Word for Windows. Setup is easy to use. Just follow the messages and prompts on the screen.

1. Start your computer.

2. Insert the Word disk labeled Setup into drive A.

3. Start Windows.

4. Pull down the File menu and select Run.

5. Type **A:Setup**, and then press ↵.

You will see a dialog box indicating that Word is initializing the setup program, then another dialog box asking you to enter your name and the name of your organization or company.

6. Type your name, and then press Tab.

7. Type your company name, and then select Continue. A dialog box will appear asking you to confirm your name and company information.

8. Press ↵ to continue the installation. You will see a dialog box asking you to confirm the Word for Windows directory, as shown in Figure A.1.

9. Press ↵ to accept the default directory, WINWORD.

If this is the first time you've set up Word for Windows, you'll see a dialog box telling you that the WINWORD directory does not yet exist. Select Yes to continue.

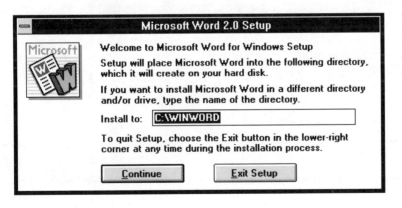

FIGURE A.1:

Confirm the default Windows directory

Word will check the amount of available disk space, and then display a dialog box listing three levels of installation, as shown in Figure A.2. The Complete Installation requires at least 15MB of hard disk space, but makes every feature of Word for Windows available. If you have less than 15MB of available disk space, select Custom Installation to designate which parts of Word you want to install, or Minimum Installation to install the basic Word functions. If you don't do a complete installation, you can rerun Setup at any time and select the Custom Installation option to install additional functions.

10. If you have the disk space, press ↵ to select the complete installation. Otherwise, select Custom Installation or Minimum Installation.

Next, you will see a dialog box asking if you want information on the WordPerfect Help system. This feature allows you to set up Word so it recognizes the command keystrokes used by WordPerfect. If you

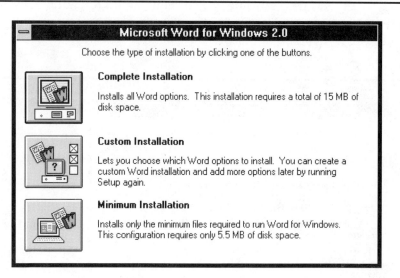

FIGURE A.2:

Installation options

select Yes, a dialog box will appear with the options Use WP Command Keys and Use Word Command Keys. Select WP command keys only if you are a WordPerfect user who wants to use the familiar keystrokes. Since all the instructions in this book use the Word command key structure, select No so that you can follow the exercises.

11. Select No. You will see a dialog box asking if you want Setup to update your AUTOEXEC.BAT file.

12. Select Update.

Setup will begin to copy the Word program onto your hard disk. A dialog box in the lower-right corner of the screen reports the file being copied and the percentage of the installation that has been completed. Messages will appear in the upper-left corner of the screen, encouraging you to mail in your registration card and reporting on some of Word's features.

Then, in a series of steps, you'll be asked to insert the Word disks in drive A.

13. Follow the prompts on the screen: insert the disk requested and select OK (or press ↵) to continue.

When all the files are copied, Word will update initialization files in the Windows directory, then create the Word for Windows group in Program Manager. Finally, a dialog box will appear to report that the installation is complete.

You have now installed Word onto your hard disk, and the program is ready to use. If you performed a minimum or custom installation and you later want to install other Word functions, restart the Setup program and select Custom Installation to add other functions.

Configuring Windows for Your Printer

Word for Windows uses the resources made available in the Windows environment. These include your specific hardware configuration, monitor, graphics adapter, and printer. If you set up Windows properly for your system, you'll be able to use Word to create and print even the most sophisticated documents.

Because Word relies entirely on Windows for its printed output, make sure that Windows is properly set up for your printer. This is especially critical if you have a laser printer or if you experience any problems when printing from Word or another Windows application.

If you have a laser printer and want to use downloadable fonts, you must also configure Windows to recognize and use the fonts. The following sections describe how to check your printer configuration and set up Windows to use downloadable fonts.

CHECKING YOUR PRINTER CONFIGURATION

Follow these steps to check your printer configuration:

1. Start Windows, not Word for Windows.

2. Double-click on Control Panel from the Program Manager Main window. With the keyboard, press Tab until you select the Control Panel icon, and then press ↵.

If the Main window is not open when you start Windows, pull down the Window menu and select Main.

3. Double-click on Printers in the Control Panel window. With the keyboard, press Tab until you select the Printers icon, and then press ↵. You'll see a dialog box with the names of printers that you've already installed for Windows, as shown in Figure A.3.

If your printer is not listed, select Add Printer to see a list of supported printers. Choose your printer, and then select the Install

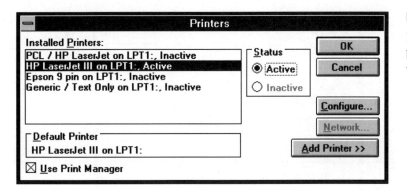

FIGURE A.3:

Printers dialog
box in
Windows 3.0

option (at the bottom of the dialog box). You'll be prompted to insert one of your original Windows disks in drive A. Insert the disk and follow the instructions on the screen until the Printers dialog box reappears.

Once the printer is installed, you have to configure it to work with your system.

4. Highlight the name of your printer in the list box, then select Configure to display the dialog box shown in Figure A.4.

5. Select the port to which your printer is connected, then select Setup to see a dialog box with options for your printer.

Figure A.5 shows an example of a dialog box that appears when a LaserJet III or compatible laser printer is being installed. Note that if you have a LaserJet III, the dialog box that you see may be different than the one shown in the figure. The dialog box that appears also depends on when you purchased your copy of Windows and the other applications you have installed.

6. Select the options that reflect your setup.

7. Select OK to confirm your settings. Continue selecting OK from the dialog boxes that appear until you return to the

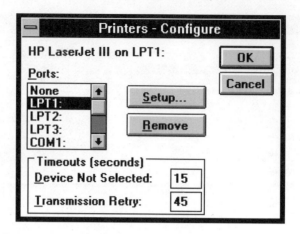

FIGURE A.4:

Use this dialog box to select your printer port

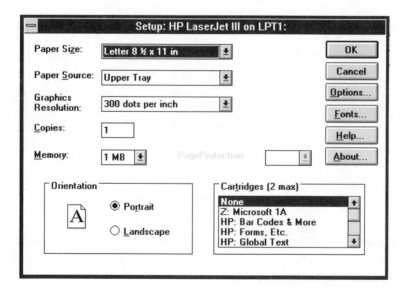

FIGURE A.5:

The Printer Setup dialog box for a LaserJet III printer in Windows 3.0

Control Panel window, and then close the window to return to the Main window.

8. If you are ready to start Word, select the applications group that contains Word, and then select the Word icon.

Using Downloadable Fonts

One of the best features of laser printers is their ability to use downloadable fonts, or *softfonts*. These are fonts that you store on disk and transfer to the printer when needed. Because downloadable fonts are purchased separately from the printer, you must configure Windows to recognize and use the fonts.

Follow these steps to set up your system for using downloadable fonts:

1. Create a directory called \PCLFONTS on the drive containing Windows. The command is **MD\PCLFONTS**.

2. Copy your font files to the PCLFONTS directory.

3. Start Windows and follow the steps given earlier to display the Printer Setup dialog box.

4. Select Fonts to display the dialog box shown in Figure A.6. Any downloadable fonts that you've already installed will be shown in the list box on the left.

5. Select Add Fonts. You'll be prompted to insert your font disk in drive A or enter the drive and path where your fonts are located.

6. Type **C:\PCLFONTS**, and then select OK. Windows will display the available fonts in the list box on the right side of the dialog box.

7. Select the fonts you want to install, then select Add. Windows will insert the fonts listed in the left list box.

By default, all fonts are given temporary status. This means that Windows will download the font each time it is called for in a document, erasing any previously downloaded temporary fonts.

If you use the same font in every document, you can save printing time by designating it as permanent. Permanent fonts are downloaded one time and remain in the printer's memory until you turn your printer off. Although this saves printing time, it also reduces the memory available for graphic images at high resolution. To set a font as permanent, select the font name in the left list box, and then select Permanent. If this is the first font you're changing to permanent, you'll see a dialog box asking you to confirm your choice. Select OK.

8. Select Exit.

If you designated fonts as permanent, you'll see a dialog box with the options Download Now and Download on Startup. Select Download Now to download the fonts immediately. Select Download on Startup to modify your AUTOEXEC.BAT file to download the fonts when you

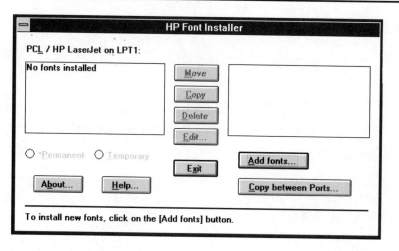

FIGURE A.6:

HP Font Installer dialog box

start your computer. If you want to use the fonts immediately and have them available whenever you start your system, choose both options. Select OK to return to the Printers-Configure dialog box.

9. Complete your configuration settings as explained previously.

As you'll learn in Lesson 4, you have to select your printer the first time you want to print a document in Word for Windows. After that, if you encounter any problems while printing, make sure your printer is turned on and properly connected to the computer. Check the port setting in the Printers-Configure dialog box and the options in the Printer Setup dialog box. If you have a serial printer, check your printer manual for the proper communications settings and make sure you're using the proper cable.

Windows Basics

ord for Windows is a Windows application. If you are new to the Windows environment, you will find it an easy and convenient way to work with your computer, especially if you have a mouse. While a mouse isn't necessary for using Word for Windows (except for creating graphics with Microsoft Draw), it is highly recommended.

In this appendix, we'll take a look at techniques you'll need to know to work with Windows and Windows applications.

Using Mouse Techniques

If you have a mouse, you will see a symbol on the screen, called the *pointer*, indicating the position of the mouse. The shape of the pointer will depend on its location on the screen. When an instruction says to *point to* something on the screen, move the mouse on your desk until the pointer is on top of the object on the screen.

An instruction to *click* the mouse, means to quickly press and release the left mouse button. If an instruction says *click on the box*, it means to point to the box referred to in the text and click the left mouse button.

The instruction to *double-click* means to perform two clicks rapidly in a row. The speed you have to click the mouse depends on your system. If you double-click to follow an instruction and nothing happens, you did not click fast enough—try again.

The instruction *drag* means to point to an option, press and *hold down* the left mouse button, then move the mouse on your desk. Instructions to drag will always tell you where to drag to, as in *drag the pointer to the bottom of the window*. When the pointer reaches the destination, you release the mouse button.

Working with Menus

Your first task in giving commands to Word will usually be to select an option from the menu bar. The menu bar is a line near the top of the screen that contains command words, such as File and Edit. Selecting an item displays a pull-down menu of additional items.

You can select a menu bar option, or *pull down a menu*, by using one of the following methods:

- Place the pointer on that option and click the left mouse button.

- Hold down the Alt key and press the underlined letter in the command, such as F for File. Notice that the underlined letter is not always the first letter in the word, as in Format. In the lessons in this book, press the letter that is boldfaced in the menu name.

- Press F10 to activate the menu bar. When the menu bar is active, you can either press the underlined letter to select the menu, or use the directional arrow keys to highlight a menu name and then press ↵ to select it.

Once you pull down a menu, you select an item from it. For example, to format characters, you pull down the Format menu and select the Character option. You can select an option in a pull-down menu in the following ways:

- Place the pointer on that option and click the left mouse button.

- Press the underlined letter in the command.

- Use the directional arrow keys to highlight a menu option and then press ↵ to select it.

Listed next to some menu options are the shortcut keys you can use in place of the menu option. For example, in the File menu, Ctrl+Shift+F12 appears next to the Print option, indicating that you can press that shortcut instead of pulling down the menu to print a document. The pluses in between the keys in the shortcut (hyphens in this book) mean that you should press the keys together. The Ctrl+Shift+F12 shortcut (Ctrl-Shift-F12 in the lessons) means to press and hold down the Ctrl and Shift keys, press the F12 function key, then release all the keys.

While a pull-down menu is displayed, you cannot type in the document. To continue entering text, click in the text region or press the Esc key.

If you pull down the wrong menu by mistake, click on another menu command, drag the pointer over the menu bar, or press the ← or → key to move from menu to menu.

In some menus, options may appear dimmed, or in a light shade of gray. These options are not available; you must perform some other function before you can select them.

When you select a pull-down menu options that has an ellipses (...), Word will display a dialog box. A *dialog box* contains additional choices that relate to the Word function you want to perform.

Working with Dialog Boxes

When a dialog box is first displayed on the screen, one of the items in it will be selected. This means that it is the option ready to be chosen, or acted upon. In most cases, the selected option will appear in reverse video, will have a blinking vertical line called the insertion point, or will contain a dotted selection box around one of its choices.

If you have a mouse, you'll simply click on options in the dialog box. With a keyboard, you can press Tab to move forward in the dialog box from option to option, and press Shift-Tab to move backward. You can also select an option by pressing Alt and the underlined letter in the option's name.

Dialog boxes may contain text boxes, list boxes, check boxes, and buttons.

TEXT BOXES

A text box is where you can type information or select options. Some text boxes will already contain an entry or setting when you display the dialog box. If the text box is highlighted, the current contents will be erased when you start typing a new entry.

To select a text box and highlight its contents, double-click or drag the mouse pointer in the box. Using the keyboard, press Tab or Shift-Tab to reach the text box. If you click once in the text box, the insertion point will appear there, but you must first delete the current contents before entering new information. (The insertion point is like a cursor; it shows where characters you type will appear.) Use the Del or Backspace key to erase the existing text.

When you have entered your information in the text box, move to another item by pressing Tab, Shift-Tab, or clicking with the mouse. Do not press ↵ after entering text in the text box unless you are done selecting options. Pressing ↵ will close the dialog box, removing it from the screen.

LIST BOXES

Some text boxes have an arrow at the end of the box. This indicates that there are additional choices for that option in a drop-down list box. A drop-down list box shows a list of available options.

To see the list, point to the arrow, and then click and hold down the mouse button. Once the list is displayed, drag the mouse down to select, or highlight, your choice. With the keyboard, press Alt-↓ to display the list box, then press the ↑ or ↓ key to select your choice. You can also press the ↓ or ↑ to cycle through the items without displaying the list. Each time you press ↑ or ↓, another item in the list appears.

When the down-pointing arrow is part of the option box, you cannot type in the box. Instead, you must select an item from the drop-down list box. If the down-pointing arrow is in a box by itself, not connected to the option box, you can either select from the drop-down list box or type your selection in the text box.

Other list boxes are already displayed on the screen. To select an option from the list box, click on it with the mouse. Using the keyboard, select the list box, then press the ↑ or ↓ key to select the option.

CHECK BOXES

A check box is a small square box next to an option that you can select. An X in the check box means that the item is selected, or turned on.

When you select a check box, an X will appear in the square. (If the function indicated by the check box is not available on your system, the square will remain empty) If there is an X already there, selecting the check box will remove the X, turning the item off.

You can check more than one check box in the same group. For example, checking both Bold and Italic when formatting characters creates a boldfaced, italic character.

RADIO AND COMMAND BUTTONS

A radio button is a circle next to an item. When you select a radio button, a black dot appears in the center, indicating it is turned on. Radio buttons come in exclusive groups. Choosing one radio button in the group automatically turns off any other button in the group that was turned on.

Command buttons carry out an action and act on the entire dialog box. Many dialog boxes have command buttons labeled OK, Close, and Cancel. Clicking on OK or Close, or pressing ↵, removes the dialog box from the screen and puts its settings into effect. Clicking on Cancel or pressing Esc removes the dialog box without accepting your changes.

Getting Help

All Windows applications have a common structure for their Help systems. To get help on a Word function, pull down the Help menu or press Alt-H to display the following options:

- Help Index: Displays the Help Index screen.

- Getting Started: Runs on-line tutorial lessons on basic Word functions.

- Learning Word: Runs on-line tutorial lessons covering all aspects of Word for Windows.

- WordPerfect Help: Shows the Word for Windows equivalent of WordPerfect 5.1 for DOS commands. You can also select to have Word recognize WordPerfect commands directly.

- About: Reports the version of Word you are using, your serial number, and the amount of memory and disk space available.

Words in Help windows that are underlined are called *jump terms*. When you point to a jump term, the mouse pointer becomes a small, pointing hand. Click on the jump terms to display detailed help information about the topic. Using the keyboard, press Tab to highlight a jump term, and then press ↵.

Words with dotted underlines are called *defined terms*. Point to the defined term and hold down the left mouse button to display a definition. Release the button when you are done. Using the keyboard, press Tab to highlight the defined term, and then hold down ↵ to display the definition.

When you need help, work through the Help menus, selecting jump terms or searching for specific topics. To get context-sensitive help when you're working with Word, press F1. *Context-sensitive* help is information about the menu, dialog box, or function from which you pressed F1. If you are working in the text region, the Help Index dialog box will appear.

From the text region, you can also get context-sensitive help by pressing Shift-F1. The I-beam becomes a small pointer connected to a question mark. Use the mouse or keyboard to select a menu option or dialog box and display specific Help information, or press Esc to return to the text region.

Help windows in Windows 3.0 also include the menu options and commands shown in Table B.1. In Lesson 2, you will practice using the Word for Windows Help system.

OPTION	FUNCTION
File	Prints the Help information or exits the Help function.
Edit	Makes a copy of the Help information, which you can insert, or *paste*, into your document.
Bookmark	Marks your place in the Help system so you can return to that location quickly.
Help	Displays information about using the Help function.
Index	Displays the Help Index.
Back	Displays the Help screen previously displayed. This button will not be active when you first start Help.
Browse ◄◄	Moves backward through a series of related Help screens.
Browse ►►	Moves forward through a series of related Help screens.
Search	Displays a list of jump terms and allows you to enter a keyword.

Draft command, 95
draft view, 94, 95, 96
drag-and-drop technique, 58–59
dragging, 41, 44, 58–59, 398
Draw button, 16, 366
drawing
    adding drawings to documents, 368–369
    arcs, 367
    circles, 367
    editing drawings, 369
    ellipses, 367
    free-form, 367
    lines, 367
    rectangles, 367
    rounded rectangles, 367
    rounded squares, 367
    squares, 367
    with text tool, 367
    tools for, 367–368
DrawPerfect file format, 348
.DRW file name extension, 348
.DXF file name extension, 348

E

Edit Copy command, 61
Edit Cut command, 60
Edit Find command, 246, 247, 249
Edit Glossary command, 173, 175, 176
Edit Go To command, 251
Edit Paste command, 61
Edit Repeat command, 87
Edit Replace command, 254, 255, 256, 257
Edit Search command. *See* Edit Find command
Edit Undo command, 53
editing, definition of, 20
{edittime} field, 209
ellipse/circle tool (MS Draw), 367, 368
Encapsulated PostScript file format, 348
End key, 43
end mark, 5
Envelope button, 16, 159, 160, 306
envelopes, printing, 162–163
    from data files, 305–307
    on laser printers, 163
    setting up for, 159–162
.EPS file name extension, 348
erasing. *See* deleting
.EXE file name extension, 29
Exit and Return command, 369, 375
Exit command, 33
exiting Word for Windows, 33
expression field type, 197, 203–204

EXT indicator, 6, 45, 46
Extend Selection key (F8), 45, 46
extensions, file name, 29, 30, 184, 348

F

F1 key (Help), 10, 404
F2 key (Move), 61
F3 key (Glossary), 175, 187–188
F4 key (Repeat), 87
F5 key (Go To), 43, 251
F6 key (Next Pane), 216
F7 key (Spelling), 67
F8 key (Extend Selection), 45, 46
F9 key (Update Field), 199, 200, 204, 205
facing pages, 101
False function, 198
fax cover page example, 210–211
field codes
    printing, 263
    viewing, 200, 206
Field Codes command, 200
Field dialog box, 196–199
fields, 205–211
    in data files, 292–293
    date, 205, 207–209
    in tables, 196–200, 204
    time, 205
    updating, 199, 200, 204, 205
File Close command, 32–33
File Exit and Return command, 369, 375
File Exit command, 33
file formats, 348
File New command, 38
File Open command, 37
File Print command, 23–24, 259, 264, 290
File Print Merge command, 293, 301
File Print Preview command, 100
File Print Setup command, 24–25
File Save All command, 228
File Save As command, 30
File Save command, 27, 29
File Summary Info command, 29
File Template command, 188
{file name} field, 211
file names
    changing, 30
    extensions, 29, 30, 184, 348
files. *See also* documents
    backing up, 30–31
    naming, 27
    read-only, 30, 38
    renaming, 27

F1	Context-senstive help
Alt-F1	Go to and select the next field
Shift-F1	Get help on a command or region of the screen
Alt-Shift-F1	Go to the previous field
F2	Move text
Alt-F2	Save as
Ctrl-F2	Increase the font
Shift-F2	Copy text
Alt-Shift-F2	Save
Ctrl-Shift-F2	Decrease the font size
F3	Insert glossary entry
Ctrl-F3	Cut text or graphics to the Spike
Shift-F3	Change the case of letters
Ctrl-Shift-F3	Insert from, then empty, the Spike
F4	Repeat the previous action
Alt-F4	Exit Word for Windows
Ctrl-F4	Close the document window
Shift-F4	Repeat the previous Find or Go To command
F5	Go to a position
Alt-F5	Restore an application window
Ctrl-F5	Restore a document window
Shift-F5	Go to the previous position
Ctrl-Shift-F5	Insert a bookmark
F6	Go to the next pane
Alt-F6 or Ctrl-F6	Switch to the next document window
Shift-F6	Go to the previous pane
Alt-Shift-F6 or Ctrl-Shift-F6	Go to the previous window